KT-504-886

The ICT Revolution: Productivity Differences and the Digital Divide

A Report for the Fondazione Rodolfo Debenedetti

Edited by

DANIEL COHEN
PIETRO GARIBALDI
STEFANO SCARPETTA

with

Bruno Amable, Philippe Askenazy, Eric Bartelsman, Andrea Bassanini,
Gøsta Esping-Andersen, Paul Geroski, Andrea Goldstein, Robert J. Gordon,
John Haltiwanger, Ronald S. Jarmin, Alan B. Krueger, John Martin,
David O'Connor, Thorsten Schank, and Jan Svejnar

OXFORD
UNIVERSITY PRESS

OXFORD

UNIVERSITY PRESS

Great Clarendon Street, Oxford OX2 6DP

Oxford University Press is a department of the University of Oxford.
It furthers the University's objective of excellence in research, scholarship,
and education by publishing worldwide in

Oxford New York

Auckland Bangkok Buenos Aires Cape Town Chennai
Dar es Salaam Delhi Hong Kong Istanbul Karachi Kolkata
Kuala Lumpur Madrid Melbourne Mexico City Mumbai Nairobi
São Paulo Shanghai Taipei Tokyo Toronto

Oxford is a registered trade mark of Oxford University Press
in the UK and in certain other countries

Published in the United States
by Oxford University Press Inc., New York

© Fondazione Rodolfo Debenedetti 2004

The moral rights of the author have been asserted
Database right Oxford University Press (maker)

First published 2004

All rights reserved. No part of this publication may be reproduced,
stored in a retrieval system, or transmitted, in any form or by any means,
without the prior permission in writing of Oxford University Press,
or as expressly permitted by law, or under terms agreed with the appropriate
reprographics rights organization. Enquiries concerning reproduction
outside the scope of the above should be sent to the Rights Department,
Oxford University Press, at the address above

You must not circulate this book in any other binding or cover
and you must impose this same condition on any acquirer

British Library Cataloguing in Publication Data

Data available

Library of Congress Cataloguing in Publication Data

Data available

ISBN 0-19-927010-4 (hbk.)
ISBN 0-19-927011-2 (pbk.)

1 3 5 7 9 10 8 6 4 2

Typeset by Newgen Imaging Systems (P) Ltd., Chennai, India
Printed in Great Britain
on acid-free paper by
T.J. International Ltd., Padstow, Cornwall

SM05004628
6/06
€27.99
338.064(Coh)

0253235

Long Loan

This book is due for return on or before the last date shown below

2 9 JUN 2007		
3 0 MAY 2008		

St Martins Services Ltd

HAROLD BRIDGES LIBRARY
ST MARTINS SERVICES LTD.
LANCASTER

0199270112

In association with the William Davidson Institute
at the University of Michigan Business School.

Acknowledgements

Both studies (Parts I and II) were originally prepared for the fourth European conference of the Fondazione Rodolfo Debenedetti, which was held in Catania in June 2002. This book draws much on the discussion in Catania, which involved a qualified audience of academicians, professional economists, representatives of unions and employers associations, industrialists, and policy-makers.

Needless to say, we are very much indebted to all those who attended that conference and contributed actively to the discussion. In particular, we wish to express our gratitude to Lucio Stanca, Italian Minister of Innovation and Technologies, who opened the conference with an insightful speech on the ongoing policy initiatives in the area of ICT investments, and to Pasquale Pistorio, President of STMicroelectronics, who illustrated to the audience how the ICT miracle in the Catania area came about in the first place. Finally, Renato Soru, President and CEO of Tiscali Corporation added some very interesting remarks on the ICT revolution seen by a successful entrepreneur.

We are obviously most grateful to Carlo De Benedetti, who allowed this event to occur and opened the Conference, and to Tito Boeri, Director of the Fondazione, who advised us and encouraged us throughout the preparation of the reports.

The event was also co-sponsored by the William Davidson Institute at the University of Michigan Business School. We are most grateful to the Director, Jan Svejnar, who accepted not only to partially fund the project, but also to act as a discussant for the second report.

Special thanks to Mauro Maggioni, Giovanna Albano, and Roberta Marcaletti who assisted in the organization of the conference and worked hard and skilfully in preparing the background material for this volume. We are also grateful to Michele Pellizzari, Saverio Scaramuzzo, and Silvia Redaelli who contributed to the final stages of the preparation of the event.

Contents

List of Figures

List of Tables

List of Maps

List of Boxes

List of Abbreviations

B2B	business to business
B2C	business to consumer
BERD	business expenditure in R&D
BI	Balassa index
CAD/CAM	Computer aided design and manufacturing
C2C	consumer to consumer
CB	Caribbean Basin
CDs	compact discs
DMOs	destination management organizations
EAF	East African Flowers
ECR	Efficient Consumer Response
EDI	electronic data interchange
EPL	employment protection legislation
F2F	fact-to-face
FHK	Foster, Haltiwanger, and Krizan
GDP	gross domestic product
GDS	global distribution system
GR	Griliches and Regev
ICT	information and communication technology
IPRs	intellectual property rights
ISIC	International Standard Industry Classification
ISM	industry-sponsored marketplace
ISO	International Standard Organization
IT	information technology
LM	labour market
MFP	multifactor productivity
OBNMs	Original Brand Name Manufacturers
OECD	Organization for Economic Cooperation and Development
OEMs	Original Equipment Manufacturers
PAP	de Particulier à Particulier
PC	personal computer
PMR	product market regulation
SCAA	Specialty Coffee Association of America
SMEs	small- and medium-sized enterprises
SSI	small-scale industry
STPI	Software Technology Parks of India
TFA	Tele Flower Auction
T&T	travel and tourism
TV	Television

Contributors

Bruno Amable, CEPREMAP, Paris, France

Philippe Askenazy, CNRS and CEPREMAP, Paris, France

Eric Bartelsman, Free University, Amsterdam, The Netherlands

Andrea Bassanini, OECD, Paris, France

Daniel Cohen, Delta, Paris, France

Gøsta Esping-Andersen, Universitat Pompeu Fabra, Barcelona, Spain

Pietro Garibaldi, Fondazione Rodolfo Debenedetti, Milan and Bocconi University, Milan, Italy

Paul Geroski, London Business School, London, UK

Andrea Goldstein, OECD, Paris, France

Robert J. Gordon, Northwestern University, USA

John Haltiwanger, University of Maryland and US Bureau of the Census, USA

Ronald S. Jarmin, Center for Economic Studies, US Bureau of the Census, USA

Alan B. Krueger, Princeton University, Princeton, USA

Richard Layard, London School of Economics, London, UK

John Martin, OECD, Paris, France

David O'Connor, OECD, Paris, France

Stefano Scarpetta, World Bank, Washington, USA

Thorsten Schank, Institut für Arbeitsmarkt und Berufsforschung and Universität Erlangen, Nürnberg, Germany

Renato Soru, Tiscali S.p.A., Italy

Jan Svejnar, William Davidson Institute, University of Michigan, USA

Introduction

TAKING STOCK OF THE ICT REVOLUTION

Over the nineties, the information and communication technology (ICT) took center stage in economic analysis, attracting a great deal of attention by economists and policy makers. Many observers attributed the pick up in output and productivity growth, observed in few countries, to the ICT revolution. Further, the emergence of the digital economy and the explosion of the internet spread the idea that the basic functioning of most markets may change for good, with far reaching consequences on the world distribution of income, and on economic distance between the advanced and developing countries.

What lies behind the idea that the spread of ICT could be a "revolution" for our economies and for our daily life? The reason is that the spread of ICT could be considered akin to the diffusion of a "general purpose technology", a technology with wide scope for improvement and elaboration; with applicability across a broad range of uses; with potential for use in a wide variety of products and processes; and with strong complementarities with existing or potential new technologies. The ICT revolution actually started almost three decades ago in the mid-seventies. At that time, the emergence of the microprocessor and the diffusion of the personal computer, with their immediate possibility of distributed information storage and processing, set the stage for a dramatic change. The new technology emerged in the world economy when a remarkable slowdown in productivity growth was taking place.

Indeed, recent estimates of the growth of computer stocks and the flow of services are consistent with the view that in the mid seventies the US economy was in the early phase of the deployment of ICT. Figures developed by Jorgenson and Stiroh (1995) reveal that in 1979, when computers had not yet evolved beyond their limited role in information processing, machinery and computer equipment were providing only 0.56 percent of the total flow of real services from the (non-residential) producer of durable equipment stock. But these measures rose at 4.9 percent in 1985, and had ballooned to 13.8 percent by 1990, and 18.4 percent few years after that.

Historically, a comparable period of diffusion of a general purpose technology took place in the 1920s, with the emergence of the dynamo and the electrification of the industrial economy (David and Wright, 1999). Indeed, the transmission of power in the form of electricity revolutionized industrial production, through a process that required much more than substitution of a new productive input for an older alternative. The electrification of the industrial economy made possible significant fixed-capital savings while simultaneously increasing labor productivity. Interestingly, the extent of computerization that had been achieved in the US economy by the late 1980s was roughly compa-rable with the degree to which the American manufacturing sector had become electrified at the beginning of the twentieth century. When the historical com-parison is narrowed more appropriately to the diffusion of secondary motors, the growth rate for 1899–1914 is almost precisely the same as that for the ratio of computer equipment services to all producers durable equipment services in the US. In the case of the emergence of dynamo, history has already unfolded itself, and we now know that the pick up in productivity growth that took place in the twenties can largely and confidently be attributed to the slow diffusion of the new general purpose technology.

For the case of ICT, history has not yet completely unfolded. All one can do at this stage is to seriously take stock of the ongoing revolution. This is the aim of this project. Throughout the book, we aim at understanding what the ICT revolution implied for productivity growth across countries, as well as for the functioning of the world markets.

Specifically, there are three key research questions that the book addresses. First, does the ICT revolution contributed to the recent widening in growth disparities across the OECD? Second, why have some countries better able to harness the potential of this technology, while others have lagged behind? Third, are internet and the ICT revolution going to reduce economic distance between industrial and developing countries? These are fundamentally diffi-cult questions. Nevertheless, this book provides an answer to each of them, and in this brief introduction, we offer a short sketch of the main logic behind the three answers.

As in previous volumes for the Fondazione Rodolfo Debenedetti, the book assembles contributions from two teams of leading economists of the field. Part One is the contribution of a team co-ordinated by Stefano Scarpetta and included Eric Bartelsman, Andrea Bassanini, John Haltiwanger, Ronald Jarmin, Stefano Scarpetta and Thorsten Schank. It focuses on the contribution that the ICT revolution has made in the advanced countries for output and productivity growth at the macro, industry and firm level. Part two of the book is the contribution of a team co-ordinated by Daniel Cohen and included Bruno Amable, Philippe Askenazy, Andrea Goldstein and David O'Connor. It assesses whether or not the digital economy will result in a more competitive and more equal world. The book includes also insightful comments by Alan Krueger and Robert Gordon, who discuss the first half of the book, and by Jan Svejnar and John Martin, who discuss the second half of the book. Finally, Gosta Esping-Andersen and Paul Geroski present their views on what they have learned from the book and what more remains to be analysed.

I: Does the ICT revolution contributed to the recent widening in growth disparities across the OECD?

If a new general technology becomes available, sooner or later it must have an impact on the growth process. And changes in the productivity process should be reflected in the growth data. In this respect, a natural starting point of our long inquiry is the analysis of aggregate output and productivity performance. Macro data clearly point to widening disparities in growth performance across the OECD countries, even using series that attempt to control for differences in the business cycle position of countries. Thus, convergence in output per capita and productivity levels can no longer be taken for granted by macro economists, not even for OECD countries that supposedly share common technologies. Indeed, significant growth divergence occurred in the 1990s across OECD countries. This is not only because the U.S., the country that was already at the productivity frontier in many industries, pulled ahead of the others, but also because some smaller economies have been able to significantly boost their economic performance (e.g. Australia, Canada, Ireland, the Netherlands).

The evidence provided in the book suggests that some of these disparities are due to "traditional economy factors" including differences in labour utilisation. But there also are important "new" factors behind them. Some countries, including the United States, have developed a sizeable ICT-production industry which has experienced over the past decade an extraordinary productivity growth. Moreover, a number of countries, whether or not with sizeable ICT industry, invested a lot in ICT equipment and this has also contributed to boost output and productivity. As often argued, ICT equipment also allows changes in work practices and could potentially lead to a faster pace of technological progress. One way to measure technological progress is by calculating the residual growth of output once the contribution of the growth of factor inputs is taken into account. This measure, often referred to as multifactor productivity, shows some interesting cross-country variation. In particular, after a prolonged period of downward trend, multifactor productivity growth accelerated in some countries, including all of those that have a sizeable ICT production industry and have adopted ICT equipment at a fast pace. And the way in which the acceleration in multifactor productivity took place appears consistent with the view of a slow diffusion of this general purpose technology. The acceleration was initially linked to productivity gains of the ICT producing industries, and was later followed by intensive productivity gains in ICT-using industries.

But the adoption of new technology interacts with a churning process at the industry level, which involves substantial rates of firm entry, firm expansion and contraction, as well as inevitable and often efficient exit of obsolete firms. Interestingly, when the book looks inside this complex churning process, it finds that a relatively stronger contribution to productivity growth in ICT-related industries came from the entry of new firms.

A careful examination of the macro, sectoral and firm turnover data, provides the tools for answer to yes to our first key question: the ICT revolution contributed to the recent widening in growth disparities across the OECD. The way in which the multifactor productivity growth picked up is consistent with a slow ICT adoption story, while the above average productivity gains of industries producing and extensively using ICT equipments suggests that, beyond the complex turnover process, ICT related industries did significantly contribute to push up productivity in a selected number of countries, such as United States, Canada, Ireland, Finland and Australia.

II. The Role of "Market Experimentation"

But how did it happen that some countries, and notably the United States, were better equipped to adopt the new general purpose technology? What was so different and so special about them? This is our second key question, and the book draws on firm and establishment level data in search for an answer. The key idea in this respect is simple, albeit original and provocative. It is *"market experimentation"*. As the report edited by Stefano Scarpetta shows, market experimentation refers to four interrelated features of firm behaviour in the United States compared to Europe. First, U.S. firms enter the market with a relatively smaller size than their European counterparts. Second, new entrants in the U.S. have on average a lower productivity relative to that of the incumbents. Third, there is greater dispersion of productivity growth amongst new entrants in U.S. than in Europe, and this dispersion tends to decline with the age of firms in the U.S. but not in Europe. Fourth, those U.S. firms who successfully enter and survive in the market, experience much stronger employment expansion relative to their European counterparts. All in all, these findings suggest that on average entrepreneurs enter each market in the U.S. with a relatively small size, test the market and, if successful expand rapidly to reach the minimum efficient scale. Those with poor productivity outcomes fail rapidly, clearing resources for others to test the market with alternative projects. Note that these findings do not come from ad hoc observations, but are obtained from a harmonized data set of firm level data for 10 OECD economies: Canada, Denmark, France, Finland, Germany, Italy, the Netherlands, Portugal, the United Kingdom and the United States.

To further test the market experimentation hypothesis, the book looks at new and original establishment level data for the U.S. and Germany. It finds that new entrants are much more heterogeneous in the U.S. than in Germany in many respects: in the level of productivity, in the skill mix of the labour force, in the degree of internet access and in the returns to investment in high technologies. All these features of new establishments are consistent with the idea of greater market experimentation in the US as compared with Germany.

Obviously, the regulatory and institutional environment and different degrees of market competitions within countries do play a role in shaping the different outcomes across industries and across countries. The book uses a new set of OECD indicators of product and labour market regulations to test whether such regulatory variables have a significant impact on sectoral multi-factor productivity and on R&D intensity, where the latter is used to proxy for the intensity of innovation. The results suggest that stringent regulatory settings in the product markets adversely affect multifactor productivity growth and R&D, even though their impact depends also on specific technological and market conditions, such as industry distance from the technological frontier. But the way in which those cross country regressions should be read is in close connection to the evidence on market experimentation. It appears that certain regulatory environments, and strict product market regulation in particular, reduce the degree of market experimentation by firms, which in turn reduces the system ability to adopt new technologies, whenever they become available. While it is not obvious that a system that facilitates market experimentation is more efficient at all times, since too much churning can lead to waste of resources and high adjustment costs for all those involved, it appears that in periods of fervid technological innovation, such as those that followed the ICT revolution, an institutional system "experimentation-friendly" may allow a quicker adoption and diffusion of new technologies, with enhancing effects on productivity.

III: ICT, *the digital economy and productivity differences between advanced and developing economies*

The first part of the book makes the case that the availability of ICT technologies was not per se a factor leading to faster convergence across industrialized countries. If anything, the ICT revolution made productivity performance across countries more heterogeneous, not least because cross-country differences in policy and institutional settings created different incentives to adopt ICT. Those findings challenge to the naïve view of the internet and the ICT revolution. Such view suggests that a fast movement toward a digital economy could create the conditions for a much more competitive world, a world that would equalize business opportunities within countries and, perhaps more importantly, across advanced and developing economies. With respect to developing countries, the view is that ICT access would lower barriers to entry of firms based in developing countries into the markets of advanced economies. This phenomenon should happen for both intermediate markets(business to business), as well as for final goods markets(business to consumer). The second part of the book argues that these equalizing forces of the ICT revolution, albeit not irrelevant, are not sufficient for reducing significantly disparities across countries, since other important features work in opposite directions. In other words, internet and the ICT revolution are not the great equalizers, and economic distance between industrial and developing countries is not going to be reduced across the board.

More specifically, there are three features of the ICT revolution that make the equalizing potential so difficult to realize in practice. The first is the fact that information is quite often not digitizable, since most business transactions require face to face (F2F) interactions. ICT equipments can certainly increase the speed at which different types of business transactions are executed, but rarely are complex transactions closed without physical connections. Relatedly, only a small fraction of the goods and services traded internationally (software, audio and video clips, books and other documents, etc...) can be fully digitized so that delivery is possible via the internet or some other communications medium. These constraints can have a major impact on the ability of developing country based firms to penetrate into the more advanced markets. An interesting case study in this respect is the world market for cut flowers, where South African exporters pay high transportation costs for sending their flowers first to trading auctions in Amsterdam, whence they are re-shipped to the final destination, which can be anywhere in the world. Flowers can be thought as an experience good for which an online image is not an adequate substitute.

The second ICT obstacle to a cross country equalization of opportunities has to do with the inherent complexity of digitally based business transactions. In practice, digital transactions are often accompanied by sophisticated side transactions. Indeed, when concluding business on line, buyers and sellers have to deal with many third parties, which specialize in technical dimensions in support of the main transaction, such as the security of the financial deal, the security of the delivery, as well as certification of what is exchanged. In other words, the Internet quite often raises the complexity of a given transaction. Consider the case of buying a book. The casual buyer goes to the bookshop, pays for instance in cash and leaves the shop carrying his book. Buying on line is more complex. The transaction now depends on a number of intermediate products which involves logistics, security of transaction, security of delivery. Paradoxically, suppliers of these products/services may see their role and their rents increased, rather than decreased, by the emergence of the digital economy. In addition, the faceless nature of digital transactions requires high levels of truth, to which brand and reputation contribute importantly. Whereas the internet technology can lower barriers to entry into certain markets, reputational costs tend to restore them. Thus, the report shows that the complementary demands placed on internet-using firms (for on-time delivery, transactions security, etc...), the limited digitizability of many commodities (hence the continued importance of traditional infrastructural and regulatory constraints), and the reputation costs of online business are important factors in explaining why producers from developing countries find ICT of limited use thus far in penetrating into the brand markets of advanced economies.

The third obstacle to cross country equalization refers to the agglomeration forces inherent in an ICT based economy. This is partly a story of increasing returns to scale, as suggested by two obvious examples: the Silicon Valley in California and the Bangalore software industry in India, the latter being an obvious success case in the developing world. But the ICT revolution is more than increasing returns to scale. A key new development in business organization, just in time production, has been greatly facilitated by ICT diffusion, e.g., in inventory and supply chain management. But delivering goods just in time imposes a constraint on the location of suppliers, who cannot be too far from consumers. One implication is that, according to a common rule of thumb, suppliers need to be within a 24 hours truck journey from the client, and in the car industry case we actually observe suppliers that co-locate with assemblers.

In terms of economic development policy, it seems that ICT in general, and the internet in particular, have changed "very little". Indeed, the policy and institutional constraints on growth emphasized by the existing development literature largely dominate the possible benefits linked to ICT adoption. In this respect, the main policy conclusion is that institutional and governance obstacles to development are still relevant in a digital world. But the book shows that for specific entrepreneurs and sectors, the impact of ICT could be relatively important. In these cases, gradually diminishing trade and other policy distortions become a necessary step for exploiting the positive effects of the ICT revolution.

In all the industries analysed, ICT and internet are affecting the forms of production and exchange, the nature of corporate behaviour, and the terms of competition. But in light of the forces analysed above, it is not clear whether the new distribution of costs and profits is unquestionably supportive of the development process. The Bangalore example shows that, provided some basic requirements are met—such as a relatively abundant and well-educated workforce and reliable telecommunications and electricity supplies—the transmission in digital form of codifiable and storable information from remote locations via computer networks is straightforward. The situation is much more complicated for production-supporting activities that make intensive use of information that requires complex, repeated face-to-face interaction for effective communication. Furthermore, e-business readiness depend on key governance dimensions—such as consumer protection, security of transactions, privacy of records and intellectual property protection—that remain weak in much of the developing world. As a result, the full exploitation of the new technology by developing countries, whatever its eventual impact, is further delayed by these institutional constraints.

Daniel Cohen, Pietro Garibaldi, Stefano Scarpetta

REFERENCES

David, P., and G. Wright (1999) General Purpose Technology and Surges in Productivity: Historical Reflections on the Future of the ICT Revolution, unpublished, Stanford University.

Jorgenson, P., and K. Stiroh (1995) Computer Investment, Capital and Productivity in the US Economics of Innovation and New Technology 4 (3–4).

PART I

THE SPREAD OF ICT AND PRODUCTIVITY GROWTH: IS EUROPE REALLY LAGGING BEHIND IN THE NEW ECONOMY?

Edited by Stefano Scarpetta

with

Eric Bartelsman, Andrea Bassanini, John Haltiwanger, Ronald S. Jarmin, and Thorsten Schank*

* Stefano Scarpetta is at the World Bank; Eric Bartelsman is at Free University, Amsterdam and Statistics, The Netherlands; Andrea is at the OECD; John Haltiwanger is at the University of Maryland and U.S. Census Bureau; Ron Jarmin is at the Center for Economic Studies, U.S. Census Bureau; and Thorsten Schank is at Universität Erlangen-Nürnberg and IAB. We thank Tito Boeri, Pietro Garibaldi, Paul Geroski, Robert Gordon, and Alan Krueger for their useful comments. Any findings, opinions or conclusions are those of the authors and do not necessarily reflect the views of the organizations of affiliation.

Introduction and Overview[1]

Understanding the sources of economic growth and how policy could affect them has always been at the heart of the debate amongst economists and policy makers. Yet, growth patterns of the past decade have raised even further the interest on these issues. This is because a number of stylized facts on economic growth have been severely challenged by recent events. For example, convergence in output per capita and productivity levels was a maintained hypothesis of macro economists, at least for OECD countries that share common technologies, have intense inter-country trade and incur substantial foreign direct investment. But significant growth divergence occurred in the 1990s across OECD countries, with some affluent economies—such as the United States, that already was at the world productivity frontier in many industries—pulling ahead of the others. Along the same lines, economists have struggled for many years to find a rationale for the so-called *productivity paradox* (generally attributed to Robert Solow): namely, why, when we are confronted by rapid changes in the quality and variety of high-tech products in our day-to-day lives, do the macro data show an inexorable slowing down in multi factor productivity (a proxy for technological progress)? Yet, in the 1990s, a number of countries, including the United States but also some smaller economies, showed clear signs of a pick up in multifactor productivity growth rates. Moreover, economists and policy makers became used, especially in Europe, to the fact that expanding the employment base comes at the expense of labour productivity growth, because the unemployed and inactive are relatively low skilled. Again, recent evidence challenges this view: in the 1990s, productivity growth was accompanied by sustained employment growth in, for example in the United States, Australia and Ireland.

Recent studies seem to agree that the observed changes in growth patterns in some countries can be attributed in part to the information and communication technology (ICT) revolution. In particular, they argue that countries where the business sector has been quick in shifting resources towards the ICT industry and in adopting highly productive ICT equipment, have been able to

[1] This study is a joint effort of all its authors. However, Chapter 1 was drafted by Andrea Bassanini and Stefano Scarpetta; Chapter 2 by Eric Bartelsman and Stefano Scarpetta; Chapter 3 by Ron Jarmin, John Haltiwanger and Thorsten Schank; Chapter 4 by Eric Bartelsman and John Haltiwanger; and Chapter 5 by Andrea Bassanini and Stefano Scarpetta.

reap higher output and productivity growth rates. In this respect, the United States and some smaller countries (e.g. Australia, Ireland) were able to benefit most from the ICT revolution, while most large European economies are still lagging behind. A possible explanation for this is that 'old institutions' have somehow slowed down the spread of ICT in Europe. For example, rigidities in product, labour and financial markets may have reduced incentives of firms to shift rapidly to ICT and to adjust production processes and other factor inputs accordingly.

The economic slowdown of 2000–2002 has added more food for thought to this discussion. It has certainly laid to rest one myth—the end of the business cycle due to the spread of ICT. Two characteristics of ICT were thought to smooth business cycles fluctuations. First, the short life of much ICT equipment was assumed to flatten investment cycles. Second, faster and broader communication amongst producers, on the one hand, and between producers and consumers, on the other hand, was expected to improve the matching between demand and supply. Neither factor has been able, at least so far, to prevent the OECD economies from experiencing an economic slow down.

More fundamentally, however, the recent weakness of most OECD economies, associated with the failure of many dotcoms and the generalized collapse of ICT stocks have reinforced the sceptical view that the ICT revolution was short lived and largely driven by unsustainable, or one-shot, factors (e.g. huge drops in computer prices, the introduction of Internet, the building up of fiber-optic telecom etc.). So the crucial question is whether, on the basis of available (albeit imperfect) data, one can identify any shift in growth trends, at least in some countries and, if so, assess whether this shift has been encouraged (or discouraged) by policy and institutional settings and reforms therein.

This study addresses this question by exploiting harmonized macro and sectoral data for the OECD countries as well as firm-level data for a sample of them and establishment-level data for the US and German manufacturing sectors. These various data allow us to examine recent growth trends and analyse the link between ICT investment and productivity at the macro, sectoral and micro levels. In particular, we use aggregate data to document widening productivity disparities and to assess contributing factors. We then use firm-turnover measures and related decompositions of industry-level productivity dynamics to explore the role of economic flexibility and adaptability for output and productivity growth. Furthermore, we use establishment-level data to examine the strategies of individual businesses in adopting ICT as evidenced by productivity, wage and skill differences across businesses. Finally, we make an attempt to link empirically differences in innovation and adoption across countries, industries and firms with specific institutional and policy settings that may have a bearing on them.

This analysis allows us to address a number of specific questions. What factors explain differences in macro and sectoral output and productivity performance across OECD countries? What roles do the ICT-producing industries and ICT-driven capital deepening play in explaining the different growth patterns of countries? Is there a relationship between innovation intensity (e.g. R&D) and the spread of ICT? Does the adoption of ICT require organizational changes and/or changes in the composition of inputs? What is the contribution of new firms to overall productivity growth in general and in ICT-related sectors? Do ICT-industries show stronger firm and employment turnover rates? In this respect, is there any relationship between the spread of ICT and institutional features of the product and labour markets? Do differences in policy and institutions explain different patterns of adoption of new technologies?

We begin our analysis (Chapter 1) by reviewing recent aggregate growth trends and decomposing growth into the main driving forces using a standard growth accounting technique. Albeit simple in theory, this task is difficult in practice. First, there are differences among countries in the statistical measures of output in some service sectors, and of quality changes in information technology products. Our study makes use of internationally harmonized price deflators for ICT equipment. Second, business cycles have been largely unsynchronized across OECD countries over the past decade, hampering comparability of international growth patterns. Our study spends considerable effort on cyclically adjusting the data series, whenever possible.

Macro data clearly point to widening disparities in growth performance across the OECD countries, even using cyclically-adjusted series. These disparities reflect differences in labour utilization rather than widening differences in labour productivity growth rates: that is, higher growth rates in output per capita observed in a number of countries have been accompanied by improvements in the utilization of labour, while sluggish employment in others (mainly in continental Europe) have not been fully compensated by higher labour productivity growth, thereby leading to a further slowdown in output growth.

There are also some new factors behind the observed disparities in growth performance across the OECD countries. In particular, multifactor productivity (MFP), a proxy for technological change, accelerated in a number of OECD countries, most notably in the United States and Canada, but also in some small economies (e.g. Australia, Ireland). The acceleration of MFP growth seems to have started initially as a pure 'disembodied' phenomenon (i.e. the productivity acceleration of the ICT-producing industry), consistent with the idea of a slow diffusion of a new general-purpose technology. As the ICT revolution progressed, intensive ICT-using industries increasingly contributed to overall productivity growth (although data limitations about the users of ICT by industry make this inference difficult). The slow diffusion hypothesis is also consistent with the fact that MFP growth accelerated somewhat later in other OECD countries that did not have a sizeable ICT-producing industry.

Why have some countries, including some small European ones, been able to develop an ICT-producing industry and, even more importantly, quickly adopt information and communications technology? To address this question, in Chapter 2 we go beyond aggregate data and look at the sectoral evolution of the OECD economies. We focus on the role of firm dynamics (the entry, expansion and exit of firms in each market) for productivity growth and adoption of technologies. Our results indicate that aggregate productivity patterns are largely the result of within-industry and even within-firm performance in most countries. Even so, ICT-related industries (both producers and users of ICT), on balance, have had stronger than average productivity growth over the past decade, and have made a major contribution to overall productivity growth in manufacturing and some service sectors. In turn, the strong productivity growth of ICT-related industries has also been driven by the entry of high performing new firms, while in other, more mature, industries the contribution of new firms has been more varied across countries.

Our sectoral analysis also reveals important cross-country differences. The US economy seems to be better able to acquire comparative advantage in rapidly growing ICT market segments than most of its trading partners. The US also has experienced a more widespread productivity acceleration of ICT-user industries, while the only notable acceleration in Europe has occurred in the finance sector. We seek to find an explanation for these cross-country differences by looking at firm and establishment level data. They suggest a higher degree of *'market experimentation'* in the United States compared with Europe, even if aggregate turnover rates are similar. We reach this conclusion by observing three interrelated features of firms' behaviour in the US compared with Europe: (i) a smaller (especially relative to industry average) size of entering firms; (ii) a lower (albeit with greater variability) level of labour productivity of entrants relative to the average incumbent; and (iii) a much stronger (employment) expansion of successful entrants in the initial years. Put in another way, our findings suggest that in the US new firms tend to be smaller (relative to average incumbent) and less productive when compared with their European counterparts, but, if successful, they also tend to grow much more rapidly.

We further test our working hypothesis of greater market experimentation in the US compared with Europe by using confidential establishment-level micro data from the US and Germany (Chapter 3). We indeed find some confirmation for this hypothesis: there is greater experimentation amongst young businesses and there is greater experimentation among businesses actively changing their technology in the US compared to Germany. The experimentation manifests itself empirically in systematic differences in the dispersion of productivity and in the related dispersion of key choices, like investment and skill mix and the role of Internet access. The evidence also indicates that the mean impact of adopting new technology is greater in US than in Germany. Putting the pieces together our evidence suggests that US businesses choose a higher mean outcome, but higher variance strategy in adopting new technology.

The next step in our analysis is to understand whether these cross-country differences in innovation, adoption of new technologies (ICT) and market experimentation are, at least partially, related to differences in underlying market and institutional framework conditions. In Chapter 4 we draw on economic theory to establish conceptually which institutional and policy factors are most likely to bear responsibility in influencing these factors. To do this, the different potential economic effects of ICT are reviewed in turn. The traditional effects of ICT can be found by tracking production of ICT goods and services, or by calculating the contribution of ICT assets. More interesting is the role of ICT in promoting MFP growth which is associated with the view of ICT investment as an explicit innovative activity. It is in context that market and institutional conditions have their greatest impact, by influencing innovation and adoption of new technologies by incumbent firms as well as the degree of market experimentation of both new entrepreneurs and existing firms. We see that product market competition affects the share of firms willing to undertake risky innovative investments. In a related manner, labour market regulations may be such that it becomes costlier up front to partake in the innovative activity. This can occur either because it is difficult or expensive to adjust the labour force to match the new technology, or because it is expensive to increase or decrease the labour force to adjust output following the uncertain outcome of the innovative gamble. Further, factor market regulations may restrict the degree to which firms are able to experiment in finding the best combination of technology, organizational structure, and relationship with customers and suppliers.

Although there is a consensus that increased product market competition and market-friendly institutional settings are likely to have positive effects on innovation and the adoption of new technologies, there is no agreement on their empirical relevance. Chapter 5 checks some of the predictions of the theoretical analysis by looking at the comparative experience of the OECD countries in terms of sectoral MFP and the intensity of innovative activity (as proxied by R&D intensity). To date, the empirical evidence on the linkages between product market competition and productivity and innovation is limited due to a lack of adequate indicators of the intensity of competition, especially in a cross-country context. Commonly used indicators of competition (such as mark-ups or concentration indexes) are typically endogenous to productivity and innovation and it is often difficult to find suitable instruments. In addition, these indicators are likely to be non-monotonic with respect to common notions of competition and, in any event, do not have a direct link to policy or regulations, making it difficult to draw clear policy conclusions from their use. In light of these problems, we take a different approach. Namely, since the degree of competition in the product market and the adaptability of labour markets are not directly measurable, we use some of their possible policy determinants as proxies, for example, regulatory provisions. This is made possible by a novel set of quantitative indicators of cross-country differences in the stringency of the product and labour market regulatory environments in OECD economies.

Our results suggest that stringent regulatory settings in product and labour markets may help explain cross-country differences in innovative activity and technology adoption, thus providing an interpretation for the growth patterns discussed in the first three chapters of our study. It should be noted, however, that the impact of regulations and institutions on productivity performance and innovation seems to depend on certain market and technology conditions, as well as on specific firm characteristics. In particular, the burden of strict product market regulations on productivity seems to be greater, the further a given country/industry is from the technology frontier. That is, strict regulation hinders the adoption of existing technologies, possibly because it reduces competitive pressures or technology spillovers, and restricts the entry of new high-tech firms. In addition, strict product market regulations have a significant negative impact on the process of innovation itself. Thus, given the strong impact of R&D on productivity, there is also an indirect channel whereby strict product market regulations may reduce the scope for productivity enhancement.

The effect of high hiring and firing costs (proxied by the strictness of employment protection legislation, EPL) on productivity and innovation is less clear cut, and largely depends on the institutional system in which firms operate and the type of technology used in the sector. Firms facing high hiring and firing costs will tend to rely more on the internal labour market (e.g. training) than on the external one if they have to adjust the workforce to exploit a new technology. However, if they cannot rely on an institutional device to tackle possible free-riding problems (e.g. in un-coordinated bargaining regimes), then investing in internal labour market is risky, because other firms may poach on the pool of trained workers. Thus, when institutional settings do not allow wages or internal training to offset high hiring and firing costs, then the latter may lead to sub-optimal adjustments of the workforce to technology changes and lower productivity performance. Consistent with this view, we find that strict EPL has a negative impact on innovation in countries lacking co-ordination, while we find no significant impact of labour market flexibility in co-ordinated countries (or even a negative impact in some industries).

Where do these findings leave us with respect to our initial questions as to the existence of a structural shift in the growth patterns in some countries and the possible role of policy and institutions in influencing this shift? We can argue that the widening of growth disparities across the OECD countries are real and cannot be fully attributed to differences in business cycle conditions. It is also comforting to see that even in the most recent years not covered in our analysis they have persisted. These disparities in growth patterns are due to a combination of 'traditional' and 'new' economy factors. Therefore, a combination of traditional and new therapies may be required for those countries, including most large European economies that are lagging behind in terms of output and productivity growth. The traditional part of the story largely refers to the inability of some countries to employ certain groups in the labour force, namely the low skilled. This has been the subject of a vast literature and policy prescriptions to overcome this problem have been formulated by many academic researchers and international institutions. The good news is that the recent experience of certain countries suggests that it is possible to widen the employment base without necessarily facing deterioration in productivity performance. It may be argued that this is because of the spread of ICT that has enhanced labour productivity potentials even amongst the low skilled segments of the workforce.

The spread of ICT has also been very different across countries and this has also contributed to widening growth disparities. Moreover, in certain industrial relations regimes, innovation and adoption of new technologies seem to be negatively affected by the stringency of certain regulations in the labour market, creating a possible synergy between labour market reforms, the spread of ICT and ultimately improvements in employment and output.

In the paper we also provide evidence that strict regulations in the product market, by reducing competitive pressures, have a negative impact on innovation and adoption of new technologies, including ICT. In particular, anti-competitive regulations seem to hamper productivity growth, and the effect is stronger in those industries where countries have accumulated significant technology gaps (possibly including ICT industries). In turn, these gaps are explained by the effects of strict product and labour market regulations on the process of innovation that, among the high-tech industries, seem to be more negative in industries with multiple technological trajectories. To the extent that important domains of the ICT industry are dominated by the frequent changes in the leading technology (e.g. in the software industry), these results may help to explain why some European countries, while enjoying leading positions in industries with cumulative technologies (such as aircrafts or motor vehicles) have been slow in moving into the ICT industry.

The micro evidence reported in the paper offers additional elements to our discussion of a growth-enhancing policy setting. Our results seem to suggest that certain institutional and regulatory settings may reduce the degree of market experimentation by firms. This, in turn, could lower the speed with which a country shifts to a new technology, thereby offering an interpretation to the observed differences in innovation and adoption across the Atlantic. For example, low administrative costs of start-ups and not unduly strict regulations on labour adjustments in the United States, may stimulate potential entrepreneurs to start on a small scale, test the market and, if successful with their business plan, expand rapidly to reach the minimum efficient scale. In contrast, higher entry and adjustment costs in Europe may stimulate a pre-market selection of business plans with less market experimentation. In addition, the more market-based financial system in the United States compared with Europe may lead to a lower risk aversion to project financing, with greater financing possibilities for entrepreneurs with small or innovative projects, often characterized by limited cash flows and lack of collateral. On the basis of available data, it is difficult for us to conclude that greater market experimentation is always good for economic growth. On the one hand, greater experimentation may strengthen innovation in new areas and quicken adoption of new technologies. On the other hand, however, it may lead to excessive dynamics, with 'stepping on toes' and business stealing also producing negative externalities. Nevertheless, in a period (like the past decade) of rapid diffusion of a new general-purpose technology (ICT), greater experimentation may allow new ideas and forms of production to emerge more rapidly. Moreover, if ICT equipment also fosters innovation activity in other areas, then having a lead in its development may generate important synergies, with additional positive effects for the economy as a whole. These are amongst the research issues that may be worth developing in future studies.

1

The Role of ICT in Shaping Growth Patterns in the United States and other OECD Countries?—Some Aggregate Evidence

This chapter presents some evidence on aggregate economic patterns in the Organization for Economic Cooperation and Development (OECD) countries and on the role of the information and communication technology (ICT). Papers from the United States have been suggesting that ICT has played an important role in boosting output growth, especially in the second half of the 1990s, and some suggest that, despite the most recent weakness of the ICT sector, it has the potential for sustaining growth over the medium term. More sceptical reports from European countries either deny the link between ICT and growth or show that they have not yet materialized. This chapter reviews cross-country evidence for several indicators of aggregate economic growth: real gross domestic product (GDP; the usual summary measure of economic activity); GDP per capita (an indicator of the average economic welfare of the population); labour productivity; and multifactor productivity (MFP; a pointer to, among other things, technological progress). Next, indicators of the production and use of ICT show how its importance varies over time and across OECD countries. Finally, the chapter concludes with an indication of how ICT impacts on the observed aggregate growth patterns.

1.1. SOME STYLIZED FACTS ABOUT GDP GROWTH AND ITS MAIN DRIVERS

To set the stage for the remainder of this chapter, and indeed this report, we need to confront our opinions and hunches on the 'new economy' with the aggregate evidence on economic performance of the past decade relative to historical patterns. Before starting our discussion on the observed growth patterns across the OECD countries, it is important to recall how difficult it is to make such comparisons. Indeed, the coverage and depth of analysis in all this report is constrained by the availability, accuracy, and international comparability of economic statistics at the different levels of the analysis (macro, sectoral, and micro).

Despite continuous efforts to improve the quality and international compar-ability of time series of outputs, inputs, and productivity, a number of meas-urement issues still arise at the aggregate and especially at the disaggregated levels. Three general issues that affect international comparisons of output measures are: (1) the independence of output from input measures; (2) the use of chain and fixed-weighted indices; and (3) the treatment of price indices of ICT products. The first issue is important especially for those industries that mainly comprise non-market producers (such as health or education), where output volume series are often based on the extrapolation of input measures, generating a downward bias within each country.[1] Moreover, annual chain-weighted indices are used in a small number of OECD countries instead of fixed base years for the construction of time series of outputs, inputs, and productivity. Annual chain-weighted indices minimize the substitution bias implicit in fixed-weight price and volume indices, which occurs in periods of rapid change of relative prices and quantities or over long time periods. Finally, the method to construct price indices of computers and peripheral equipment varies between OECD countries (see Box 1.1).

In our analysis, we use data provided by the national authorities and included in the OECD *Economic Outlook* database. However, adjustments were necessary to improve international comparability, especially with respect to the way in which changes in the quality of ICT is taken into account (see Box 1.1).[2] Notwithstanding the efforts made, statements about relative growth performance, in particular at the sectoral level, have to be read with these caveats in mind, and results should be interpreted with the necessary care.

A final issue that is important in an international comparison of growth performance in the short to medium term is that cross-country differences in output growth rates and levels may reflect differences in cyclical positions as well as underlying differences in performance (e.g. see Gordon, 2000, 2002). This problem was particularly relevant in the 1990s when business cycles were largely unsynchronized across OECD countries. In order to account for differences in the cyclical position of countries, we largely rely on *trend series* as opposed to actual series. Trend series were estimated at the OECD (see Scarpetta *et al.*, 2000 for more details) using an extended version of the Hodrick–Prescott filter (Hodrick and Prescott, 1997) where the well-known end-of-sample problem is minimized by prolonging the time series out of the sample using OECD medium-term projections. Given the assumptions included in the OECD projections, this can be considered as a prudent approach, insofar as it underestimates sharp deviations from the historical pattern in the neigh-bourhood of the end of the sample. This is particularly important for this analysis, since the significant slowdown in the US economy in 2000–2002 has

[1] The extent of the underestimation is difficult to determine, although The Bureau of Labor Statistics suggests that the order of magnitude is unlikely to be very large (Dean, 1999).
[2] Details are discussed in Scarpetta *et al.* (2000).

raised concerns as to the sustainability of the growth patterns of the late 1990s over the medium term.[3]

Bearing these caveats in mind, our first pass at the data is to look at the development of GDP per capita over time to see whether there is any evidence of shifts in the growth path of OECD countries owing to increased penetration of ICT throughout the economy. Figure 1.1 suggests that, for the OECD area as a whole, trend GDP per capita growth rates slowed down in the 1990s compared with the previous decade. However, there has been a fairly widespread pickup in growth in the second half of the decade (with the exception of Korea, Japan,

---

Box 1.1. *Price indices for ICT goods*

One element that is particularly important for our analysis is the treatment of price indices of information technology products, in particular, computers. The significant quality improvements associated with technological advances in ICT have to be taken into account in the construction of ICT price indices. The use of hedonic deflators is generally considered as the best way to address this problem, and a number of OECD countries use them to deflate output in the computer industry.[1] In the case of the United States, hedonic deflation methods are applied to most components of ICT investment. Other countries (e.g. Canada, Japan, and France) have recently introduced some hedonic adjustment for the measurement of real computer investment and sometimes base their deflators on the US ones. Other countries make no adjustment for quality changes in ICT investment.

Any international comparison of ICT cannot overlook this problem but, at the same time, the harmonization of deflators is not an easy task, not least because there are differences in industrial specialization; that is, only few countries produce computers or semiconductors, many only produce peripheral equipment. Bearing this caveat in mind, our analysis uses 'harmonized' price indices for ICT products to control some of the international differences in deflation methods that might affect the comparability of the results. The 'harmonized' series assumes that price ratios between ICT and non-ICT products have the same time patterns across countries, with the United States as the benchmark. For more details on this approach, see Schreyer (2000). The Figure below shows the actual and harmonized price deflators for computers used in this study for the eight countries for which details on different types of capital are available.

---

[1] Hedonic deflators are not the only measurement problem for the ICT manufacturing sector. The correct measurement of input prices for these industries is also quite complicated, and demands detailed input–output tables as well as hedonic deflators for certain inputs.

---

[3] A detailed sensitivity analysis of trend series using variants of the extended H-P filter and different approaches to deal with the end-of-sample problem yielded broadly similar results. In particular, Scarpetta *et al.* (2000) experimented with a multivariate filter in which structural employment is obtained via a Philips curve and trend output is obtained by estimating an Okun-type relation. Moreover, they tested the robustness of results by prolonging actual data out of the sample using average growth rates (observed over the 1980s and 1990s) instead of the OECD medium-term projections.

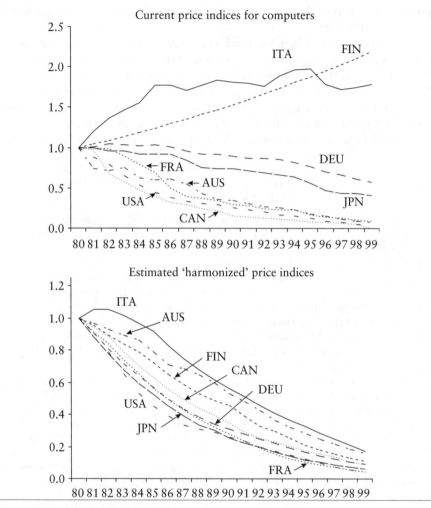

Current price indices for computers

Estimated 'harmonized' price indices

Source: Colecchia and Schreyer (2002).

and Turkey). This aggregate pattern, however, hides persistent differences across countries. Amongst the G-7, Canada and to a lesser extent the United States were able to reverse the slowdown in growth performance observed since the early 1970s, while the other countries experienced declining growth (particularly Japan and Italy). Outside the G-7, however, several smaller OECD countries also were able to reverse the slowdown in GDP per capita growth. It is noticeable that disparities in growth performance were particularly marked within Europe, with most of the large countries experiencing a significant slowdown in GDP per capita growth and some (mainly small) economies showing acceleration in growth. Overall, however, better performance in these small

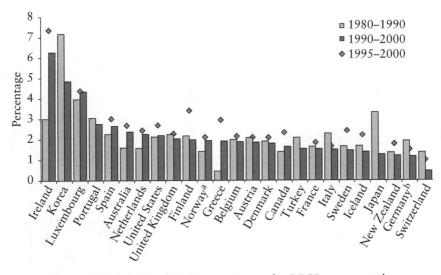

Figure 1.1. *Growth of GDP per capita in the OECD area over the 1980s and the 1990s*

ᵃ Including offshore activities.
ᵇ 1991–2000 instead of 1990–2000, western Germany in 1980s.

Source: Bassanini and Scarpetta (2002*a*).

economies has not fully offset declines in the other countries, and growth in the EU15 area declined in the 1990s.

1.1.1. *Labour utilization and productivity lay behind widening growth disparities*

Table 1.1 presents a decomposition of GDP growth in the business sector into its main drivers, mainly total hours growth and the growth rate of hourly labour productivity.[4] Moreover, it further decomposes labour productivity growth into a capital deepening effect (due to a change in the capital/labour ratio) and technological progress, the latter proxied by the growth rate in MFP.

Labour productivity growth accounts for at least half of GDP per capita growth in most OECD countries and considerably more than that in many of them. Notwithstanding differences in labour productivity growth rates across

---

[4] The focus on the business sector is due to the inherent difficulties in measuring output and capital stock for the government sector. Moreover, trend series avoid picking up idiosyncratic movements in output and inputs. Moreover, since the focus of the table is on the 1990s, we did not include the effects on GDP growth of demographic changes. Indeed, for most countries, the share of the working-age population in the total population changed only marginally over the 1990s. Countries with significant changes are those with a rapidly evolving age structure due to strong population growth (Korea) and changes in migration flows (e.g. Ireland).

Table 1.1. *Decomposition of growth performance 1990–2000 (summary of business sector GDP growth and its components)*

	GDP			Total hours			Labour productivity			Capital deepening			MFP		
	1980–1990[a]	1990–2000[b]	1996–2000[c]	1980–1990[a]	1990–2000[b]	1996–2000[c]	1980–1990[a]	1990–2000[b]	1996–2000[c]	1980–1990[d]	1990–2000[e]	1996–2000[f]	1980–1990[d]	1990–2000[e]	1996–2000[f]
United States	3.3	3.6	4.1	2.0	2.2	2.5	1.3	1.4	1.6	2.9	2.5	3.0	0.9	1.1	1.3
Japan	4.1	1.7	1.0	0.7	-0.6	-0.9	2.3	2.3	1.9	6.5	5.1	4.3	2.2	1.0	0.7
Germany	2.3	1.8	2.1	-0.2	-0.1	-0.5	2.5	1.9	1.6	3.7	3.2	3.0	1.5	0.9	0.8
France	2.3	2.1	2.6	-0.9	0.1	0.8	3.2	2.0	1.8	4.0	3.1	2.7	1.9	1.0	1.1
Italy	2.5	1.9	2.1	0.1	-0.1	0.5	2.4	2.0	1.6	3.2	3.0	3.0	1.5	0.7	0.7
United Kingdom	3.1	2.0	2.6	0.7	0.7	1.2	2.3	1.4	1.5	2.8	2.8	2.8	1.0	0.7	1.0
Canada	2.7	3.1	4.0	1.5	1.6	2.4	1.2	1.5	1.6	3.5	1.4	0.9	0.6	1.3	1.7
Australia	3.5	4.1	4.5	2.1	2.0	2.2	1.4	2.1	2.2	4.4	4.1	4.5	0.6	1.3	1.4
Austria	2.4	2.7	2.6	0.2	0.1	0.0	2.7	2.6	2.7	4.4	4.4	4.3	1.8	1.6	1.5
Belgium	2.6	2.1	2.2	0.0	-0.1	0.1	2.6	2.3	2.2	3.4	3.8	3.8	1.7	1.2	1.2
Denmark	2.2	2.6	3.1	0.3	0.3	1.0	1.9	2.3	2.1	3.8	2.5	2.4	1.0	1.5	1.4
Finland	2.6	2.9	4.9	-1.0	-0.7	1.5	3.7	3.7	3.3	3.2	0.8	0.7	2.4	3.2	3.6
Greece	0.7	2.1	2.8	0.2	0.7	0.8	0.6	1.4	2.0	0.4	2.2	3.5	0.6	0.8	0.9
Ireland	4.4	7.4	8.7	0.1	2.8	4.1	4.3	4.5	4.4	2.7	3.3	—	3.6	4.4	—
Netherlands	2.2	3.1	3.4	-1.1	0.9	1.7	3.3	2.1	1.6	3.6	3.4	3.5	2.3	1.6	1.2
New Zealand	1.3	2.9	3.3	-0.1	2.1	2.3	1.4	0.7	0.9	3.1	2.2	2.5	0.2	0.8	0.9
Norway	1.4	2.5	2.9	-0.5	0.2	1.0	1.9	2.2	1.8	2.7	2.1	2.9	1.2	1.7	1.3
Portugal	3.7	2.1	—	0.7	-0.4	—	3.0	2.5	—	—	—	—	—	—	—
Spain	2.4	2.9	3.5	-1.0	1.1	2.4	3.5	1.8	1.1	4.4	4.2	3.9	2.1	0.7	0.5
Sweden	2.1	2.4	3.4	0.5	0.2	1.5	1.6	2.2	1.9	2.0	1.5	—	1.0	1.4	—
Switzerland	1.7	0.5	—	—	0.1	0.1	—	0.3	—	—	2.7	—	—	—	—
Korea	9.2	6.1	4.1	2.0	1.0	0.3	7.0	5.0	3.8	—	—	—	—	—	—
Weighted average															
EU15[g]	2.5	2.2	2.6	-0.2	0.3	0.9	2.7	1.9	1.6	3.4	3.1	2.9	1.5	1.0	0.9
OECD24[h]	3.1	2.7	3.0	0.9	1.0	1.3	2.1	1.7	1.7	3.7	3.1	3.1	1.3	1.1	1.1
Standard deviation															
EU15[g]	0.84	1.40	1.77	0.64	0.85	1.09	0.93	0.84	0.89	1.09	1.01	0.96	0.77	1.07	0.82
OECD24[h]	0.91	1.31	1.59	0.92	0.99	1.15	0.99	0.89	0.79	1.21	1.08	1.06	0.81	0.90	0.68

[a] 1983–1990 for Belgium, Denmark, Greece, and Ireland, 1985–1990 for Austria and New Zealand, 1986–1990 for Portugal.

[b] 1991–1996 for Switzerland, 1990–1997 for Austria, Belgium, and New Zealand, 1990–1998 for Ireland, Korea, and Netherlands, 1990–1999 for Denmark, Greece, Japan, and United Kingdom.

[c] 1996–1997 for Austria, Belgium, and New Zealand, 1996–1998 for Ireland, Korea, and Netherlands, 1996–1999 for Denmark, Greece, Japan, and United Kingdom.

[d] 1983–1990 for Belgium, Denmark, Greece, and Ireland, 1985–1990 for Austria and New Zealand, 1987–1990 for United Kingdom.

[e] 1991–1996 for Switzerland, 1990–1996 for Ireland and Sweden, 1990–1997 for Austria, Belgium, New Zealand, and United Kingdom, 1990–1998 for Netherlands, 1990–1999 for Australia, Denmark, France, Greece, Italy, and Japan.

[f] 1996–1997 for Austria, Belgium, New Zealand, and United Kingdom, 1996–1998 for Netherlands, 1996–1999 for Australia, Denmark, France, Greece, Italy, and Japan.

[g] Excluding Luxembourg.

[h] Excluding Czech Republic, Hungary, Iceland, Korea, Luxembourg, Mexico, Poland, Slovak Republic, and Turkey.

Source: OECD (2003).

countries, it is noticeable that the overall dispersion (proxied by the standard deviation across countries) did not change in the 1990s as compared with the 1980s, despite the significant widening of GDP per capita growth rates discussed above.

A key factor to reconcile growing disparities in GDP growth rates in a context of broadly stable differences in labour productivity growth is a divergence in the growth rates of employment and average hours worked. Significant increases in labour utilization (employment plus hours) in Ireland, Netherlands, Spain, United States, and Australia contrast sharply with slumps in Japan, Germany, Finland, and Portugal and, to a lesser extent, Italy and Belgium.[5] Notably, the United States is the only clear case where both hours worked and employment rates increased in the 1990s by a significant amount.

Labour productivity growth can be further decomposed into changes in the capital/labour ratio—which in turn depends upon the rate of growth in fixed capital formation and/or changes in employment—and the efficiency with which factor inputs are used in the production process, that is MFP growth. The estimates of MFP growth reported in Table 1.1 are computed using total hours worked and gross capital stock as factor inputs (*i.e. without any adjustment for* changes in the quality and composition of labour and capital inputs). This is the broadest measure of productivity growth that incorporates the effects of progress in human capital as well as embodied (in physical capital) and disembodied technological progress.[6]

Table 1.1 suggests that a number of countries, during the 1990s, were able to raise labour productivity by fostering technical progress rather than by substituting labour with capital. Indeed Ireland, Australia, Canada, Norway, and New Zealand experienced acceleration in the average growth rates of MFP of at least 0.5 percentage points over the 1990s (in most cases from relatively low levels in the 1980s) together with a high or even rising pace of employment growth. In contrast, in Sweden and Finland, increases in MFP growth rates have been accompanied by significant falls in employment rates.[7] At the same time, the United States recorded a somewhat smaller recovery in MFP growth, which however reversed a longstanding downward trend. Conversely, labour productivity growth, while decelerating, remained fairly high in a number of European countries, thanks to a high pace of capital deepening rather than acceleration in MFP

---

[5] These patterns resulted from generally negative changes in hours worked in most countries (Sweden and the United States being exceptions) and wide differences in the growth of the employment rate.

[6] For countries that use hedonic (or similar) price indices for certain investment goods (e.g. ICT), this measure of MFP growth rate does not incorporate technological progress embodied in them (as the capital stock is augmented by the improvements in quality of ICT goods).

[7] In these latter cases, severe crises in the early 1990s (in Finland largely due to the collapse of the Soviet market) most likely led to cleansing the least productive activities not only with major employment losses but also with an increase in the recorded average MFP growth. Hence, their pattern of MFP growth does not reflect only an acceleration of technical change but also a one-shot reduction of inefficiencies.

growth, and the capital deepening effect was largely driven by poor employment growth rather than strong accumulation of physical capital.[8] MFP growth rates decreased significantly in a number of countries, including all the other G-7 countries. During 1995–2000, MFP seems to have accelerated more strongly in Canada, United States, Australia, and Finland.

To summarize, our examination of recent trends in output and labour productivity indicates that the OECD have experienced quite different growth experiences over the 1990s. GDP growth disparities have tended to widen, and stable hourly labour productivity in some European countries has been associated with low or falling employment levels. Amongst the major economies, the United States and Canada were the exceptions in the 1990s, combining significant acceleration in labour and MFP growth rates with rising labour utilization.

1.2. THE ROLE OF ICT

Most of the debate about the 'new economy' has been centred around the continuous technological advances in ICT, largely relying on evidence for the United States. Here we would like to assess evidence on the role of ICT in influencing aggregate growth for a broader set of countries. Conceptually, ICT can raise output or output growth via several routes: (1) an increase in productivity growth in the ICT-producing sectors themselves,[9] and/or an increase in size of the fast-growing ICT-producing sectors in the economy;

---

[8] Moreover, in most European countries, sluggish employment growth and falling hours worked have been accompanied by a significant up-skilling of the workforce. This raises the suspicion that productivity gains have been achieved in part by dismissing or not employing low-productivity workers. By contrast, in other countries with greater labour utilization (e.g. Ireland and Netherlands) the skill upgrading has played a relatively modest role in total labour productivity growth. Improving labour market conditions and structural reforms have widened the employment base in these countries, especially in the 1990s, allowing low skilled workers to get a foothold into employment, but reducing the overall process of skill upgrading (see OECD, 2003).

[9] The ICT-producing sector includes the following industries according to the International Standard Industry Classification (ISIC) Revision 3: within *Manufacturing* (ISIC Rev3 3000): Manufacture of office, accounting, and computing machinery; (ISIC Rev3 3130) Manufacture of insulated wire and cable; (ISIC Rev3 3210) Manufacture of electronic valves and tubes and other electronic components; (ISIC Rev3 3220) Manufacture of television and radio transmitters and apparatus for line telephony and line telegraphy; (ISIC Rev3 3230) Manufacture of television and radio receivers, sound or video recording or reproducing apparatus, and associated goods; (ISIC Rev3 3312) Manufacture of instruments and appliances for measuring, checking, testing, navigating, and other purposes, except industrial process control equipment; (ISIC Rev3 3313) Manufacture of industrial process control equipment. In *Services* (ISIC Rev3 5150): Wholesale of machinery, equipment, and supplies; (ISIC Rev3 7123) Renting of office machinery and equipment (including computers); (ISIC Rev3 6420) Telecommunications; (ISIC Rev3 7200) Computer and related activities. See OECD (2000b).

(2) capital deepening driven by high levels of investment in ICT equipment; and (3) increases in efficiency in ICT-using sectors that successfully adopt this new technology.

1.2.1. *The ICT-producing industry is generally small, but has grown rapidly over the 1990s*

The ICT sector accounts for a relatively small share of the total value added in the OECD business sector (Fig. 1.2): from less than 5 per cent in Australia to more than 8 per cent in Finland, United Kingdom, United States, Sweden, and Korea. More interestingly, the composition of the broad ICT-producing industry varies considerably across the board: differences in the size of telecommunication industry are rather modest, while countries differ significantly in the size of ICT-manufacturing and in ICT-related services.

Notwithstanding the small share in the total value added, the ICT-producing industry contributed significantly to a surge in productivity in a number of countries, especially in the latter part of the 1990s. Figure 1.3 shows the contribution of the broad *electrical equipment* industry—which comprises most of the ICT-producing industries—to the total manufacturing labour productivity growth in the 1990s and the previous decade. The contribution of this industry to aggregate labour productivity has increased in the 1990s in most countries. More generally, the services part of the ICT sector tended to have more rapid

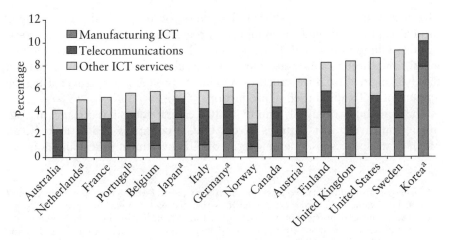

Figure 1.2. *The share of the ICT sector in total GDP, 1998*

[a] Excluding all the wholesale of machinery, equipment, and supplies (ISIC 5150).
[b] Including all the wholesale of machinery, equipment, and supplies (ISIC 5150).

Source: OECD (2000c), *Measuring the ICT Sector*.

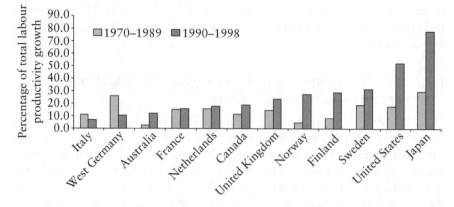

Figure 1.3. *Contribution of the electrical machinery industry to total labour productivity in manufacturing*

Source: Calculations on the basis of the OECD STAN database.

productivity growth than the service sector as a whole.[10] Other studies for the United States and a few European countries suggest that there has been a further substantial increase in contributions from ICT-producing industries in the second half of the 1990s.[11]

1.2.2. *There has also been a strong process of capital deepening boosted by falling prices of ICT*

The next channel through which ICT operates on output and productivity is through capital deepening. Technological progress has manifested itself, in part, through falling prices of ICT equipment. Falling prices have boosted the real investment, through a mixture of income and substitution effects resulting from the changing relative price structure of inputs to production; thus increasing the amount of ICT capital used in production.

The availability of rapidly improving ICT capital goods has certainly had an impact on investment patterns across OECD countries. Unfortunately, no official data sources provide time series of ICT investment in real and nominal

[10] There is also additional evidence on the role of the ICT-producing industry in country studies. For example, Forsman (2000) suggests that the mobile telephone producer Nokia accounted for more than one-fourth of GDP growth of 4% in Finland in 1999. Moreover, the Bank of Korea find that about 40% of recent GDP growth in Korea came from the ICT sector, five times its 1999 share in GDP (Yoo, 2000).

[11] OECD data only allow to assess the role of ICT-producing industries in Denmark, Finland, and Germany (see Pilat and Lee, 2001). In Finland and Germany, the contribution of the ICT-producing sector increased dramatically in the second half of the 1990s compared to the first half the 1990s. For the United States, see Jorgenson and Stiroh (2000) and Oliner and Sichel (2000).

terms for the OECD countries. The following makes use of work done at the OECD to collect and analyse cross-country ICT investment on the basis of data from statistical offices national accounts (Colechia and Schreyer, 2002).[12]

In the G-7 countries, the share of information technology (IT) capital goods in total investment expenditure rose steadily over the 1990s, and ranged from 3 per cent to more than 8 per cent of total non-residential gross fixed capital formation in 2000 (Table 1.2). The share of communication equipment also increased, though less rapidly (with the exception of Finland where it rose dramatically), and accounted for around 4–8 per cent of total non-residential investment.[13] Software investment also rose rapidly: from being a marginal component of total investment in the 1980s to one main driving force (especially in the United States).

Moreover, at constant prices, volume growth rates of IT capital investment progressed at an annual rate from 20 per cent to more than 30 per cent over the 1995–2000 period, while communication equipment and software investment progressed at an annual rate generally above 10 per cent over the same period. This fast growth is due to an annual decline in IT price indices of about 20 per cent (much less for communication equipment and software), reflecting rapid quality improvements and technical progress embodied in these capital goods.

This strong ICT-led process of capital deepening has contributed to boost output growth in most OECD countries for which data are available (Fig. 1.4). The contribution of ICT equipment and software to output growth of the business sector has been between less than 0.4 (France, Italy, and Japan) and almost 0.9 percentage points a year over the second half of the 1990s. In terms of shares in overall output growth this translates in an average contribution that ranges between 12 and 35 per cent across countries in the sample (see Fig. 1.4). The contribution on the second half of the 1990s was particularly high in absolute terms in the United States, more than doubling with respect to the 1980–1985 period. However, strong contributions also emerged in Australia, and Finland.

It is also worth noting the increasing contribution of software capital to output growth. Over the second half of the 1990s, the accumulation of software capital accounted for a third of the overall contribution of ICT capital to output growth. What is remarkable is that this result holds across all OECD countries in the sample, with the exception of Japan.[14] In particular, the

[12] Other sources of ICT investment data are Daveri (2002), Schreyer (2000), and Van Ark (2001).

[13] Methodologies to measure the price change in ICT capital goods vary a great deal across the OECD countries. The figures reported are based on a harmonized deflator constructed on the assumption that the differences between price changes for ICT capital goods and non-ICT goods are the same across countries. See Colecchia and Schreyer (2002) for more details.

[14] This is partly due to the fact that software investment in Japan is underestimated.

Table 1.2. *Percentage share of ICT investment in total non-residential investment, current prices, 1980–2000*

		Australia	Canada	Finland	France	Germany	Italy	Japan	United Kingdom	United States
IT equipment	1980	2.2	3.9	2.0	2.5	4.6	4.1	3.3	2.9	5.1
	1990	5.5	4.5	3.6	3.5	5.5	4.2	3.8	6.0	7.0
	1995	8.4	5.7	4.0	3.9	4.6	3.5	4.6	8.6	8.7
	2000	7.2	7.9	2.9	4.4	6.1	4.2	5.2	8.4	8.3
Communication equipment	1980	4.0	3.0	3.2	2.9	3.9	4.0	3.4	1.6	7.1
	1990	3.8	3.8	3.9	3.2	4.8	5.7	4.0	2.0	7.5
	1995	4.7	4.0	9.3	3.5	4.2	6.7	5.3	3.6	7.3
	2000	5.6	4.2	15.3	3.9	4.3	7.2	6.9	3.6	8.0
Software	1980	1.1	2.2	2.6	1.3	3.6	1.7	0.4	0.3	3.0
	1990	4.6	4.9	5.2	2.6	3.7	3.8	3.1	2.1	8.0
	1995	6.4	7.1	9.2	3.5	4.5	4.3	4.0	3.5	10.1
	2000	9.7	9.4	9.8	6.1	5.7	4.9	3.8	3.0	13.6

Source: Colecchia and Schreyer (2002).

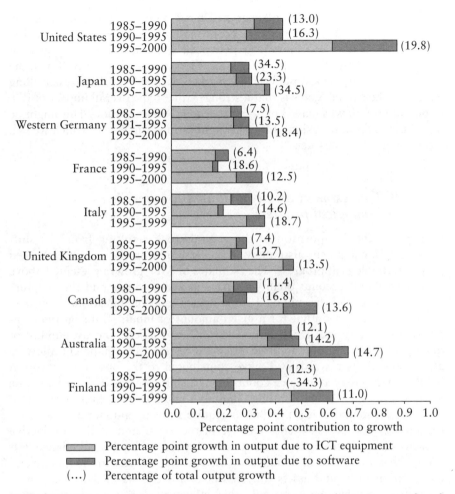

Figure 1.4. *The contribution of ICT capital to output growth (business sector, based on harmonized ICT price index)*

Source: Authors' calculations from Colecchia and Schreyer (2002).

percentage contribution of software capital to output growth almost doubled from the second half of the 1980s to the second half of the 1990s in the United States, and increased significantly also in Germany and France.[15]

---

[15] It should be stressed that measurement on software capital differs greatly across countries and in some countries it is likely that existing figures grossly underestimate it. In addition, the price indices of software equipment do not fully account for quality improvements in this asset. In summary, the contribution of software capital to output growth should be considered as a lower bound estimate of the real contribution. Jorgenson and Stiroh (2000) perform some simulations with three alternative scenarios for software price indices (baseline, moderate price decline, and rapid price decline). They find that the contribution of software to capital

All in all, these results indicate that the United States was not alone in experiencing an ICT-led growth in the second half of the 1990s: in particular, Australia, Canada, and Finland experienced some acceleration in growth because of a strong ICT capital deepening. However, the impact of ICT in the other countries in the sample was less marked. If anything, the distinguishing feature of the United States is that a stronger role to the overall impact of ICT to output growth was played by software capital accumulation. This might be linked to the rapid diffusion of Internet applications, an issue to which we will return later in this chapter.

1.2.3. ICT investment also contributed to embodied technological progress

Changes in the composition of the capital stock resulting from the shift towards ICT equipment also allow us to shed light on the role of embodied part of technological progress. The estimates of MFP growth presented above do not take into account quality changes in factor inputs and thus capture both embodied and disembodied technological and organizational improvements that increase output for a given amount of inputs. Data on the composition of the capital stock into seven different assets, and availability of quality-adjusted and non-adjusted price indices for ICT equipment allow to assess how shifts towards ICT have contributed to the observed pickup in MFP growth observed in some countries. The shift towards ICT assets, whose relative prices have been falling, implies that with the same amount of foregone consumption it is possible to acquire a greater amount of productive capital services. We can tentatively term the expansion of the productive capacity resulting from this process as 'embodied' technological change.[16] It should be stressed that in doing so we assume that changes in the quality and composition of capital assets fully reflect improvements in the productivity capacity of new vintages and not other influences, for example, changes in consumer preferences.

In the same vein as the correction for changes in the composition and quality of physical capital, the evolution of the total labour input can be decomposed into changes in the quality-constant hours worked and quality changes due to

accumulation in the United States in 1995–1998 would increase from 0.17% in the *baseline* scenario to 0.37 and 0.48% in the *moderate* and *rapid decline in price* scenarios, respectively.

[16] In particular, embodied technological change includes both changes in the composition of physical capital and changes in the quality of the different assets. From the discussion above, a proxy for total (embodied and disembodied) technological change can be computed as the residual from a growth accounting exercise in which we use the standard measure of capital stock (deflated at real acquisition prices). This can be justified from a theoretical point of view on the basis of the work of Solow (1960) and Fisher (1965). For a more detailed discussion on this issue see Bassanini *et al.* (2000).

shifts towards more skilled workers.[17] Indeed, improvements in human capital can be seen as reflecting a widening of the knowledge base that could be added to the embodied part of technological change. However, as discussed above, the observed changes in the skill composition of the workforce do not only represent a progress in the knowledge base of the working age population but also a skill-biased evolution of employment that has left out relatively low skilled work.

From these considerations, we complement the measure of MFP growth presented above with two alternative measures. The first shifts back changes in labour quality from MFP to the labour input. The second measures fully disembodied technological change and is computed by subtracting growth in factor inputs that are fully adjusted for changes in quality and composition from output growth (this is what Jorgenson, 1966, would consider as the only identifiable component of technological progress).

Table 1.3 suggests that one-third of the acceleration in MFP in the United States from the first to the second half of the 1990s was due to embodied technical progress, while the contribution of this factor was generally smaller (with the exception of Finland) in the other countries. However, for the United States the contribution of embodied technical progress was also strong in the second half of the 1980s. To better assess the role of the different components, Fig. 1.5 plots the different measures of MFP growth for the United States. The first point to notice is that the end of the productivity slowdown should be dated back to the early 1980s and not to the 1990s as often stressed on the basis of unadjusted series. This holds whatever measure of MFP growth is considered. Moreover, the contribution of ICT to embodied technological progress has increased over time to peak in the second half of the 1990s, as a result of a faster pace of ICT adoption.

Table 1.3 also suggests an acceleration in MFP growth in a number of countries even in fully disembodied technical progress. This is encouraging because it suggests that even countries without a sizeable ICT-producing industry have benefited from the spread of ICT, by shifting towards this more productive technology. Indeed, if the acceleration in fully adjusted MFP growth due to ICT were merely a reflection of rapid technological progress in the production of computers, semiconductors and related products and services, there would be no visible effects of ICT on MFP in countries that do not have a sizeable ICT-producing industry. For ICT to have visible effects on MFP in countries that do not produce ICT goods, it requires to have spillover effects—or network externalities—linked to its use in other sectors of the economy.

---

[17] The effect of changes in the composition of the labour input are assessed by considering six different types of labour, based on gender and three different educational levels: below upper-secondary education; upper-secondary education, and tertiary education. Relative wages are used to proxy for relative productivity. See OECD (2003) for more details.

Table 1.3. *Estimates of MFP growth rates (average annual growth) 1980–2000*

	Australia	Canada	Finland	France	Germany	Italy	Japan	United Kingdom	United States
Broad measure (technical change + human capital)									
1980–1985[a]	0.68	0.49	2.46	2.00	1.15	1.53	1.92	–	0.82
1985–1990[b]	0.46	0.77	2.36	1.71	1.46	1.57	2.38	1.01	1.03
1990–1995[c]	1.18	1.00	2.76	0.92	0.65	1.22	1.22	0.63	0.95
1995–2000[d]	1.50	1.45	3.11	1.02	0.84	0.72	0.62	0.93	1.28
Adjusted for human capital (embodied + disembodied technical change)									
1980–1985[a]	–	0.32	2.20	1.82	–	–	–	–	0.67
1985–1990[b]	–	0.61	2.01	1.36	–	–	–	0.66	0.87
1990–1995[c]	1.12	0.79	2.37	0.44	0.67	0.76	–	0.02	0.79
1995–2000[d]	1.36	1.24	2.79	0.60	0.87	0.27	–	0.29	1.12
Fully adjusted (disembodied technical change)									
1980–1985[a]	–	0.12	2.01	1.66	–	–	–	–	0.47
1985–1990[b]	–	0.40	1.82	1.18	–	–	–	0.46	0.65
1990–1995[c]	0.79	0.58	2.12	0.26	0.47	0.58	–	–0.19	0.50
1995–2000[d]	1.01	0.97	2.52	0.41	0.66	0.08	–	0.04	0.72
Memorandum item (embodied technical change)									
1980–1985[a]	0.22	0.20	0.19	0.16	0.14	0.17	0.14	–	0.20
1985–1990[b]	0.28	0.21	0.19	0.18	0.17	0.19	0.20	0.20	0.22
1990–1995[c]	0.33	0.22	0.26	0.18	0.19	0.17	0.23	0.21	0.29
1995–2000[d]	0.35	0.28	0.38	0.20	0.22	0.19	0.23	0.25	0.40

[a] 1982–1985 for Finland.
[b] 1987–1990 for the United Kingdom.
[c] 1991–1995 for Germany.
[d] 1995–1997 for the United Kingdom, 1995–1999 for Australia, France, Italy, and Japan.

Source: Bassanini and Scarpetta (2002*a*).

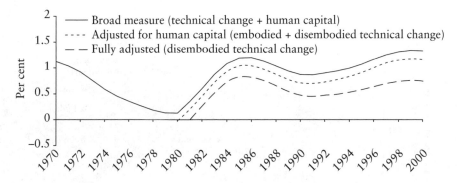

Figure 1.5. *Different measures of the trend MFP annual growth rates for the United States, 1970–2000*

Source: Bassanini and Scarpetta (2002a).

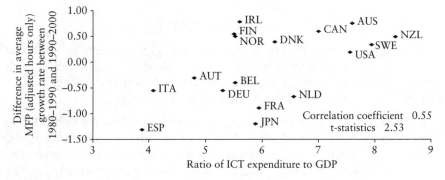

Figure 1.6. *Change in MFP growth and ICT expenditure, 1990–1999. ICT intensity is the average of the ratio of ICT expenditure to GDP in the 1990s.*

Source: OECD (2001a).

Figures 1.6 and 1.7 show some additional light on this issue. They indicate some *prima facie* evidence of a possible relationship between the acceleration of MFP growth and the overall intensity of ICT, the latter proxied by either total ICT expenditure or by a more specific indicator of the intensity of use of personal computers (PCs) by the population. Indeed, countries with greater expenditure in ICT and greater PC intensity were also those characterized by acceleration of MFP growth over the past decade.

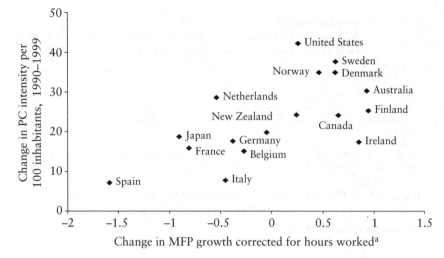

Figure 1.7. *Change in MFP growth and change in PC intensity, 1990–1999*
[a] Correlation coefficient: 0.63.

1.3. SUMMARY

In this chapter we have shed some light on recent growth trends in the OECD countries and, in particular, in our comparison of the United States with Europe. We have identified a number of stylized facts that will guide our empirical investigation in the following chapters, including:

1. Per capita GDP growth was uneven across the OECD in the 1990s. While some economies experienced an acceleration of growth (e.g. Ireland, Australia, Netherlands, United States, and Canada) others, including the large ones in continental Europe, persisted along the slow growth path observed since the 1970s.

2. Compared to GDP, differences in labour productivity growth rates across countries remained fairly stable from the 1980s to the 1990s. The explanation for these seemingly conflicting patterns is the diversity in the trends in labour utilization: in general, acceleration in GDP growth rates has been accompanied by improvements in the utilization of labour. By contrast, most countries with low or falling employment rates have experienced a slowdown in GDP growth because labour productivity growth was not able to fully offset the reduced productive capacity. In this context, the United States stands out with respect to large Continental European countries not much in terms of labour productivity, but as having an acceleration in labour productivity growth being accompanied by growth in hours and employment.

3. There are also some new factors behind the observed disparities in growth performance across the OECD countries. In particular, MFP, taken as

a proxy for technological change, accelerated in a number of countries, most notably in the United States and Canada, and also in some small economies (e.g. Ireland and Australia). In the United States, the acceleration of MFP growth seem to have started initially as a pure 'disembodied' phenomenon, consistent with the idea of a slow diffusion of a new general purpose technology. Later on, an increasing contribution to the overall productivity growth seems to result from greater use of highly productive ICT equipment by other industries. The slow diffusion hypothesis is also consistent with the fact that MFP growth accelerated somewhat later in other OECD countries that did not have a sizeable ICT-producing industry.

4. The intensity of investment in ICT (either relative to GDP or to total investment) has increased in most countries, but still varies across the board. The United States does not stand out in this respect, as a number of (small) European countries have been experiencing a surge. What distinguished the United States from most of the large European economies is the larger (and more productive) ICT-producing industry.

5. In an attempt to further link the spread of ICT to recent growth trends we also showed a positive correlation between the overall ICT expenditure and the acceleration of MFP growth across countries. Needless to say, simple bivariate correlations cannot be taken as proof of a causal relationship between ICT and productivity. Nevertheless, they strengthen our motivation for further exploring these issues in the following chapters.

2

Scraping the Surface: What Lies Behind Aggregate Growth Patterns? Industry- and Firm-level Evidence

As discussed in the previous chapter, the spread of information and communication technology (ICT) may influence aggregate economic growth via three main channels: (1) the rapid growth of the broadly defined ICT industry; (2) the ICT-induced process of capital deepening; and (3) the improvements in efficiency in ICT-using sectors. We aim at shedding further light on why ICT has had a very different impact on growth along all these three channels in the Organization for Economic Cooperation and Development (OECD) countries, although in this chapter we will not be able to disentangle the latter two paths. We use industry-level data, which are available for several OECD countries, as well as firm-level data for a selected sample of countries. First, we assess how shifts of resources across industries have contributed to the observed productivity performance. Recalling from Chapter 1 that ICT-producing industries consistently boosted aggregate productivity growth, we look at cross-country differences in the ability to reallocate resources to such fast growing markets. We then descend to firm-level data and assess how firm dynamics (entry, exit, and post-entry growth) has contributed to manufacturing and industry-specific performance with a particular focus on ICT industries.

2.1. THE COMPOSITION OF AGGREGATE PRODUCTIVITY GROWTH: THE ICT SECTOR AND BEYOND

Structural change has certainly been an important factor in explaining long-run trends and cross-country differences in labour productivity. However, evidence for the most recent period suggests that the most important contribution to overall productivity growth patterns comes from productivity changes within industries rather than as a result of significant shifts of employment across industries. This is illustrated in Fig. 2.1 that shows that within-industry labour productivity growth accounted for a large share of overall productivity growth over the 1990s.[1] The net-shift effect did not make an important contribution

---

[1] Figure 2.1 is based on a decomposition of labour productivity growth in the business sector into: (1) a within-industry effect, that measures productivity growth within industries;

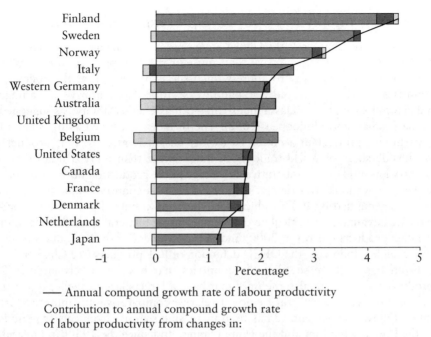

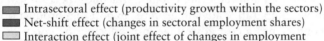

— Annual compound growth rate of labour productivity

Contribution to annual compound growth rate
of labour productivity from changes in:

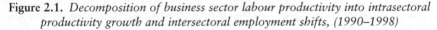 Intrasectoral effect (productivity growth within the sectors)
Net-shift effect (changes in sectoral employment shares)
Interaction effect (joint effect of changes in employment
shares and sectoral productivity)

Figure 2.1. *Decomposition of business sector labour productivity into intrasectoral productivity growth and intersectoral employment shifts, (1990–1998)*

during this period, and the interaction effect was negative for most countries, implying that industries that boosted productivity were also shrinking in size.[2]

Even though aggregate productivity growth has been largely driven by within-industry performance, the differences across countries in the size of the ICT-producing sector, and the intensity of ICT use in other sectors, make it important to analyse the sectors separately. These are treated in turn in Sections 2.1.1 and 2.1.2.

(2) a between-industry effect, that measures the impact on productivity of the shift in employment between industries; and (3) a residual third effect, the 'interaction effect'. A contribution for the within-industry effect greater that 100% in some countries is due to a negative contribution from the interaction effect: when industries with growing relative productivity decline in size or when industries with falling productivity grow in size. The data are from the OECD STAN database (2-digit ISIC for services and a 3–4-digit ISIC for manufacturing).

[2] The net-shift effect was more significant over the 1970–1979 and 1979–1990 periods.

2.1.1. *How rapidly do countries shift to expanding sectors*

As discussed in Chapter 1, the United States and a few smaller economies have a larger ICT-producing industry than most of the European countries. Why is this the case? One way to address this issue is by looking at the ability of countries to shift to rapidly expanding sectors. Comparative advantage indicators—such as the Balassa index (BI)—can assess this 'ability', as suggested by Bartelsman and Hinloopen (2002). The BI index is defined as the share of a particular product in a country's export basket relative to that product's worldwide share of world trade. A BI index larger than unity denotes that a country has a relative comparative advantage in the production of that product. In Fig. 2.2 we look over time at the percentage of a country's value of exports that are generated by ICT products for which the country has a relative comparative advantage. We calculate these figures using bilateral trade flow data for detailed products (Feenstra, 2000) and our assignment of these products to the ICT category following the OECD definition of ICT products (see Chapter 1).

From Fig. 2.2, we see that the countries that have relatively large ICT-producing sectors are also the ones that have a large share of their exports in ICT products for which they enjoy a relative comparative advantage. More interestingly, this percentage has been increasing steadily from earlier periods in the United Kingdom and the United States, and since the 1980s in Finland. Having a relative comparative advantage in the export of a product often indicates that a country has a cost advantage in producing the good, or that the quality of the good is appreciated in international markets. If the distribution of the BI for a certain product is near uniform worldwide, then it has become a commodity that everyone has the ability to produce: likely profit margins will be small. In contrast, if the distribution of BIs for a product is highly skewed, then margins are likely to be large. For the many ICT products for which the United States has a comparative advantage, few other countries

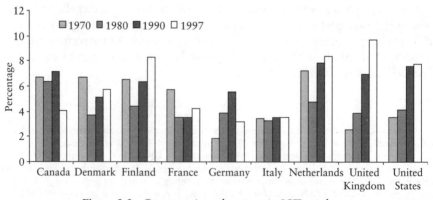

Figure 2.2. *Comparative advantage in ICT products*

have a BI above unity. In contrast, the other countries that have high and rising comparative advantage in ICT products, are more narrowly specialized in a smaller segment (such as mobile phones in Finland) of the ICT market.

2.1.2. *The role of ICT-using industries*

ICT is readily available in the world market and, in theory, all firms can acquire the equipment at fairly similar prices, wherever they are located. Therefore the ability of the firms in a country to use these technologies should not depend, to a first approximation, on the location of the producing sector. In Chapter 1 we saw that, however, the degree of ICT adoption varied significantly across countries in the 1990s. Is this reflected in different productivity performance of sectors that can exploit this technology the most? Here we focus on ICT-using industries and in particular on ICT-using services. We further detail the performance of wholesale and retail trade, finance, insurance, and business services. As stressed by the Council of Economic Advisors (2001), more than two-thirds of all information technology products in the United States are purchased by these two broad sectors.

Figure 2.3 suggests that in most countries for which data are available, the contribution of ICT-using industries to overall labour productivity growth has increased, most notably in the United States. If we then look at the two detailed sectors separately (i.e. *trade* and *financial and business services*, Fig. 2.4), we

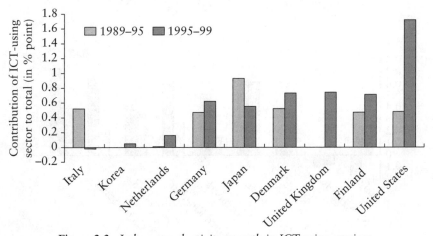

Figure 2.3. *Labour productivity growth in ICT-using services, 1989–1995 and 1995–1999*[a]

[a] 1991–1995 and 1995–1997 for Germany; 1995–1998 for Japan. Employment-based labour productivity growth is used for the United States since hours worked is not available for ICT-using industries.

Source: Calculations on the basis of the OECD STAN database.

observe that both sectors contributed substantially to the acceleration in labour productivity in the United States over the second half of the 1990s, while for the other countries the contribution mainly came from finance and business services. All in all, the evidence suggests that, amongst the large OECD economies, the United States has been better able to move resources to supply the rapidly expanding market for ICT products and has thereby enjoyed a direct boost to overall productivity growth. Moreover, there is evidence to suggest that the United States as well as some smaller economies (e.g. Finland) have experienced a stronger increase in productivity of ICT-using sectors, most likely because of a stronger process of ICT-driven capital deepening. Is there

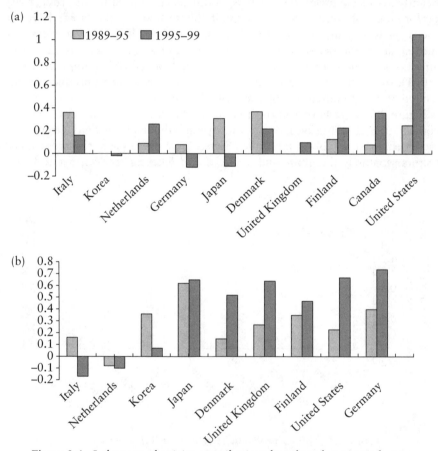

Figure 2.4. *Labour productivity contributions by selected service industries (in % point).[a] (a) Wholesale and retail trade, repairs; (b) finance, insurance, real estate, and business services*

[a] 1991–1995 and 1995–1997 for Germany; 1995–1998 for Japan.

Source: Calculations on the basis of the OECD STAN database.

something inherent in the characteristics of manufacturing and ICT-user service industries in the United States that make them more able to develop and adopt these new technologies? We try to shed some further light on this issue by reporting some firm-level evidence in Section 2.2.

2.2. FIRM DYNAMICS AND PRODUCTIVITY GROWTH: EVIDENCE FROM FIRM-LEVEL DATA

As suggested by growing micro evidence, industry performance (especially in a highly dynamic context) may hide a wide heterogeneity of individual firms' behaviour, and it is precisely the different features of this firm heterogeneity that may explain cross-country difference in industry-wide performance. In particular, various formal models have emphasized the importance of a 'Schumpeterian' process of 'creative destruction' for innovation and adoption of new technologies (see Box 2.1).

Box 2.1. *Creative destruction and economic growth*

Various explanations have been offered to explain the wide heterogeneity of individual firm's behaviour. One class of these models focuses on the learning process (either active or passive) due to experimentation under uncertainty. In the *passive learning model* (Jovanovic, 1982) a firm enters a market without knowing its given potential profitability *ex ante*. Only after entry does the firm start to learn about the distribution of its own profitability, based on (noisy) information from realized profits. In a process of continuous updating of information, the firm decides to expand, contract, or exit. This model implies that smaller and younger firms should have higher and more variable growth performance. Ericson and Pakes (1995) suggested that firms explore the market actively and invest to enhance their profitability under competitive pressure performance. Its potential and actual profitability changes over time in response to the stochastic outcomes of the firm's own investment, and those of other actors in the same market. A successful firm will expand rapidly, while it will shrink or exit otherwise. This inherent uncertainty would imply that, even an entrant who turn out to be successful *ex post*, will typically enter small. The accumulation of experience and assets, in turn, reinforce the position of survivors and reduces the probability of failure.

One variant of the creative destruction process is described by vintage models of technological change. These models stress that new technology is often embodied in new equipment and the full exploitation of the latter requires a costly restructuring of existing plants. In this context, new firms may have an advantage in the adoption of leading technologies. Related to this idea are models that emphasize the potential role of entry and exit: at the extreme, if new technology can only be adopted by new establishments, growth occurs only via entry of new units of production, which displace outpaced establishments. The existence of sunk costs implies that high-tech new firms coexist with older and less productive firms generating the observed heterogeneity.

Despite the clear attractiveness of firm-level analyses of technological innovation and adoption, their implementation has often been constrained by the lack of cross-country comparability of the underlying data. While many studies exist for the United States, evidence for most other countries is often scattered and based on different definitions of key concepts or units of measurement (see Caves, 1998 and Ahn, 2001 for surveys). In this section we use a specially constructed firm-level data for ten OECD countries (United States, Germany, France, Italy, United Kingdom, Canada, Denmark, Finland, Netherlands, and Portugal; see Box 2.2). In particular, we look at certain features of firm dynamics (entry, exit, and survival) and how they influence industry-wide productivity growth in total manufacturing and in ICT-related industries.[3]

Box 2.2. *The OECD firm-level study*

Firm-level data have been assembled by national experts as part of a 2-year project, coordinated by the OECD, in which one of the key aims was to minimize inconsistencies along different dimensions (e.g. sectoral breakdown, time horizon, definition of entry and exit, etc.). Notwithstanding the efforts made to harmonize the data, there remain some differences that have to be taken into account in the international comparison.

SOURCES OF MICRO DATA

Available data at the firm level are usually compiled for fiscal and other purposes and, unlike macroeconomic or industry-level data, there are few internationally agreed definitions and sources (see Bartelsman *et al.*, 2002 for more details on the OECD firm-level project). The analysis of firm demographics is based on business registers for (Canada, Denmark, France, Finland, Netherlands, United Kingdom, and United States or social security databases Germany and Italy). Data for Portugal are drawn from an employee-based register containing information on both establishments and firms. These databases follow firms over time because addition or removal of firms from the registers (at least in principle) reflects their actual entry and exit. The decomposition of aggregate productivity growth requires a wider set of variables and has been based on production survey data, in combination with business registers.

DEFINITION OF VARIABLES

The *entry rate* is defined as the number of new firms divided by the total number of incumbent and entrant firms in a given year; the *exit rate* is defined as the number of firms exiting the market in a given year divided by the population of origin, that is, the incumbents in the previous year.

---

[3] For more details see Bartelsman *et al.* (2002), Barnes *et al.* (2003) and OECD (2003).

Labour productivity growth is the difference between the output growth rate of and the employment growth rate and, whenever possible, controls for material inputs. Available data do not allow the control for changes in hours worked, nor do they distinguish between part- and full-time employment.

Multifactor productivity (MFP) growth is the change in gross output less the share weighted changes in materials, capital, and labour inputs. Changes are calculated at the firm level, but income shares refer to the OECD-wide industry average in order to minimize measurement errors. The capital stock is based on the perpetual inventory method and material inputs are also considered. Real values for output are calculated by applying 2–4-digit industry deflators.

COMPARABILITY OF MICRO DATA

Two prominent aspects of the data have to be borne in mind while comparing firm-level data across countries.[1]

Unit of observation

The data used in this study refer to 'firms' rather than 'establishments'. More specifically, most of the data used conform to the following definition (Eurostat, 1995): 'an organizational unit producing goods or services which benefits from a certain degree of autonomy in decision-making, especially for the allocation of its current resources'. Nevertheless, business registers may define firms at different points in ownership structures; for example, some registers consider firms that are effectively controlled by a 'parent' firm as separate units, whilst others record only the parent company.[2]

Size threshold

Some firm registers include even single-person businesses, while others omit firms smaller than a certain size, usually in terms of the number of employees but sometimes in terms of other measures such as sales (as is the case of the data for France and Italy). Data used in this study exclude single-person businesses. However, because smaller firms tend to have more volatile firm dynamics, remaining differences in the threshold across different country datasets should be taken into account in the international comparison.[3]

---

[1] For more detail on the comparability of the firm-level data, see Bartelsman *et al.* (2003).

[2] In a sensitivity analysis, the decomposition of productivity growth has been repeated for the United States, on the basis of establishment data instead of firm data. The results are largely unchanged, at least with respect to the sign and broad magnitude of the different components.

[3] However, a sensitivity analysis on Finnish data, where cut-off points were set at five and twenty employees, reveals broadly similar results for the productivity decomposition and aggregate entry and exit rates.

2.2.1. *The role of firm dynamics in industry productivity growth*

We use two alternative approaches to decompose labour productivity growth: the approach proposed by Griliches and Regev (1995, GR henceforth); and that proposed by Foster, Haltiwanger, and Krizan (1998, FHK henceforth) (see Box 2.3). The analysis is based on 5-year rolling windows for all periods and industries for which data are available.

Figure 2.5 presents the decomposition of labour productivity growth in manufacturing sectors for two 5-year intervals, 1987–1992 and 1992–1997. Both the GR, and especially the FHK decomposition method, suggest that overall labour productivity growth was largely driven within-firm productivity

---

Box 2.3. *The decomposition of productivity growth*

One approach used to decompose productivity growth is from Griliches and Regev (1995): in this decomposition, each term is weighted by the average (over the time interval considered) market shares as follows:

$$\Delta P_t = \sum_{\text{Continuer}} \bar{\theta}_i \Delta p_{it} + \sum_{\text{Continuers}} \Delta \bar{\theta}_{it} (\bar{p}_i - \bar{P})$$
$$+ \sum_{\text{Entries}} \theta_{it}(p_{it} - \bar{P}) - \sum_{\text{Exits}} \theta_{it-k}(p_{it-k} - \bar{P}) \tag{1}$$

where Δ means changes over the k-years' interval between the first year $(t-k)$ and the last year (t); θ_{it} is the share of firm i in the given industry at time t (it could be expressed in terms of output or employment); p_i is the productivity of firm i and P is the aggregate (i.e. weighted average) productivity level of the industry.[1] A *bar* over a variable indicates the averaging of the variable over the first year $(t-k)$ and the last year (t). In eq. (1), the first term is the *within component*; the second is the *between component*, while the third and fourth are the *entry and exit components*, respectively.

Another decomposition has been proposed by Foster *et al.* (1998). It uses base-year market shares as weights for each term of the decomposition, and includes an additional term (the so-called 'covariance' or 'cross' term) that combines changes in market shares and changes in productivity (it is positive if enterprises with growing productivity also experience an increase in market share) as follows:

$$\Delta P_t = \sum_{\text{Continuers}} \theta_{it-k} \Delta p_{it} + \sum_{\text{Continuers}} \Delta \theta_{it}(p_{it-k} - P_{t-k}) \sum_{\text{Continuers}} \Delta \theta_{it} \Delta p_{it}$$
$$+ \sum_{\text{Entries}} \theta_{it}(p_{it} - P_{t-k}) - \sum_{\text{Exits}} \theta_{it} - k(p_{it-k} - P_{t-k}) \tag{2}$$

One potential problem with this second method is that, in the presence of measurement error in assessing market shares and relative productivity levels in the base year, the correlation between changes in productivity and changes in market share could be spurious, affecting the within- and between-firm effects. The averaging of market shares in the GR method reduces this error. However, the interpretation of the different terms of the decomposition is less clear-cut in the GR method. If market shares indeed change significantly over the 5-year interval, the 'within' effect in fact also includes a reallocation effect.

---

[1] The shares are based on employment in the decomposition of labour productivity and on output in the decomposition of total factor productivity.

(from 50 to 85 per cent of the total). Consistent with our sectoral analysis above, the impact on productivity via the reallocation of output across existing enterprises (the 'between' effect) is typically small especially if one does not consider the 'cross-effect' in the FHK decomposition. The cross effect is mostly negative, implying that firms experiencing an increase in productivity were also losing market shares, that is, their productivity growth was associated with restructuring and downsizing rather than expansion. Lastly, the combined contribution to overall labour productivity growth of the entry

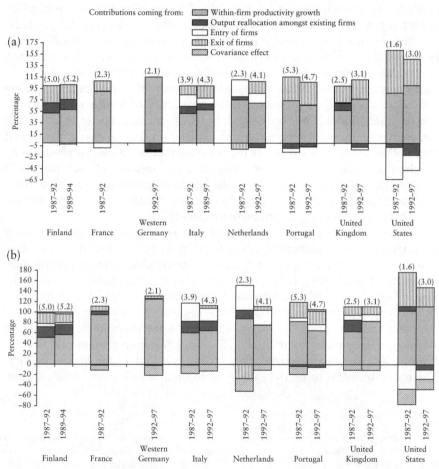

Figure 2.5. *Decomposition of labour productivity growth in manufacturing (percentage share of total annual productivity growth of each component[a]). (a) GR decomposition[b]; (b) FHK decomposition[b]*

Note: Figures in brakets are overall productivity growth rates (annual percentage change).
[a] Components may not add up to 100 because of rounding.
[b] See main text for details.

Source: OECD (2003) and author's calculations.

and exit of firms (net entry) is positive in most countries (with the exception of western Germany over the 1990s), typically accounting for between 20 and 40 per cent of total labour productivity growth.

There are significant differences in the contribution of entries to productivity growth. Leaving aside France and Italy, where data are to some extent problematic,[4] data for the other European countries show that new firms generally make a positive contribution to overall productivity growth, although the effect is generally of small magnitude. By contrast, entry in the United States for most industries makes a negative contribution to industry productivity growth. Less surprising, the exit contribution to productivity growth is typically positive across the data for all countries (Fig. 2.5), indicating that exiting firms usually have below-average levels of productivity. However, the contribution of exiting firms in the United States is larger than in all other countries. Differences in the role of entry and exit to overall productivity in the United States compared with European countries are probably related and point to a somewhat different nature of firm dynamics in the United States. Indeed, by analysing cohorts of entrants, Foster *et al.* (1998) shows that many weak recent entrants exit the market rapidly in the United States. This tends to boost the estimated contribution of exit to productivity for the United States but, at the same time, the presence of such firms also weakens the contribution of entry in the US decomposition at short horizons. Over a longer horizon, the same selection and learning effects increase the contribution of net entry to productivity growth.

The contribution made by entry and exit to productivity growth varies considerably across industries. Most notably, in ICT-related manufacturing industries, the entry component makes a stronger than average contribution to labour productivity growth (Fig. 2.6).[5] This is particularly the case in the United States, where the contribution from entrants to total labour productivity is strongly positive, in contrast to the negative effect observed in most of the other manufacturing industries (see Fig. 2.6 for an example of the *office and computing machinery* industry). This suggests an important role for new firms in an area characterized by a strong wave of technological change. The opposite seems to be the case in more mature industries, where a more

---

[4] The French data refer to firms with at least twenty employees or with a turnover greater than €0.58 million. They are not likely to be representative of the total population. The Italian data refer to firms with a turnover of at least €5 million. Sample size is maintained by deleting firms falling below the threshold and adding new firms in. Thus, the Italian data are likely to overstate the true entry and exit rates. See Bartelsman *et al.* (2003) for more details.

[5] The industry group is '*electrical and optical equipment*'. In the United States, most 3–4-digit industries within this group had a positive contribution to productivity stemming from entry. In the other countries, there are cases where, within this group, the contribution from entry is very high, including the *office, accounting, and computing machinery* industry in Finland, the United Kingdom, and Portugal and *precision instruments* in France, Italy, and the Netherlands.

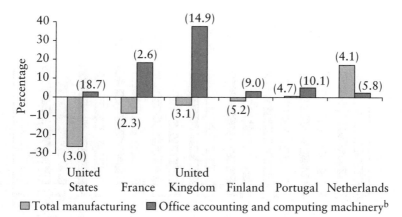

Figure 2.6. *Contribution of new entry to labour productivity growth in manufacturing and selected ICT industries (percentage share of total productivity growth[a])*

[a] Total productivity growth in parenthesis.
[b] Electrical machinery and apparatus n.e.c. for France, Netherlands, and Portugal.
Source: OECD (2003).

significant contribution comes from either within-firm growth or the exit of presumably obsolete firms.

2.2.2. *Firm dynamics in manufacturing and the ICT industry*

Based on a considerable amount of research using disparate firm-level datasets, the micro literature has collated some stylized facts about firm dynamics (see Geroski, 1995; Caves, 1998). Using relatively harmonized methodology, the OECD firm-level data sources allow us to review these facts. Figure 2.7(a) seems to confirm a significant churning of firms in all countries. Over the first half of the 1990s, firm turnover rates (entry plus exit rates) were in the range of 15 per cent to more than 20 per cent in the business sector: that is, a fifth of firms are either recent entrants, or will close down within a year. The process of entry and exit of firms involves a proportionally low number of workers: that is, only about 10 per cent of employment is involved in firm turnover, and in Germany and Canada, employment-based turnover rates are around 5 per cent (Fig. 2.7(b)). The difference between firm turnover rates and employment-based turnover rates arises from the fact that entrants (and exiting firms) are generally smaller than incumbents. For most countries, new firms are only 40–60 per cent the average size of incumbents, and in the United States, Germany, and Canada their average size is less than 30 per cent of that of incumbents. The relatively small size of entrants in these countries reflects either the large size of incumbents (e.g. United States) or the small average size

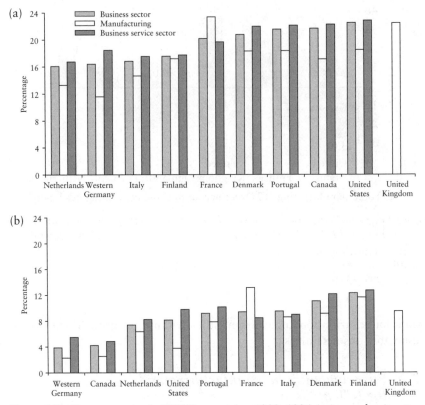

Figure 2.7. *Turnover rates in OECD countries, 1989–1994 (entry and exit rates, annual average[a]). (a) Overall firm turnover in broad sectors; (b) employment turnover due to entry and exit in broad sectors*

[a] The entry rate is the ratio of the entering firms to the total population. The exit rate is the ratio of the exiting firms to the population of origin. Turnover rates are the sum of entry and exit rates.
[b] Total economy minus agriculture and community services.

Source: OECD (2003).

of entrants compared with that in most other countries (Germany and Canada). This would suggest that, in these countries, entrant firms are further away from the average size in a given industry (what could be interpreted as the minimum efficient size).

The main conclusion from Fig. 2.7 in the context of our international comparison is that there seem to be no significant differences between Europe and North America in terms of firm dynamism using annual turnover rates. If the latter is taken as a proxy for the ability of industries to innovate and adopt leading technologies—as the different models in the tradition of the creative destruction hypothesis seem to imply—we can tentatively conclude that such ability may not differ on the two sides of the Atlantic.[6] However, we will see below that annual turnover rates without taking into account differences in post-entry dynamics may mask the differences across countries.

Despite their cross-country similarity, turnover rates vary significantly across industries, confirming a potential link between firm churning and technological characteristics of each industry. To shed light on this issue, Fig. 2.8 shows differences in entry rates across industries, once country and size effects are controlled for. Values in the figure are relative to the overall business sector (unweighted) average. Notably, high-tech manufacturing industries and some business service industries, and in particular those related to ICT, have higher entry rates than average.[7] This evidence ties in with earlier discussion about the role of entry in productivity growth in high-tech industries, and lends some support to the vintage models of technological change whereby rapid technological change is associated with greater firm churning where new innovative units replace outpaced ones.

All in all, there is no evidence in our sample of countries, of strongly differences in the degree of firm turnover rates across countries at annual frequencies. At the same time, however, we have seen different contributions of this dynamism to industry-wide productivity performance. The additional piece of the puzzle is the analysis of post-entry performance, another aspect of firm dynamism.

Looking at overall survivor rates, almost 60–70 per cent of entering firms survive the first 2 years in the countries for which we have data (Fig. 2.9). Those that remain in business after the first 2 years have a 50–80 per cent chance of surviving for five more years. But, in the countries considered, only about 40–50 per cent of firms entering in a given year survive on average beyond the seventh year.

Failure rates in the early years of activity are highly skewed towards small units, while surviving firms are not only larger, but also tend to grow rapidly. Thus, in most countries the size of exiting firms is broadly similar to that of entering firms. Moreover, the average size of surviving firms increases rapidly to approach that of incumbents in the market in which they operate. On this latter point, there are significant differences across countries (Fig. 2.10): in the United States, surviving firms on average double their employment in the

---

[6] This similarity in turnover rates may hide a composition bias due to structural differences across countries. However, Bartelsman *et al.* (2003) estimate country-specific effects on firm turnover, over and above those possibly stemming from the sectoral composition of the economy and the different time period covered by the data. Their results suggest that, with the exception of western Germany and Italy, all countries have higher entry rates than the United States.

[7] The very high positive dummy for post and telecommunication is likely to be due to two factors: (1) the privatization of telecoms in a number of countries, which has led to the entry of a number of new private operators; and (2) the rapid increase in the number of firms operating in the communication area, related to the spread of Internet and e-commerce activities.

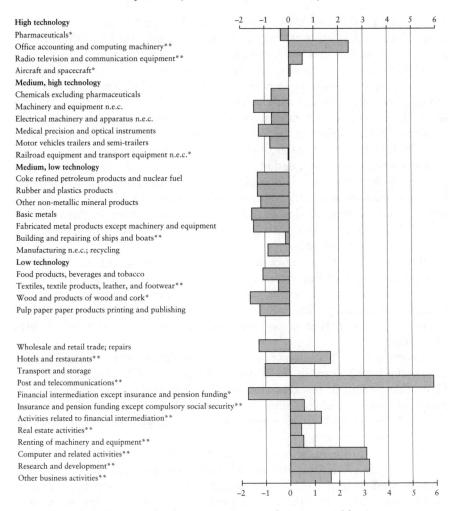

Figure 2.8. *Estimated industry[a] entry rates relative to total business sector*

Note: *indicates significance at 5%; **at 1%.

[a] Figures reported are the industry fixed effects in an entry equation that includes country, size, and time fixed effects. (See Table 2.6.)

Source: OECD (2003).

first 2 years, while employment gains amongst surviving firms in Europe are in the order of 10–20 per cent.[8] This substantial difference in post-entry growth for surviving firms suggests that the entry and exit dynamics across the Atlantic are indeed different.

---

[8] Audretsch (1995*a,b*) found similar results for the United States are consistent with the evidence in. He found that the 4-year employment growth rate amongst surviving firms was about 90%.

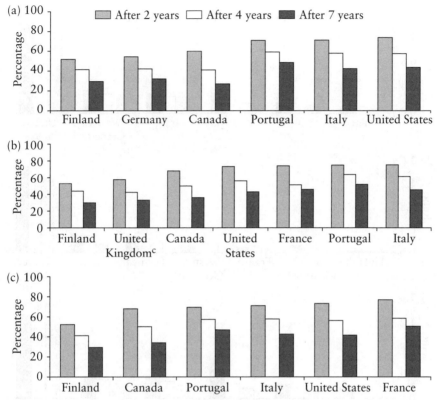

Figure 2.9. *Firm survivor rates at different lifetimes*[a]*, 1990s. (a) Total economy;*
(b) total manufacturing; (c) business services sector

[a] The survivor rate at duration (*j*) is calculated as the probability that a firm from a population of entrants has a lifetime in excess of (*j*) years. Figures refer to average survival rates estimated for different cohorts of firms that entered the market from the late 1980s to the 1990s.
[b] After 6 years for the United Kingdom.
[c] Data for the United Kingdom refer to cohorts of firms that entered the market in the 1985–1990 period.

Source: OECD (2003), and Baldwin *et al.* (2000) for Canada.

The distinct development of *high-technology* industries is once again exemplified by the marked employment growth amongst surviving firms (Fig. 2.11). In particular, firms in ICT-related industries (*office accounting and computing machinery* and *radio, TV, and communication equipment*) generally experience rapid post-entry growth in all countries for which data are available. However, even in these highly dynamic industries, surviving US firms show a stronger employment expansion, compared with those in most of the other countries. The marked difference in post-entry behaviour of firms in the United States compared with the European countries is partially

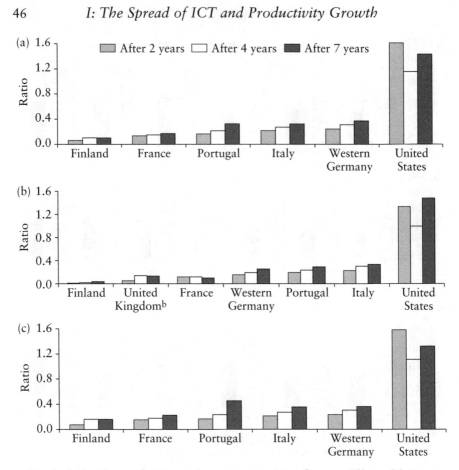

Figure 2.10. *Net employment gains among surviving firms at different lifetimes, 1990s (net gains as a ratio of initial employment). (a) Total economy; (b) total manufacturing; (c) business services sector*

[a] After 6 years for the United Kingdom.
[b] Data for the United Kingdom refer to cohorts of firms that entered the market in the 1985–1990 period.

Source: OECD (2003).

due to the larger gap between the size at entry and the average firm size of incumbents, that is, *there is a greater scope for expansion amongst young ventures in the US markets than in Europe*. In turn, the smaller relative size of entrants can be taken to indicate a greater degree of experimentation, with firms starting small and, if successful, expanding rapidly to approach the minimum efficient scale. These differences in the firms' performance can only partly be explained by statistical technicalities or business cycles conditions, and seem to indicate a greater degree of *experimentation* amongst entering

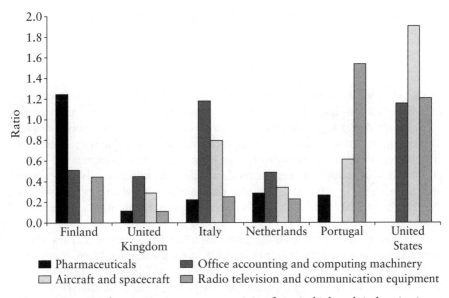

Figure 2.11. *Employment gains among surviving firms in high-tech industries (net gains as a ratio of initial employment)*

Source: OECD (2003).

firms in the United States. This greater experimentation of small firms in the US market may also contribute to explain the evidence of a lower than average productivity at entry, as discussed above.[9] Putting the pieces together, the evidence is consistent with the view that there is greater market experimentation in the United States. The new entrants in the United States are small and less productive relative to the incumbents. Many of the new entrants fail but the more productive survive and grow rapidly. This evidence for selection and learning effects playing a more important role also suggests that measurement of the contribution of net entry to growth needs to take into account the role of post-entry growth dynamics. The contribution of net entry to productivity growth will be disproportionately greater in the United

[9] The other additional factors that could contribute to explain the observed differences in post-entry behaviour include: (1) firms with plants spreading into different US states are recorded as single units, while establishments belonging to the same firm, but located in different EU countries are recorded as separate units: available evidence for the United States and Finland reveals only marginal differences in the average number of plants per firm in the two countries (1.2 and 1.1 in total business sector); (2) business-cycle influences could also possibly explain the distinct growth of surviving firms in the United States: estimates of post-entry growth in Italy and Portugal in an expansionary period (the second half of the 1980s) are only marginally higher than those in the early 1990s. See Bartelsman *et al.* (2003) for more details.

States over a longer horizon given the high post-entry growth of successful survivors.[10]

2.3. SUMMING UP

In this chapter we have explored further recent growth patterns by exploiting industry- and firm-level data. The emerging picture enhances our understanding of the main driver of economic growth and helps to focus our policy-oriented discussion. In particular, we have shown that aggregate productivity patterns are largely the result of within-industry and even within-firm performance in most countries. This should not neglect the fact that some industries (both producers and users of ICT) have had stronger than average productivity growth over the 1990s and have significantly boosted manufacturing and service overall productivity.

In terms of our international comparison, we have shown that the United States have been notably better than most of its trading partners in acquiring a comparative advantage in rapidly growing ICT market segments. The United States has also experienced a more widespread productivity acceleration of ICT-user industries, while in Europe notable acceleration generally occurred only in the finance sector. So, there seems to be evidence to suggest a different pace of development by both ICT producers and ICT users across the Atlantic.

A number of theoretical studies and some anecdotal evidence suggest that new, innovative, firms may play a key role in the diffusion of a general purpose technology as the ICT. We have investigated this issue by means of firm-level data. The picture that emerges is one in which, overall, there is a similar degree of firm churning in Europe as in the United States. The distinguishing features of the firms' behaviour in the US markets compared with their EU counterparts can be summarized as follows:

1. In the United States, entrant firms are more heterogeneous in terms of both size and productivity than in Europe.
2. However, selection effects work quickly so that weak recent entrants exit the market and this is associated with a stronger contribution of exits to total labour productivity in the United States compared to Europe.
3. Moreover, selection and learning effects imply that successful, surviving entrants expand rapidly, generating stronger post-entry growth. This is consistent with the evidence of a much stronger (employment) expansion of successful entrants in the initial years in the United States compared with Europe.

---

[10] The evidence in Foster *et al.* (1999) shows that over a longer horizon (e.g. 10 years), the contribution of net entry to productivity growth in the United States is disproportionately larger than over shorter horizons.

We have advanced the hypothesis that these differences may indicate a *different degree of market experimentation* in the United States as compared with Europe. The more market-based financial system may lead to a lower risk aversion to project financing in the United States, with greater financing possibilities for entrepreneurs with small or innovative projects, often characterized by limited cash flows and lack of collateral. Moreover, low administrative costs of start-ups and not unduly strict regulations on labour adjustments in the United States, are likely to stimulate potential entrepreneurs to start on a small scale, test the market, and if successful with their business plan, expand rapidly to reach the minimum efficient scale. In contrast, higher entry and adjustment costs in Europe may stimulate a pre-market selection of business plans with less market experimentation.

3

Productivity, Investment in ICT, Human Capital, and Changes in the Organization of Work: Micro Evidence from Germany and the United States

3.1. INTRODUCTION

In the firm-level analysis presented in Chapter 2, we were somewhat limited in the number of issues that we could address with internationally comparable data. There is a trade-off between the number of countries that can be covered in the analysis and the comparability of information across them. In this chapter we seek to shed further light on some of our key findings from Chapter 2 (that US businesses appear to engage in more market experimentation than do their European counterparts, and that selection and learning effects are more important in the United States) using detailed establishment-level data for two countries: Germany and the United States. As shown in Chapter 2, these two countries represent two prototypes in terms of the firms' behaviour, in general, and market experimentation, in particular. They also are characterized by different institutions, regulatory settings, and industrial relations regimes and thus their comparison may shed light on the possible role of such factors to explain the differences in the firms' behaviour.

We examine the theme of potential differences in experimentation between the United States and Germany in two distinctive ways. First, experimentation may be present in the entry and exit process as new businesses adopt new technologies (broadly defined to include the use of advanced technologies and also organizational structure) and concurrently learn whether the technology chosen is suitable and whether the ownership/management team is suitable as well. This form of experimentation is closely linked to the ideas in Jovanovic (1982) where new businesses are uncertain of their type (which can be defined in a variety of ways including managerial ability and/or the appropriate business practices for a specific production unit) and learn about it in the first several periods of operation. Such experimentation suggests that dispersion on a variety of dimensions (productivity, size, wages, skill mix, and the use of technology) is likely to be especially large for entrants and young businesses. In what follows, we explore this hypothesis by examining the nature of such experimentation across the United States and Germany. Again, the working hypothesis from earlier chapters is that the market and institutional environment in the United States encourages such experimentation so that we should observe a stronger relationship between establishment age and the dispersion of various outcomes in the United States.

An alternative but related idea is that each time a business (whether new or mature) adopts a new technology the experimentation process begins anew. This idea, that learning is an 'active' ongoing process as businesses adopt new technologies, is based on the model of Pakes and Ericson (1995). Under this view, it is at businesses that are most actively changing their technology where we should observe the greatest dispersion in choices and outcomes reflecting the underlying experimentation. Here again, we are interested in exploring whether the patterns that emerge in the data differ between the United States and Germany.

We focus on cross-sectional micro data for the years 1999 and 2000 in the United States, and 2000 and 2001 in Germany (see Box 3.1). While the data are cross-sectional, we know the age of the establishments so that we can explore the differences in investment in information and communication technology (ICT) and the outcomes for different cohorts. The micro data permit us to examine the relationship between investment in computers, employee Internet access, the skill mix of the workforce, and the outcomes such as productivity and wages. While there have been studies conducted at the micro level on these topics for both the United States and European countries, our advantage is that we conduct the study for a virtually identical time period using harmonized measurement and methodology.[1]

The chapter proceeds as follows. Section 3.2 presents the key features of the establishment-level data for the United States and Germany. Section 3.3 presents the results of simple regressions relating labour productivity and wages to measures of use of advanced technology in both countries. Section 3.4 examines the evidence on 'experimentation' across countries—first by looking at the results by establishment age and then exploring the active learning model by examining the differences across businesses depending on how actively they are changing their technology. Section 3.5 concludes with interpretation of the results.

---

[1] For the US studies using micro data include Doms *et al.* (1997, 2002), Dunne *et al.* (2001). For Germany the only micro study we know of, which analyses the impact of ICT on productivity, is Hempell (2002). This study, however, is based on the German service sector.

Box 3.1. *Establishment-level data for the United States and Germany*

US DATA

The US data come from two surveys of US manufacturing establishments: the Computer Network Use Supplement (CNUS) to the 1999 Annual Survey of Manufacturer (ASM) and the 2000 ASM. We also draw information on establishment age from the Longitudinal Business Database (see Jarmin and Miranda, 2002), a research data file maintained by the Center for Economic Studies. Since both surveys are based on the ASM sample frame, we first discuss the general features of the ASM.

Both the 1999 ASM (from which the 1999 CNUS is drawn) and 2000 ASM are part of the 1999–2003 ASM panel. The panel is drawn from the 1997 Economic Census with allowances for new establishment births and replacement for sample deaths. The design for the 1999–2003 panel initially contained approximately 52,000 of the over 380,000 US manufacturing establishments with paid employees. Manufacturing companies with more than $1 billion in manufacturing shipments are selected into the ASM with certainty. There are just over 500 of these certainty enterprises, and all of their over 14,000 establishments are included in the 1999–2003 ASM panel.

Also selected with certainty are remaining establishments meeting at least one of the following conditions: have at least 500 paid employees, produce (electronic) computers, or produce in certain 'small' industries. The number of certainty cases in the 1999–2003 ASM panel is approximately 16,600. The remaining portion of the sample is chosen randomly from the remaining establishments with five or more employees. Selection probabilities are proportional to size, according to a procedure that minimizes sample size while satisfying quality constraints within industry and product strata.

For the analysis, we require a number of data items from the ASM and CNUS. Table 3.1 lists the data items and their source. We also use establishment identifiers and industry codes from the ASM and CNUS files. The CNUS data on e-business processes are available only for reference year 1999. The computer investment data are available for reference years 1992 and 2000. We examine the 2000 cross-section only. We match the 1999 CNUS to the 2000 ASM. Since both surveys are drawn from the 1999–2003 ASM panel, differences in the samples are minimal. There will be some difference due to entry and exit. However, the largest difference in the establishment composition of the two files is due to non-response to the 1999 CNUS.[1] The 1999 CNUS contains just fewer than 40,000 establishment observations. After matching the 1999 CNUS, the 2000 ASM, and the LBD, we are left with 31,265 establishment observations.

THE GERMAN DATA

The German data we use are from the Establishment Panel Data Set collected by the Institut für Arbeitsmarkt- und Berufsforschung (IAB), Nuremberg, Germany.[2] This yearly survey has been conducted since 1993 in Western Germany, and since 1996 in Eastern Germany. Information is obtained by personal questioning carried out by Infratest Sozialforschung, Munich, with voluntary participation by the plant managers. Altogether, the (unbalanced) IAB panel comprises 79,000 observations and 26,000 plants. Detailed descriptions of the IAB Establishment panel can also be found in Kölling (2000).

The sample is drawn from the employment statistics register of the German Federal Office of Labour, which covers all plants with at least one employee (or trainee) subject to social security.[3] All plants included in the population (i.e. all plants included in the employment statistics register) are stratified into 400 cells, which are defined over ten plant sizes, twenty industries, and two regions (Western vs. Eastern Germany), from each of which the observations of the establishment panel are drawn randomly. Large plants are over-represented in the IAB panel. In the first wave (1993), for example, the probability of being drawn was on an average 91 per cent for plants employing more than 5000 employees, but only 3 per cent for plants employing between 100 and 200 employees, and as small as 0.1 per cent for plants with less than five employees. The over-sampling of large plants implies that the survey covers about 0.7 per cent of all plants in Germany, but 10 per cent of all employees.[4]

Interviewers ask about eighty questions each year on topics including: detailed information on the decomposition of the workforce (gender, skill, blue-collar vs. white-collar, part-time employees, apprentices, civil servants, and owners) and its development through time; business activities (total sales, input materials, investment, exports, profit situation, expectations, whether the plant does R&D, product and process innovations, organizational changes, technology of machinery, adopted plant policies/strategies); training and further education; wages; lots of information on working time (standard working time, overtime, and percentage of employees working overtime, and percentages of employees working on Saturdays, working on Sundays, working on shifts, and working with a flexible working time schedule); and general information about the plant (whether the plant is a subunit of a firm, ownership, birth year, existence of works council, whether the plant applies bargaining agreement, whether the plant has been merged with or split from another plant in the last year, three-digit industry affiliation, region). While most questions are asked yearly (or on a 2-year/3-year basis), some topics have been surveyed only once.[5]

This study uses observations from the manufacturing sector of the 2000 and 2001 waves of the IAB panel. The regression analysis, however, is only carried out with the latter wave, since we do not observe information on Internet access in 2000. This leaves approximately 7700 observations for the descriptive statistics and 3500 observations for the regression analysis. Altogether, in 1999, there were 336,000 plants (which employed at least one employee subject to social security) covered in the German manufacturing sector.[6] Our sample accounts for approximately 1 per cent of these plants, but for 12 per cent of its workforce and for 11 per cent of its value added.

[1] More details on the 1999 CNUS are in US Census Bureau (2001), '1999 E-business Process Use by Manufacturers: Final Report on Selected Processes', available at www.census.gov/estats

[2] The IAB (in English Institute for Employment Research) is the research institute of the Federal Employment Services in Germany.

[3] For 1995, the employment statistics cover about 79% of all employed persons in western Germany and about 86% in eastern Germany (Bender *et al.*, 2000).

[4] Population weights, which are the inverse of the sample selection probabilities, are available for empirical analysis.

[5] Information on Internet access, for example, is only available for 2001.

[6] *Source*: IAB-Betriebsdatei, own calculations.

3.2. DATA DESCRIPTION

Table 3.1 presents the definitions of the key measures used in this study, while Table 3.2 presents summary statistics for the key variables. As shown in Table 3.1, for the most part, the measurement methodology has been harmonized so that the measures are comparable across the countries. Moreover, in order to compare value figures between the two countries, we have converted German measures into dollars using an aggregate Purchasing Power Parity measure (Organization for Economic Cooperation and Development (OECD), *Main Economic Indicators* 2002). There is only one notable exception where comparability between the two countries is problematic: the access of employees to Internet— the German dataset has a categorical variable on the proportion of workers with Internet access (none, some, half, most, all) instead of a measure of the percentage of workers with access to Internet, as in the US data.

The first item that emerges from the data for the two countries is the significant heterogeneity in main characteristics of establishments (see the standard deviations of key variables). These differences reflect both within- and between-industry differences (the latter are shown in Table A.1 in Appendix).[2] Moreover, confirming the finding of the previous chapter, the average size of US establishments tends to by much larger than in Germany (Table 3.2). We also find that the share of non-production workers (an indirect measure of skill) is larger in Germany relative to the United States, but this level comparison may not warrant much attention given the potential differences in how production and non-production workers are defined (e.g. in Germany the distinction is based upon hourly wage workers vs. salaried workers while the US definition refers more to the type of activity).

Productivity and payroll per worker are higher in the United States but there is greater dispersion in productivity and payroll per worker in Germany (see cautions below about simple comparisons of dispersion measures across countries). Total equipment investment per worker is higher in the United States but computer investment per worker is higher in Germany. However, the United States exhibits much greater dispersion for both measures of investment relative to Germany. For the most part, the industry rankings on the various measures are similar across the countries although there are some notable exceptions (See Table A.1 in Appendix).

While these summary statistics are useful, we base our subsequent analysis on a difference in difference approach (e.g. difference between low- and high-tech businesses in the United States vs. difference between low- and high-tech in Germany). The level comparisons across the countries may be plagued by a variety of measurement problems (e.g. the appropriate price deflator conversion

---

[2] For example, in the United States (Table A.1.a in Appendix) computer investment per worker is lowest in the non-metallic minerals industry but highest in the computer and office equipment industry. The gap in computer investment between these two industries is about $1600 per worker, which is substantial. However, this gap is relatively small compared to a one standard deviation difference in computer investment per worker reported in Table 3.2 (which is $5100 per worker).

Table 3.1. *Primary US and German data items*

Variable	Source	Notes
US data		
Shipments	ASM	Total value of shipment. We adjust for changes in inventories to get a concept closer to actual production.
Value added	ASM	Adjusted shipments minus materials, energy, and the costs of resales and contract work.
Employment	ASM	Number of full and part-time workers at the plant (production and non-production).
Production workers	ASM	Number of full and part-time production workers.
Payroll	ASM	Total salaries and wages paid.
Total machinery and equipment investment	ASM	Total investment in new equipment and machinery, including vehicles.
Computer investment	ASM	Total investment in computers and peripheral equipment (software not included).
Percentage of employees with Internet access	CNUS	Percentage of employees at establishment with access of any kind to the Internet.
STAN industry	Derived	Using SIC codes available on ASM.
Age	LBD	Categorical age variable taking on values 0–10 for plants aged 0–10 and 11 for plants aged 11+.
German data		
Shipments	IAB	Total value of shipment in the previous business year. No adjustment for changes in inventories.
Value added	IAB	Total shipments minus materials and services received from other plants.
Employment	IAB	Number of (production and non-production) employees (excluding apprentices) at the plant on 30 June of the current year. Adjusted for part-time workers.
Production workers	IAB	Number of full- and part-time workers (as opposed to salaried employees) on 30 June of the current year.
Payroll	IAB	Total salaries and wages paid in June of the current year (excluding social insurance payments by the employer).
Total machinery and equipment investment	IAB	Total investment in the previous business year (buildings, equipment, machinery, vehicles).
Computer investment	IAB	Total investment in ICT in the previous business year.
Percentage of employees with Internet access	IAB	Percentage of (office) jobs at establishment with access of Internet/Intranet (categorical: 1 = all, 2 = most, 3 = half, 4 = a few, 5 = none). Information for 2001 only.
STAN industry	IAB	Thirteen categories.
Age	IAB	Categorical age variable taking on values 1–12 (in 2000: takes the value 11 for plants aged 11+; in 2001: takes the value 12 for plants aged 12+).

Table 3.2. *Descriptive statistics*

Statistic	Mean	Standard deviation	Tenth percentile	Ninetieth percentile
US data—Matched ASM/CNUS sample (weighted by sample weights)[a]				
Age (years)	9.45	3.024	4	11+
Employment	140.1	402.50	15 (freq = 121)	288 (freq = 19)
Skill (proportion of non-production workers)	0.277	0.191	0.071	0.540
Employee Internet access (percentage)	0.210	0.263	0.000	0.600
Total equipment investment per worker ($1000)	7.927	41.380	0.344	14.938
Total computer investment per worker ($1000)	0.455	5.113	0.000	0.925
Log labour productivity: VA per worker ($1000)	4.325	0.758	3.536	5.173
Log payroll per worker ($1000)	3.480	0.402	2.972	3.973
German descriptive statistics (weighted by sample weights)				
Age (years)	9.7	2.99	5	12
Employment	28.95	229.75	2	47
Skill (proportion of non-production workers)	0.32	0.34	0	1
Employee Internet access (categorical: 1 = all, 5 = none)	2.83	1.7	1	5
Total equipment investment per worker ($1000)	7.05	23.6	0	14.61
Total computer investment per worker ($ 1000)	0.78	2.71	0	1.97
Log labour productivity: VA per worker ($1000)	3.63	0.9	2.49	4.59
Log payroll per worker ($1000)	2.92	0.63	2.05	3.61

[a]Statistics for the matched ASM/CNUS sample differ from population values. First, ASM establishment are on average larger and more productive than the average manufacturing establishment, as measured by the Census of Manufactures—the typical ASM establishment has eighty-one workers in 2000 and the average employment from the 1997 Census of Manufactures is forty-four. Second, plants matching the CNUS data are larger still.

across the countries) and thus we have much greater confidence in the results that rely on differences in differences. In this regard, we especially note that the differences in dispersion across the countries may reflect differences in the degree of measurement error as well as differences in the size distribution or other factors across countries. Thus, we do not put much emphasis on the differences in the levels of dispersion, in say, productivity between the United States and Germany reported in Table 3.2.

In what follows, we seek to relate the use of advanced technology to outcomes like productivity and wages at the micro level. Given limitations of available data, we rank establishments on the basis of their equipment investment per worker and computer investment per worker. Since both of these measures are only proxies of what we would like (which instead might be a measure of the stock of high-tech capital per worker), we use them to create a set of technology groups similar to that used in Doms *et al.* (2002). Specifically, for each measure we create three groups: (1) zero investment; (2) low investment (below the seventy-fifth percentile); and (3) high investment (above the seventy-fifth percentile).[3] We choose to classify high investment establishments as those to the right of the seventy-fifth percentile since the investment distributions are very skewed. In turn, these three groups interact to give seven possible combinations.

One point that is worth emphasizing in this context is that the computer investment, by itself, is likely to be an inadequate measure of the use of advanced technology beyond the obvious problem that we have a flow rather than a stock measure. The computer investment measure only captures the direct spending on computers but does not include the spending on equipment with imbedded advanced technology (e.g. semiconductors). Prior research using the Survey of Manufacturing Technology (e.g. see Dunne, 1994) finds that direct spending on computers misses a substantial amount of the investment in high technology equipment. Accordingly, we focus on both total equipment expenditures as well as computer investment expenditures.

Given that our proxies for the intensity of advanced technologies are imperfect, we check whether our results for so-called advanced technology investment also apply to other equipment investment. Namely, we replicate the analysis for investment in *highway vehicles* (i.e. cars and trucks—which, like computers, are components of equipment investment) by US establishments. Obviously, if similar results also hold for vehicles this would raise substantial questions as to whether our measures of information technology (IT) investment are capturing advanced technology.[4]

Another limitation worth emphasizing is that using establishment-level data for wages is inadequate along a number of dimensions. Clearly, the relationship between advanced technology and wages should be conducted at the individual worker level. Having said that, a number of micro studies have shown that (1) a large fraction of the dispersion in wages across workers is accounted for by between-establishment differences as opposed to within-establishment differences; (2) the between-plant differences in wages largely reflect differences in the skill mix across workers; (3) the differences in the skill mix across establishments is closely linked to differences in technology use across businesses.[5]

---

[3] These non-parametric measures also have the advantage of being more comparable across the two countries.

[4] This experiment is similar to that performed by DiNardo and Pischke (1997).

[5] See, for example, Davis and Haltiwanger (1991), Doms *et al.* (1997), and Dunne *et al.* (2002).

Thus, there is considerable information content in exploiting the cross-plant variation in wages in this context. Moreover, checking the cross-plant variation in wages is a useful robustness check on the results using the cross-plant variation in measured output per worker since there are undoubtedly measurement problems in the latter.

3.3. THE RELATIONSHIP BETWEEN PRODUCTIVITY, WAGES, AND ADVANCED TECHNOLOGY

We begin our micro comparison of the United States and Germany by examining the empirical relationship between labour productivity and technology choices at businesses, including investment in advanced technology and in human capital (using the skill mix of the workforce). In a like manner, we examine the relationship between payroll per worker and these same factors.

The left column of Table 3.3 presents the results from simple descriptive regressions with labour productivity (log value added per worker) as dependent variables and measures of the use of technology, and the skill mix as right-hand-side variables. As discussed earlier, we define technology groups in a non-parametric fashion using the equipment investment and computer investment per worker measures. We also include the skill mix (share of non-production workers), a measure of Internet access, and the interaction of the skill mix and the Internet access variable as right-hand-side variables. Also, all regressions include controls for size, age, multi-unit status (a dummy variable indicating whether or not the establishment is owned by a multi-location company), two-digit STAN industry dummies, and (for Germany) a dummy indicating that the plant is located in Eastern Germany. The regression results reported are weighted estimates, where the weights are constructed by multiplying the appropriate survey sample weight by employment.[6]

In both countries, the use of advanced technology and more skilled workers are associated with higher labour productivity. Also, in the United States, the interaction of Internet access and the skill mix is (somewhat surprisingly) negative while the interaction effects in Germany are more difficult to interpret, as the effects are not monotonic and often statistically insignificant.[7] Still, at first glance, it is striking that the overall patterns are so similar across the two countries.

While the patterns across the countries are broadly similar, the quantitative effects are different in some interesting ways. In particular, the use of advanced

---

[6] We also estimated the regression models unweighted and with survey sample weights alone. The results are broadly similar regardless of the weights used. The employment-weighted results are the most relevant to the analysis in other chapters, so we focus on them here.

[7] The surprising negative interaction effect may in part be related to the fact that the non-production worker mix is a poor proxy for the skill mix. For example, the non-production worker mix includes clerical workers. Put differently, the interaction effect may be picking up composition effects within the two broad categories of workers that we measure.

Table 3.3. *Cross sectional regressions*

Variable	Dependent variable: log(value added per worker)	Dependent variable: log(payroll per worker)
A: US results[a]		
Investment class: total equipment/IT		
0/0	−0.669	−0.288
	(0.160)	(0.077)
Low/0	−0.461	−0.240
	(0.018)	(0.008)
High/0	−0.157	−0.045
	(0.023)	(0.011)
Low/Low	−0.513	−0.261
	(0.017)	(0.008)
Low/High	−0.414	−0.165
	(0.019)	(0.009)
High/Low	−0.074	−0.067
	(0.021)	(0.010)
High/High		
	0.524	0.219
Percentage of employees	(0.028)	(0.014)
with Internet access	0.154	0.349
Percentage of non-production	(0.037)	(0.018)
workers (skill)	−0.451	−0.006
Interaction effect (percentage of	(0.069)	(0.033)
non-production workers)		
(Internet access)		
Number of observations	22,704	22,947
R^2	0.259	0.408
B: German results[b]		
Investment class		
0/0	−0.287	−0.111
	(0.068)	(0.036)
Low/0	−0.434	−0.104
	(0.077)	(0.035)
High/0	−0.176	0.018
	(0.096)	(0.042)
Low/Low	−0.393	−0.141
	(0.055)	(0.031)
Low/High	−0.31	−0.032
	(0.058)	(0.024)
High/Low	−0.172	−0.030
	(0.062)	(0.027)
High/High	Omitted	Omitted
Internet access (all omitted)		
Most	0.165	0.124
	(0.098)	(0.056)

Table 3.3. (Continued)

Variable	Dependent variable: log(value added per worker)	Dependent variable: log(payroll per worker)
Half	−0.053	0.068
	(0.149)	(0.115)
A few	0.163	0.107
	(0.076)	(0.061)
None	0.09	0.055
	(0.104)	(0.069)
Percentage of non-production workers	0.978	0.582
	(0.133)	(0.103)
Interaction effect (percentage of non-production workers) (Internet access)		
Most	−0.333	−0.17
	(0.229)	(0.122)
Half	0.029	−0.173
	(0.322)	(0.231)
A few	−0.585	−0.183
	(0.201)	(0.140)
None	−0.828	−0.713
	(0.257)	(0.170)
Number of observations	3,121	3,121
R^2	0.315	0.342

Notes: Standard errors in brackets; A: All regressions also control for size, age, STAN industry, and multi-unit status; B: All regressions also control for size, age, STAN industry, multi-unit status, and Eastern Germany.

Source: A: Authors' calculations using the 1999 CNUS and 2000 ASM (Center for Economic Studies); B: Authors' calculations from the 2001 wave of the IAB Establishment Panel.

technology yields a greater increase in labour productivity in the United States compared to Germany. We base this inference on the difference between the labour productivity of the highest technology group (High/High) and the lowest technology group (0/0). In the United States, the productivity premium for being 'High/High' is 67 log points, while it is only 29 log points in Germany. In a like manner, the productivity premium for being 'High/High' relative to 'Low/Low' is 51 log points in the United States and 39 points in Germany.

Some of the intermediate comparisons are less clear-cut. For example, conditional on the level of total equipment investment, there is an additional productivity premium for US establishments with high computer investment per worker of approximately 7–10 log points. These effects are estimated less precisely for Germany. According to the point estimates, a business with high computer investment per worker has, conditional on the level of total equipment investment, a productivity premium of between 8 and 17 log points. Alternatively, conditional on computer investment, there is a bigger productivity premium from an increase in total equipment per worker in the

United States relative to Germany. That is, conditional on computer investment per worker, the productivity premium in going from low to high equipment investment is between 41 and 44 log points in the United States and 14 and 31 log points in Germany. We think these intermediate/conditional comparisons are interesting but place more emphasis on the comparisons based upon using the combined impact of total equipment and computer investment spending (e.g. High/High vs. 0/0) given the limitations of the measures. Moreover, even though there are less clear-cut patterns for some intermediate comparisons, it is apparent from Table 3.3 that the broad patterns are such that the impact of investment is greater in the United States than Germany.

Internet access has a slightly larger quantitative effect in the United States than Germany. The differences in the measurement of the variables make this a bit difficult to compare. However, consider that in the United States, moving a plant from the tenth to the ninetieth percentile of the Internet access distribution is equivalent to an increase in Internet access from 0 to 60 per cent of the plant's workforce. Using the coefficients from Table 3.3 suggests that this is associated with an increase in productivity of approximately 24 log points (this calculation takes into account the negative interaction effect). In Germany, an increase in Internet access by a plant's workers from 'none' to 'half' or 'most' (which is roughly equivalent in going from 0 to 60 per cent in the United States) yields an increase in productivity of between 13 and 23 log points.[8]

Turning to other effects of interest, we see that in both countries an increase in the skill mix is associated with an increase in productivity and, in this case, the quantitative effect is much larger in Germany.[9] Also, as noted, the interaction between Internet access and the skill mix is negative[10] in the United States while the effect is not monotonic in Germany. Going from 'none' to 'all' Internet access does yield a positive interaction effect in Germany.

The right columns of Table 3.3 present analogous results based on payroll per worker for the two countries. Interestingly, the findings suggest that productivity differences are also reflected in wage differences along the same dimensions (i.e. the right-hand-side variables in the regressions), especially

---

[8] The interaction effects for Germany are imprecisely estimated; so appropriate caution is required about this comparison. However, we have estimated these specifications without the interaction effects and the quantitative estimated impact is still approximately the same.

[9] This measure of skill is quite crude but the only one we have available readily for both countries. For Germany, there are alternative measures of skill and somewhat surprisingly we find that when we include these alternative measures of skill instead of this measure, there is less of an impact of a change in skill on productivity.

[10] Interestingly, the negative interaction term for the United States implies that the marginal impact of increased skill, as measured by the share of non-production workers on productivity is negative for a significant number of establishments with high levels of Internet access. Our prior hypothesis was that Internet access and skill would interact positively. This may yet be the case and our finding may be due to imperfections in our measures—especially for skill as noted above. An alternative and somewhat whimsical interpretation is that the web surfing by the non-production workers is decreasing productivity.

in the United States. As is typically the case in these types of regressions, appropriate caution needs to be given to the interpretation. It is likely the case that US high-tech firms are especially high skill firms and the production/ non-production distinction only captures part of the skill differences across firms. Existing studies (e.g. Doms *et al.*, 1997; Abowd *et al.*, 2001) suggest that this pattern holds in the United States. Alternatively, it may be that there is some rent sharing of 'success' from adopting advanced technology. In looking at the quantitative patterns, the wage gaps tend to be smaller than productivity gap. For example, the wage gap between the 0/0 group and the High/High group is 0.288 for the United States, and only 0.111 for Germany. One possible explanation for the apparent greater compression of wages relative to observables in Germany is that this is due to the wage setting institutions in Germany (and Europe more generally), which reduce the flexibility of relative wages and thus reduce experimentation in Europe.

As stressed above, we checked for the validity of our results concerning the impact of investment in advanced technologies on the plants' outcomes by replacing it with investment in 'low-tech' equipment—highway vehicles (cars and trucks). Reassuringly, we find no productivity or wage premium at establishments with high investment in highway vehicles. As such, this gives us more confidence that there is information content in the computer investment data we are exploiting in this analysis.

In sum, while the overall patterns in the data reveal striking similarities across the two countries, there are some notable differences in the relationships between outcomes like productivity and payroll per worker and measures of the use of advanced technology such as expenditures on computers and equipment, and Internet access. In both the United States and Germany, the high productivity workplaces are the high skill and high-tech workplaces. In the United States, the differences in technology use account for more variation across businesses in productivity and payroll per worker than in Germany. In what follows, we treat these results as a backdrop and investigate whether there is a different degree of market experimentation in the United States relative to Germany.

3.4. EXPERIMENTATION? DIFFERENCES ACROSS GERMANY AND THE UNITED STATES

3.4.1. *The role of establishment age*

As discussed in the introduction of this chapter and in earlier chapters, a key theme/hypothesis is that the United States exhibits greater market experimentation, which might help explain its stronger growth performance in a period of rapid diffusion of the new general purpose technology (ICT). Here we look at the nature of experimentation for entrants and young businesses. New businesses are inherently experimenting as they are beginning to produce goods or

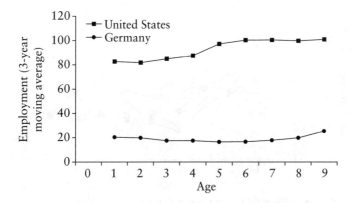

Figure 3.1. *Average employment by age*

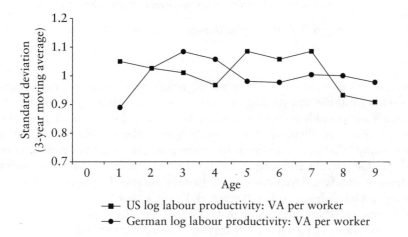

Figure 3.2. *Productivity dispersion by age*

services at a new location. However, the incentives for experimentation may vary across institutional environments. In environments that especially encourage experimentation, we would expect to see greater dispersion in both choices and outcomes for young and new businesses.

Figures 3.1–3.3 show how some of our key indicators vary with plant age.[11] Figure 3.1 confirms the finding of Chapter 2 that while the average size of US businesses increases significantly with plant age, no such age effect is found

---

[11] The figures highlight some of our more interesting results, and additional detailed statistics are available in Tables A.2 and A.3 in the Appendix. The results depicted in Figs 3.1–3.3 are computed from the Appendix tables using a 3-year moving average and excluding the final age categories that include all establishments with age 10 or more.

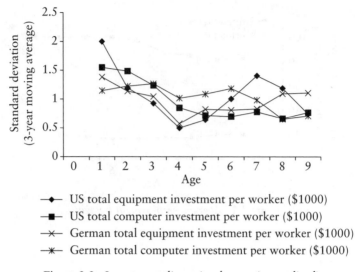

Figure 3.3. *Investment dispersion by age (normalized)*

amongst German plants. Note that these results are based on a cross-section of existing establishments and not on the size evolution of a given cohort (which is not possible on the basis of available data). Moreover, Fig. 3.2 shows that productivity dispersion falls with age in the United States but not in Germany.[12] While the decline is not monotonic, the magnitude of the change in dispersion over the entire age range is substantial in the United States with the within-age standard deviation for age 9 establishments 13 per cent below that for age 1 establishments. Finally, Fig. 3.3 shows that both the United States and Germany exhibit decreasing dispersion in investment per worker over the age distribution. The decreased dispersion is more marked in the United States, consistent with the notion that young businesses in the United States experiment with a wider range of strategies than do their counterparts in Germany.

---

[12] In unreported results, we have calculated similar statistics using industry controls to remove the effect of different industrial structures across the two countries. That is, before calculating the statistics, we deviate each measure from the relevant industry-specific two-digit STAN mean. We find the same basic patterns in those results. In particular, even controlling for industry, we find that productivity dispersion falls systematically with age in the United States but it does not fall in Germany. For example, for the United States, the standard deviation of log productivity decreases from 0.92 (compare with Tables A.3a and A.3b in Appendix) for the youngest plants to 0.67 for the most mature plants while the equivalent statistics for Germany are 0.54 (youngest) and 0.59 (most mature). The patterns for other variables are similar as well. We also repeated the exercise using the employment weighted distribution and found similar patterns.

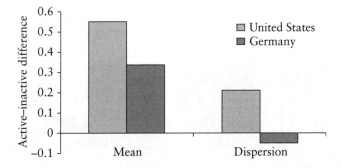

Figure 3.4. *Active vs. inactive gap in mean and dispersion of productivity*

3.4.2. *The role of active learning—Differentiating between businesses actively changing their technology and others*

Businesses that are actively changing their technology are also inherently experimenting. There is uncertainty about the best way to implement a new technology and/or whether the business in question is capable of implementing the new technology in a successful manner. Again, different market and institutional environments may provide different incentives for experimentation. If adjustment costs from institutional factors limit flexibility then businesses may choose a lower mean, lower risk strategy of implementation.

For this analysis, we use the technology groups that we used in the simple regression analysis in Section 3.3. For example, businesses that are most actively engaged in changing their technologies are the 'High/High' group—those businesses that are above the seventy-fifth percentile in both equipment investment per worker and computer investment per worker.

We summarize the results of this analysis in Figs 3.4 and 3.5 that are based upon the analysis by more detailed technology groups that are in Tables A.4 and A.5 in the appendix. For illustrative purposes, in Figs 3.4 and 3.5, we collapse the seven technology groups into two that we designate as active and inactive. The active group consists of groups 'High/High', 'High/Low', 'Low/High', and 'High/0'. The inactive group consists of groups '0/0', 'Low/Low', and 'Low/0'. In other words, the active group has at least one of the investment indicators in the high category (i.e. above the seventy-fifth percentile in either or both the total or computer investment intensity distributions) and the inactive group has neither investment indicator in the high group.[13]

---

[13] The appendix tables make clear that these summary patterns are robust to alternative cut-offs of the respective groupings. For example, if the 'High/0' group is made part of the 'low' summary group the patterns in Figs 3.3–3.5 remain the same.

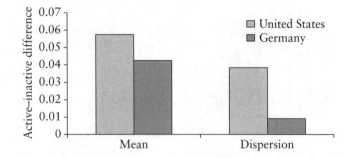

Figure 3.5. *Active vs. inactive gap in mean and dispersion of skill mix*

Figure 3.4 shows the difference in the mean productivity and the dispersion of productivity between the active and inactive groups. Figure 3.5 shows the analogous statistics for the skill mix. The detailed statistics in Tables A.4 and A.5 show that in terms of means, businesses that are more actively changing their technology in both countries have higher productivity, higher payroll per worker, a higher skill mix, and have more workers with access to the Internet (an alternative technology measure in its own right). These patterns are more pronounced in the United States. Figures 3.4 and 3.5 highlight this finding as they show that the difference in the mean productivity and mean skill across the tech groups is greater in the United States.

The striking difference between the United States and Germany is in the dispersion across the technology groups. In the United States, Tables A.4 and A.5 show that businesses most actively changing their technology have greater dispersion in productivity, payroll per worker, the skill mix of workers, computer and equipment investment per worker, and the Internet access relative to those businesses less actively changing their technology. The differences in dispersion are substantially larger and more systematic in the United States relative to Germany as illustrated in Figs 3.4 and 3.5. For example, Fig. 3.4 shows that the increase in productivity dispersion from the inactive to the active tech groups is more than 20 log points. Figure 3.5 shows that the increase in dispersion in the skill mix from the inactive to active tech is about 4 log points. These patterns are less pronounced and less systematic for Germany. For example, Fig. 3.4 shows that there is slightly lower dispersion in productivity in the active tech group and the detailed statistics in the appendix tables show that this reflects the lack of a systematic relationship between productivity dispersion and technology groups in Germany.

To explore these findings further, we use the results from Section 3.3 above that relate the characteristics of the business to the productivity differences. In particular, we use the regression results in Table 3.3 to examine how much of the changes in productivity dispersion across technology groups can be accounted for by changes in the dispersion of characteristics across businesses

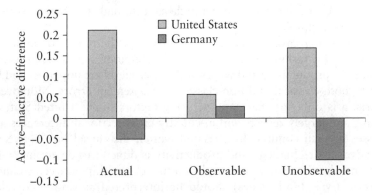

Figure 3.6. *Active vs. inactive gap in productivity dispersion: observable and unobservable factors*

(e.g. skill mix, Internet access, and computer investment and equipment investment per worker) and how much is accounted for by unobservable factors. Figure 3.6 presents the results of this exercise (and results by detailed technology group are in Table A.6 in Appendix). Interestingly, both observable and unobservable factors help account for the increasing dispersion with the pace of technology change in the United States. These results are consistent with the view that experimentation occurs over both observable and unobservable dimensions. That is, the contribution of observables may reflect the role of experimentation as businesses try different ways of conducting business. Alternatively, the role of the unobservables might be interpreted as suggesting that those businesses most actively changing their technology face considerable uncertainty about how best to change the technology and whether they have the 'ability' to change the technology successfully. Apparently, both observable and unobservable factors are important in the United States. For Germany, given that there is not a large or systematic relationship between the pace of technology changes and dispersion, it is harder to interpret the results.

3.5. SUMMARY AND INTERPRETATION

The evidence presented in this chapter provides further support to the idea that US businesses engage in experimentation in a variety of ways not matched by their German counterparts. In particular, there is greater experimentation amongst young US businesses and among those actively changing their technology. This experimentation is evidenced in a greater dispersion in productivity and in related key business choices, like the skill mix and Internet access for workers. We also find that the mean impact of adopting new technology is greater in the United States than in Germany. Putting the pieces together suggests that US businesses choose a higher mean, higher variance strategy in adopting new technology.

There are many caveats and cautions that must be noted for interpreting the results in this fashion. Our measures of technology as well as measures of outcomes like productivity and wages at the micro level are imperfect and likely subject to both classical and non-classical measurement errors. Moreover, the comparison is only for the manufacturing sectors in the United States and Germany, and largely reflects within-country cross-sectional differences across businesses in each country. In a related matter, the causal link between the use of advanced technology and productivity is difficult to determine without longitudinal data and, thus, our results on the relationship between technology and productivity (and wages) should be interpreted as simple correlation between the variables of interest. Bearing these caveats in mind, the covariance structure between productivity and measures of changing technology differ systematically at the micro level across the United States and Germany in a manner that is clearly suggestive of the United States exhibiting a greater degree of experimentation in the adoption of new technologies.

There are many areas of research that we have only touched upon that deserve further exploration. For one, the micro-based results in this chapter on experimentation seem to line up well in broad terms with the micro- as well as aggregate-based analysis in prior chapters. However, the analysis is not fully integrated as the sample periods and countries differ across the different parts of the analysis. Full micro and macro reconciliation of the statistics and analysis is beyond the scope of this study but should be an objective for analysis and development of such statistics in the future. In addition, we have only touched on the many different sources of heterogeneity across businesses in this analysis that may underlie the role of experimentation. One of the most policy-relevant is the differences in the demand for skills and the associated differences in internal labour market and human resource practices across businesses. The type of experimentation we stress in this study obviously has implications for labour market dynamics given the implied reallocation of labour. However, beyond these obvious implications, there may be even more far-reaching implications. Relevant open questions include: Is market experimentation across businesses closely linked to the demand for skills and human resource practices? Are the successful businesses those that not only adopt advanced technologies on the 'hard' side of technology (i.e. IT) but also on the 'soft' side of technology? Analysis by Bresnahan *et al.* (2002) suggests, for example, that successful adoption of IT is closely related to the human resource and organizational practices of businesses. To explore such ideas, the micro data that we have used in this analysis must be augmented with richer data on the mix of workers at businesses as well as richer measures of the hard and soft sides of technology. Developing the micro datasets that permit such analysis should be another priority for the future.

4

ICT and Growth: The Role of Factor and Product Markets

4.1. INTRODUCTION

The economic model needed to understand the role of ICT is not unified and different theories are needed to explain how growth occurs through different channels (namely, through capital deepening and technology shifts, or through growth in the ICT producing sector). On the one hand, neoclassical investment theory and more modern versions incorporating uncertainty are needed to understand the process of capital deepening associated to the spread of ICT. On the other hand, theories of endogenous growth may shed some light on growth within firms in the ICT producing sector. Likewise, strategic industrial organization theory can help explain how firms use innovation as a competitive weapon, and how resources move between competing firms and sectors of the economy. Finally, growth models with an evolutionary flavour emphasize that firms grope for the proper configuration of inputs, outputs, and technology in an attempt to profitably serve the market. As an illustration, Table 4.1 below shows the main channels through which ICT is expected to boost growth, along with the theory needed to understand the mechanisms, and the institutional or policy environment that impinges on the mechanism.

The various models used to shed light on the mechanisms underlying the effects of ICT on growth need to be consistent with the stylized facts displayed in the previous chapters. These include the findings that the US had higher ICT investment intensity than the EU on average during the 1990s. Further, the European countries did not enjoy the productivity boom in the late 1990s. At the micro level, entrants are relatively smaller in the US but grow much faster, conditional on survival. Entrants exhibit more dispersion in productivity and ICT investment in US relative to Germany. Also, the dispersion in a range of indicators among firms with high ICT intensity is larger in US than in the German manufacturing sector. These micro patterns suggest a greater degree of market experimentation in the US via the net entry process as well as among those actively changing their technology. A full model that explains all the features cannot be pulled off the shelf, although the different models described

Table 4.1. *Growth channel, theory, and policy*

Channel	Driving force/ Theoretical	Area of possible policy
Capital deepening	Investment; growth accounting	Factor markets
MFP		
Innovative adoption of ICT within firms		
Process/product	R&D; strategic industrial organization	Product markets
Internal organization	Experimentation; labour	Factor markets
Resource reallocation	General equilibrium; strategic	Factor and product markets
Knowledge creation	R&D; endogenous growth	Science and technology policy
ICT producers		
Within firm	R&D; endogenous growth	Factor and product markets
Resource reallocation	General equilibrium; strategic	Factor and product markets

below in turn, exhibit features that can help explain some of the emerging facts.

The role of market experimentation helps reinforce the view, as stressed by Baily (2002), that the adoption of ICT requires explicit innovative actions. Firms producing ICT goods, or making use of ICT both must experiment with their production processes and the characteristics of goods and services produced in order to find a combination that is successful in the market place. Productivity and profitability differences driven by differential efficiencies, costs and customer preferences yield a selection mechanism that sorts out the good from the bad implementations of ICT in the 'research laboratory' that is the market.

In this chapter, we first discuss alternative perspectives on the role of ICT for economic growth—in particular as an investment good and as an innovative activity. Using this discussion, we then describe each of the growth channels in turn in a relatively brief fashion. Our primary objective is to provide a framework to assess how market institutions may affect incentives for firms to innovate and adopt ICT and therefore influence the process of economic growth.

4.2. ICT AS AN INVESTMENT GOOD

In Table 4.1, investment theory offers a tool to interpret how the process of capital deepening associated to the shift to ICT equipment can boost growth. The importance of this channel for the total expected growth effect of ICT is, however, an empirical issue. Growth accounting quantifies the effect by treating ICT investment in the same way as other asset purchases and the hiring of other productive inputs. As seen in Chapter 2, the contribution of ICT to growth is much smaller in EU countries than in the US. Most of the difference derives from a lower stock of ICT assets, and thus a lower expenditure share on this input into production, although growth rates of ICT capital services continue to lag somewhat in the EU as well.

The variables that determine the contribution of ICT capital services to growth in the accounting framework include tax rates, asset depreciation, and asset prices, as well as the rate of return on investment. The allocation of resources between ICT capital services and other factors of production also depends on asset prices for other investment types, as well as the wage rate. For this reason, framework conditions in the factor markets are important for investment in ICT. In recent studies (e.g. Caballero and Hammour (1998) and Blanchard, 2001), bargaining power of workers, or stringent labour market (LM) regulations may push firms away from labour and towards more capital-intensive technologies. There is enough evidence that LM regulations tend to be stricter in most EU countries than in the US but there is much less information on how regulations affect the relative share of ICT in total capital input. From the micro-level manufacturing data we do see that investment per worker in individual industries is higher in Germany than in the United States, but that the ratio of ICT investment to total equipment investment is about the same.

Another variable that plays a role in investment decision is the uncertainty surrounding returns to investment in high-tech equipment. With small modifications to standard theory, the option value of waiting before committing to sunk investment can be incorporated into the investment function. In general, investment will be lower in a more volatile environment (Dixit and Pindyck, 1994). The effect of this type of uncertainty on the choice between ICT and other equipment is not clear. On the one hand, the general-purpose nature of ICT provides exactly the kind of flexibility in future production that options theory calls for. On the other hand, the technological uncertainty of ICT-related investment projects is likely to be higher than tried-and-true equipment, which would justify a wait and see strategy concerning ICT investment choices. Although it is proper to consider technological uncertainty as a cause of slow diffusion, this path is not able to explain the differences in ICT intensity across countries, nor the differences in firm-level heterogeneity seen in the micro-level manufacturing data.

4.3. ICT ADOPTION AS AN INNOVATIVE ACTIVITY

Describing ICT investment through use of neoclassical investment theory does not appear to be able to account for the differences across countries, sectors or firms, and does not explain fully how ICT use may affect growth. Seeing

ICT adoption by a firm as an innately innovative activity is an alternative perspective that can potentially help in this regard. How do these two views of ICT adoption differ, and why does business spending on innovative activities (e.g. R&D), require such different theory from investment in buildings or traditional equipment?

Expenditures on traditional capital (structures and equipment) and expenditures on ICT have costs and benefits associated with them, with associated factor prices, and marginal revenue products. Both types of expenditures are characterised by benefits that occur over time and by timing differences in the flow of benefits and costs, thus requiring some method of expectations formation and of discounting to determine optimal current expenditures. However, the effects of uncertainty may differ between the two types of expenditures. The chance of a successful outcome is related to the effort spent on innovation. Further, with innovative activities, the outcome of the search for a better mousetrap may be uncertain, but once a successful discovery is made, the result may be used elsewhere by the firm at relatively little extra cost. These characteristics are consistent with viewing ICT as a general purpose technology (see Bresnahan and Trajtenberg, 1995). Also, they underlie the predictions emerging from endogenous growth models.

ICT may be used by firms in many different ways and for many different purposes, but it is unknown a priori how best to implement the technology. Unfortunately, the search for improvements through adoption of ICT is not yet formalized in the manner that R&D laboratories are. In an R&D lab, trial and error takes place in a controlled environment, at an experimental scale. No such laboratory exists in implementing ICT to improve business processes or products. Instead, the laboratory for figuring out and developing good implementations of ICT must be the market itself. To some extent, this uncertainty on how to implement ICT is shared for any change in how a business operates and thus applies to changes in the mix and scale of any of the factors of production. However, it is reasonable that changes in the way of doing business using cutting edge technologies (like ICT) involves a greater degree of trial and error and associated learning.

The search for a successful implementation of ICT is not restricted to finding ways to substitute away from labour or other productive inputs. As will be discussed below, ICT changes transactions costs within firms, and between firms and their customers and suppliers. As such, areas for improvement will involve search over strategies to increase 'organisational capital', by experimentation with various schemes such as performance pay, flexible job requirements, and workforce training (e.g. Bresnahan, Brynjolfsson and Hitt, 2002; Black and Lynch, 2001, 2002). Also firms will experiment with strategies within the supply chain, such as make-or-buy decisions, strategic alliances and customer relation management (examples from management literature, e.g. Hax and Wilde, 1999 or Duysters and Hagedoorn, 2000). In addition, firms may experiment with product characteristics using the 'mass customisation' (increased product variety without increased marginal cost) that is made possible through use of ICT. According to most theoretical accounts of innovation, the chance of success depends positively on the amount of experimentation. Because a successful ICT implementation, once found, may be replicated by the firm for not much more than the direct capital and labour input costs, firm profitability increases with scale. In an environment that changes over time, firm profitability increases if the firm can adjust its scale up or down, depending on the apparent success in the market of its particular implementation strategy.[1]

By broadening one's view of 'technology' to include the implementation through internal organization and management of supply chain as well as the physical ICT (e.g. Pavitt, 1998), the problem of within-firm innovation may be analysed through more standard growth models. For example, in models of learning, the amount of experimentation increases the learning rate and boosts the present value of profit flows (Wieland, 2000). While some of the models attempt to characterize the optimal amount of experimentation (e.g. Moscarini and Smith, 2001), they do not explicitly state how the experimentation is to take place. In the management literature, advice is given on how to infuse a firm with the desire to experiment and innovate (e.g. Hamel, 1999), but the exact methodology for experimentation is left to specialized literature.

In considering the experimentation process, the learning and selection effects emphasized by Jovanovic (1982) and Ericson and Pakes (1995) (and discussed briefly in earlier Chapters 2 and 3) are relevant. Each cohort of new entrants will face uncertainty about many facets of the way to do business but in the recent era especially how best to adopt and implement ICT. Existing businesses will also face uncertainty as they restructure and retool their production and organization as they implement ICT. Failure to adopt the new technology implies falling behind but failing to adopt the new technology successfully may be just as bad. Those entrants and those adopting businesses that have implemented poorly will have lower profits and productivity and as such will contract and exit. Those businesses that implement successfully (and/or through learning by doing learn how to implement successfully) will have profitability and productivity advantages and expand. The market selection and learning effects this perspective suggests have obvious policy implications that we discuss below.

Beyond the trial and error aspects of experimentation, another important set of factors are those that imply a possible wedge between social and private returns to innovative activities. Endogenous growth theory (e.g. Jones and Williams, 1999), describes the effect at the macro level of the market failures

---

[1] This effect is well known in the card game of black jack, where a player can make positive profits despite unfair odds overall, if he can change the size of the bet as the probability of having a winning hand changes over the course of the game.

associated with R&D. Incomplete appropriability of the benefits leads to under-investment in a decentralised equilibrium. On the other hand, 'stepping on toes' or a congestion externality occurring between firms competing for a prize leads to over-investment, as does the neglect of socials losses owing to 'business stealing' away from the incumbents using a previous generation of technology.

It does not seem likely that firms that purchase existing ICT technology and then experimentally arrive at a successful implementation have the same problem in appropriating the benefits as they would have, had they acquired truly non-rival knowledge. However, externalities associated with additional users in a communications network may hamper adoption at early stages of such networks. Likewise, the 'stepping on toes' externalities may describe problems associated with first-mover advantages inside ICT producing sectors, but less in ICT-using sectors. On the other hand, the 'business stealing' externality may be particularly relevant for ICT adopters, where the quality and variety of products or services made possible by successful implementation of ICT may rapidly erode the incumbents' market share. Differences across countries in the smoothness with which resources (both in factor and product markets) are reallocated among competing suppliers may therefore provide a possible explanation for the observed differences in the pace of ICT adoption.

It is important to note that the possible welfare externalities associated with ICT adoption are not clear-cut. There is always the possibility of excessive dynamics (Bresnahan and Reiss, 1987; Berry and Waldfogel, 1999; Jones and Williams, 1998). Negative externalities of 'stepping on toes' and business stealing may outweigh the positive externality of knowledge spillovers and create excessive investment in innovative activities. Although hard empirical proof is lacking, Jones and Williams (1998) gather circumstantial evidence that overall R&D investment is sub-optimal in a decentralised economy.

4.4. THE GROWTH CHANNELS

With the two views of ICT adoption—as an asset investment or as an innovation process—highlighted above, we now turn to the channels through which ICT adoption could lead to higher growth. First, labour productivity and output grow as a result of capital deepening. Growth accounting in Chapter 1 shows how investment in ICT that increases the real flow of services attributable to the stock of ICT assets contributes to output growth. This direct channel of ICT adoption to output is well understood, theoretically and empirically. More interesting are the possibilities that the adoption of ICT provides efficiency gains over and above the contribution of capital deepening. Even when quality improvements in ICT assets are controlled for (see Chapter 2), the measured multifactor (MFP) residual still shows rates of 'technical change' that varies across countries. An open question is whether ICT is contributing to this residual 'technological' growth. The following sketches out how ICT adoption may end up boosting MFP growth.

4.4.1. *MFP growth*

As emphasized above, investment in ICT can be viewed as adoption of a new general purpose technology with potentially far reaching implications for how businesses do business. To reiterate the points made above, ICT potentially contributes by increasing the efficiency of communication and information processing throughout parts of the economy where many actors successfully have implemented the technology. The improvements in communication and information processing have direct consequences for (at least) two aspects of economic processes: (i) transaction cost will go down and (ii) the productivity of knowledge workers will increase.[2] In a related manner, ICT implementation is associated with changes in the organizational capital of firms (as emphasized for example by Bresnahan *et al.*, 2002). All of these channels offer scope for investment in ICT to increase multifactor productivity growth (i.e. to have an impact on growth beyond the traditional channel of capital deepening).

Economic transactions, whether they take place among people, between firms and customers, or between firms are accompanied by transaction costs. These include transport costs and search costs, but also the costs incurred to check whether contracts are carried out properly (see Milgrom and Roberts, 1994 for a detailed discussion). The distorting effects of these costs are well known: they place a wedge in the match-up of demand and supply. It is indeed possible that economically desirable transactions do not occur because of excessive transaction costs.

The use of ICT could yield more efficient communication between economic parties. For instance, to better match demand and supply in the labour market, but also to aid in the logistics of production processes, with the purchase of final consumer products (e-commerce) or with the transaction between firms (business-to-business commerce). Indeed, examples abound of internet-based markets, such as the market for real estate or for automotive parts. Unfortunately, factual estimates of the magnitude of the reduction in transactions costs due to ICT are scarce.

Less clear are the quantitative economic consequences of the emergence of new markets and/or the growth of existing markets as a result of decreasing transaction costs. In the former situation an entirely new market comes into existence with concomitant surplus. In the latter case existing producers' and consumers' surplus can increase. An example of such a situation is the market for second-hand commodities. On-line auctions make it possible that buyers and sellers don't have to be at the same physical place. Millions of transactions

---

[2] A third effect is that the supply and demand curves can change through increased ICT uptake; supply curves tilt since marginal costs fall relative to fixed costs because of the non-rival nature of knowledge as a production factor, while demand curves tilt due to the increased frequency and force of (network) externalities (see Shapiro and Varian (1998)). For the story we develop here these consequences are of less importance.

can be handled real-time. Indeed, this market has experienced a spectacular growth in recent years, leading to a more efficient allocation of the stock of existing goods.

Another possible implication of the penetration of ICT is that ICT intensity and competition in a market are positively correlated. If markets become more transparent firms have to resort to enhancements of their products and processes in order not to loose market share. Put differently, ICT investments by firms react to market structure, and in turn affect market structure. What this means is that the penetration of ICT into economic processes is ruled, to some extent, by a snowball effect, where the incentive to adopt ICT increases with the penetration rate.

The second consequence of ICT use throughout the economy is its possible impact on the efficiency of knowledge creation and innovation. Knowledge workers conduct R&D in order to come up with new products (product innovations) or enhance the efficiency of existing production processes (process innovations). Due to the use of ICT in research it is quite possible that the number of successful product and/or process innovations increases for the same R&D efforts. Besides the use of ICT to provide useful scientific and technical information for knowledge workers, the effectiveness of R&D may increase because ICT allows more rapid feedback on customer desires.

All of these effects are associated with potential changes in the organizational structure of firms. The manner in which firms interact with each other (through changes in the supply-chain structure and management) and the manner in which firms organize and locate their production facilities, capital and workforce inputs are all potentially impacted by the implementation of ICT. The work of Bresnahan, Brynjolffson and Hitt (2002), for example, suggests that those businesses that also changed their organizational capital exhibited the largest productivity gains from ICT. Thus, it may be that the contributions of ICT to the measured residual technology growth are also (or even mostly) associated with the accompanying changes in organizational capital.

4.4.2. *ICT production*

Improvements in the efficiency and quality of ICT production can also contribute directly to growth. One of the contributing factors here is that one of the largest users of this technology is the ICT-producing sector itself: in this context, both the traditional capital deepening channel as well as the multi-factor productivity channel may play an especially large role in the ICT sector itself. The trial and error process of using ICT to enhance the production of ICT may be even bigger than the average, given that businesses in the producing sector are among the first users of the very latest advances in the technology. Changes in the organization structure of the ICT producers have been profound over the last several decades, with both large producers and small producers playing an important role. In like manner, both mature businesses and start-ups have played an important role and the location of production of key components of the ICT products has changed dramatically. For example, much of semiconductor production of chips has been shifted to Pacific Rim countries.

4.5. MARKET INSTITUTIONS: THE ROLE OF PRODUCT AND FACTOR MARKETS

The incentives to innovate in the ICT and adopt this technology depend critically on the structure of product markets. Moreover, the rapid changes in the organizational structure required by the adoption of this technology implies that the structure of product and factor markets plays a critical role in its evolution. In this section, we discuss briefly how market institutions and the regulatory setting may influence both ICT-producing and ICT-using businesses. It is beyond the scope of this chapter to provide a comprehensive survey of the literature on the role of market institutions and policies for promoting growth via the channels discussed above. Instead, we discuss some of the key points that have emerged in the literature that will help guide the empirical analysis of the role of policy in the next chapter. The basic hypothesis relating policy and regulations to incentives for innovation and adoption is non-controversial, that is, policy barriers to resources being allocated to their highest valued use may have an adverse impact on economic performance in general, and on productivity growth in particular. While this view is not controversial, it is an open question as to what specific policies and regulations act as main barriers to innovation and adoption.

The following discussion focuses on the effect of product market competition and the product and factor market environment on the incentives for development, adoption and experimentation of new technologies. The discussion pays less attention to the effect of stable macro policies on capital accumulation in general and on growth through the traditional capital deepening channel of ICT in particular. Our lack of attention to macro policies does not imply that these policies are unimportant but rather that such a perspective is already reasonably well understood and agreed upon. Further, it does not seem that the differences in the contribution of ICT to growth between the US and Europe lie in the differences in macro policies across these countries.

4.5.1. *Product and factor markets and within firm growth*

Starting with the role of product market competition, the theoretical literature has yielded ambiguous results about the sign and the magnitude of the impact of competition on innovation. The standard Schumpeterian argument is that the relationship between competition and innovation is negative, due to the hypothesized negative impact of competition on the appropriability of innovation profits. In general, the statement that post-innovation rents should be high enough to cover the cost of innovation is relatively uncontroversial (see e.g. Kamien and Schwartz, 1982 and Geroski, 1990). The policy implication is that some protection of intellectual property rights is needed (IPRs hereafter).

Pre-innovation market power may be a requisite for innovation. Nelson and Winter (1982), among others, point to the role of retained profits in financing innovation in a world of imperfect capital markets. Levin (1978) emphasizes the role of pre-innovation barriers to enforce post-innovation monopoly power. Others argue that, in certain industries, to the extent that future innovations complement past ones, incumbents may have higher returns from innovation than entrants.

In contrast to these views, textbook microeconomic theory suggests that competition brings about allocative efficiency gains by forcing price to converge to marginal costs. The role of competition in raising efficiency may not, however, be limited to such static gains; additional potential gains—much larger in magnitude—arise from 'dynamic efficiency'. Dynamic efficiency is likely to bring about additional gains because firms will continue to improve their performance in ways they would not have were competitive pressures weak (Winston, 1993). Moreover, taking a dynamic perspective on competition allows to understand better new forms of competition observed in 'dynamically' competitive industries (Evans and Schmalensee, 2001).

Models focussing on dynamic efficiency need a premise as to why monopolistic firms do not minimize costs or the present value of costs. Much of the literature takes recourse to information asymmetry and the associated agency problems. In these models, monopoly rents are captured by managers (and workers) in the form of managerial 'slack' or reduced work effort, and product market competition disciplines firms into efficient operation. At least three different channels can be identified (Nickell et al., 1997). First, competition creates greater opportunities for comparing performance, making it easier for the owners or the market to monitor managers (Lazear and Rosen, 1981; Nalebuff and Stiglitz, 1983). Next, since more competition is likely to raise the likelihood of bankruptcy at any given level of managerial effort, managers may work harder to avoid this outcome (Schmidt, 1997; Aghion and Howitt, 1998). Also, if product market rents are partly shared with workers in the form of higher wages or reduced effort, then competition probably influences workers' behaviour too (Haskel and Sanchis, 1995).

It should be stressed that theoretical predictions of the effects of greater competition on managers' incentives are often 'subtle and ambiguous' (Vickers, 1995). For example, models using *explicit* incentives under information asymmetry do not lead to clear-cut implications (see e.g. Holmström, 1982), while intertemporal models using *implicit* (i.e. market-based) rewards suggest a positive link between competition and managerial effort if productivity shocks are more correlated across competitors than managerial abilities (Meyer and Vickers, 1997). But, competition could also lead to more slack if managers are highly responsive to monetary incentives (Scharfstein, 1988).

As we have emphasized in the analysis in the first three chapters, the role of the trial and error of the innovation and adoption process and therefore the need for market experimentation does provide an argument in support of the view that competitive pressures yield greater dynamic efficiency. Market power permits inefficient producers who should contract or exit to continue to survive and maintain market share. If such inefficient producers/innovators survive because of market power then average within firm growth (due to innovation and adoption) may be lower as well.

Turning to factor markets, factor market regulation and the specific employment contracts resulting from the labour bargaining setting, may restrict the domain over which firms may experiment. If changing the size of the overall labour force is difficult, firms may not want to experiment too much in make-or-buy decisions. If pay scales and job description are written in stone, firms may not be able to play with incentive schemes that induce employees to undertake new initiatives. Overall, with a restricted domain of configurations to choose from, theory would predict less within firm productivity growth from the channel of organization and supply chain management.

4.5.2. *Factor and product markets and resource reallocation*

Factor and product market policies also play an important role in determining innovative activity and growth through the channel of resource reallocation from less to more productive firms (including reallocation through firm entry and exit).[3] The arguments here are different in nature from those that rely on asymmetric information. If competitive pressure is lacking, not only are managers able to avoid extra effort for the reasons given earlier, but the overall rewards to the firm from innovative effort may be lower as well, because the market does not respond by shifting demand to firms with better price or quality. In a more competitive market, buyers will more rapidly shift their expenditures to a firm that has made a successful product or process innovation. If factor markets are flexible, firms will be able to adjust factor inputs to match the demand for their products and the most efficient producers will expand while the less efficient producers will contract and potentially exit.

The overall effect of competition on incentives to innovate through the resource reallocation channel is not unambiguous. Although demand may shift more rapidly to the better firms, overall mark-ups and profit margins may decline with heightened competition. Yet, what is important to a firm is the difference between expected profit following innovation, versus profit if it falls behind technologically. Further complications in the link between competition

---

[3] It should be noted that the channel called resource reallocation here includes more than what is captured in the 'between' term in productivity decompositions. This channel also includes the incentive effect that resource reallocation has on inducing firms to increase their own productivity, which is captured in the 'within' term in decompositions.

and incentives to innovate relate to relative technological positions of firms in the market. A firm that is far ahead in its technology may sit back while innovative efforts by competitors do not lead to large movements in market share. Overall, recent theoretical work find a hump-shaped relationship between competition and innovation, while recent empirical work show a positive relationship.

Modelling the effect of product market competition on resource reallocation is not straightforward. First, endogenous growth models with entry, exit, and reallocation of resources between firms are only recently being developed (Klette and Kortum, 2002). Next, the literature is still groping towards a generally accepted indicator of the degree of product market competition (Boone, 2000*a,b*). Finally, only recently are the various pieces being put together (Aghion *et al.*, 2002; Bartelsman and Hinloopen, 2002). Although a full model has not been developed to explain the role of factor and product markets in reallocation, we will give a description of the requirements for such a model, by pulling together pieces from the existing literature.

The Klette and Kortum model provides a framework for studying endogenous growth in a setting with heterogeneous firms. The model is able to account for many of the stylized facts emerging from firm-level empirical studies and yields results at the aggregate level that coincide with quality ladder models (Grossman and Helpman, 1991). In the model, the heterogeneity of innovation intensity across firms is imposed by assuming that firm profitability varies across firms.[4] Further, the model assumes monopolistic competition across differentiation products, but assumes the innovator takes all in the quality ladder for each particular differentiated product. Extensions of this model could allow multiple suppliers of each product, with the degree indicator of competitiveness determining how the profit shares move with technological state of the supplier. A reasonable indicator of the degree of competitiveness of an industry has the property that it moves monotonically with the profit share of the efficient firms, as argued by Boone (2001*a,b*).

Models that capture both the heterogeneity among firms, entry, exit, and reallocation of resources between incumbents, innovative activity, and the degree of competition, must take into consideration some of the following effects. First, when considering the incentive to innovate, the expenses of the innovative activity should not be balanced against the expected profit flows, but against the difference in expected profit flows between this case, and the case in which no innovative activities where undertaken. With stronger competition, mark-ups may be lower, but the loss of market share and rents for firms without successful innovations may be larger than under weak

---

[4] Further research will be needed to extend the model such that experimentation by firms causes heterogeneity in profits and innovation intensity.

competition. Next, the effect of heightened competition on the incentive to innovate may depend on how close the competing firms are technologically. Aghion *et al.* (2001*a*) argue that, for any given level of protection of IPRs, fierce competition between firms with similar technological competencies (neck-and-neck competition) may force them to innovate in order to escape competitive pressure. Boone (2000*a*) shows how incentives vary depending on state of efficiency relative to competitors, and distinguishes the effects of competition on product and process innovation. Based on results in Aghion *et al.* (2002), it is generally thought that the relationship between competition and innovative activity is hump-shaped. The intuition is that the expected profit from a risky investment increases with more competition, up to a point, because the gains from a higher market share for successful innovator are not outweighed by the reductions from the decline in mark-up.

The above discussion deals primarily with product market competition. Because the costs of resource reallocation increase with less flexible factor markets, the incentive for innovation should increase monotonically with more flexibility. Further, the ease of reallocation boosts growth through the direct arithmetic channel of increasing the share of more productive firms, but also through the incentives it creates firms to innovate and boost their own productivity level. In an environment where innovation and experimentation are closely linked, barriers to reallocating capital and labor inputs can have a very adverse impact on productivity and growth.

4.6. SUMMARY

In this chapter, we sketched the main links between factor and product market policies, innovation, and growth. In particular,

- We outlined three possible channels through which ICT can affect growth: (i) the 'traditional' process of capital deepening; (ii) ICT as an instrument for innovative activity; (iii) the contribution of the ICT-producing sector to aggregate growth. Since we consider ICT as a general-purpose technology, we have placed considerable emphasis on the role of experimentation in the development of new ICT products as well as in the implementation of ICT. For the latter, we stressed that ICT has changed (and will change in the future) the manner in which businesses organize themselves internally and interact externally with other businesses and consumers.

- The emphasis on experimentation raises a variety of questions regarding the appropriate market institutions for promoting growth via ICT. Incentives for the development of an ICT-production industry seems to be affected by market structure and externalities in complex ways raising difficult questions about the appropriate market policy interventions (if any).

In terms of both innovation and adoption, experimentation suggests that market selection and learning effects are likely to be important. As such, barriers to the reallocation of capital and labour inputs across sectors and firms can adversely influence the successful development and adoption and diffusion of innovative technologies like ICT.

5

Do Policy and Regulatory Settings Help to Explain Industry Differences in Productivity and Innovation Activities Across OECD Countries?

5.1. INTRODUCTION

In Chapters 1–3, we described the impact of information and communication technology (ICT) on productivity and growth, both at the aggregate and micro levels, highlighting differences between Organization for Economic Cooperation and Development (OECD) countries. One is naturally led to conjecture as to what generates these differences, especially given that the capabilities and costs of ICT are more or less the same across countries. In Chapter 4, drawing from different theoretical models, we then advanced the hypothesis that these differences may be related to the institutional and policy settings characterizing the OECD countries. Theory, however, does not give clear indications as to the magnitude of the effects, or to the specific aspects of the institutional and policy settings that are of foremost importance for performance. This final chapter of Part I provides some empirical evidence on this issue by relating industry-level performance in different countries with a set of OECD indicators of product and labour market policy and institutions.

Ideally, we would like to trace the link between market institutions, the investment in and adoption of ICT, and differences in productivity dynamics and innovation activity across countries. However, data limitations make this analysis rather difficult, at least on a cross-country basis (i.e. the relevant dimension to study policy and institutions). Instead, we take an indirect approach and look at the broader links between policy, productivity, and innovation, after controlling for a set of other possible influences. The implications of the empirical results for our ICT discussion are, however, straightforward. First, we explore the links between policy and industry performance during the 1980s and 1990s, when the ICT shock offered many new opportunities to boost internal efficiency and innovation. In this respect, we are looking at a 'natural experiment' in which differences in policy and institutional settings may have been particularly important in influencing the firms' decisions.

Second, the focus on individual industries in manufacturing allows taking into account possible differences in their patterns of innovation and adoption of new technologies. This enables us to identify ICT-producing industries and industries that are heavy users of ICT equipment and check for any difference in performance with respect to other industries.

In the chapter, we will confine ourselves to regulatory settings in the product and labour markets, thereby leaving aside other relevant macroeconomic and structural policies (e.g. financial systems, education policies, or migration rules for high skilled workers) that can be of paramount importance in the process of diffusion of ICT. As a consequence, the conclusions of the analysis may not be exhaustive of all potential influences of policy and institutional settings. The chapter is organized as follows. We first review the empirical literature linking policy and institutions with innovation and productivity. Second, we conduct our own empirical exploration along two separate dimensions. First, we explore the role of policy and institutions on productivity, while controlling for technological catch-up across countries and innovation efforts (proxied by R&D). Second, we look at whether policy and institutions also affect innovation itself and, via this channel, further contribute to shape productivity performance. If one sees the investment and adoption of ICT as a form of innovative activity, then these results may provide a direct explanation for the observed differences in the spread of ICT across countries.

5.2. EXISTING EMPIRICAL EVIDENCE

5.2.1. *Product market competition, innovation, and productivity*

The empirical evidence on the links between product market competition and productivity growth is limited and not always conclusive. Some studies focus on trade liberalization with estimated positive effects on both the level and growth rates of productivity (Van Wijnbergen and Venables, 1993; MacDonald, 1994). There have also been attempts to link *technical efficiency* to competition. For example, Caves and Barton (1990), Caves *et al.* (1982), and Green and Mayes (1991) suggest that, above a certain threshold, market concentration leads to a reduction in technical efficiency. Other studies look at specific industries across different countries and assess the role of domestic and global competition (Porter, 1990; Baily and Gersbach, 1995; McKinsey Global Institute, 1997; and several articles in OECD, 2001*b*). These studies tend to conclude that domestic competition is the key for productivity and for gaining world market shares, although Baily and Gersbach (1995) also point to the importance of 'global competition'—that is, exposure to the best producers wherever they are located—for productivity growth. Finally, there are a number of firm-level studies that report a positive effect of competition (proxied by concentration rates, size of rents, etc.) on productivity in the United Kingdom

(Blanchflower and Machin, 1996; Nickell, 1996; Nickell *et al.*, 1997; Disney *et al.*, 2000). In contrast with the empirical studies mentioned above, Nickell (1996) simultaneously uses different measures of competition (Lerner index, concentration ratio, and a measure of the number of competitors). Less competition is found to be associated with less multifactor productivity (MFP) growth for all variables except the dummy on the number of competitors, which is found to have a negative and significant effect only when the Lerner index is not included in the equation.

Evidence on the links between product market competition and innovation is even more scant, although a number of empirical studies have found a positive association using sector- and firm-level data for the United Kingdom (e.g. see Geroski, 1990 and Blundell *et al.*, 1995, 1999).[1] These studies suggest that incumbents are pushed to innovate in order to pre-empt rivals. Conversely, Aghion *et al.* (2001*b*) find a hump-shaped relationship between patents and competition, the latter measured by price–cost mark-up in a panel of British firms. Still, for a large portion of the range of variation of the mark-up, they find an upward sloped relationship, which becomes downward sloped only in the neighbourhood of perfect competition. They also find evidence supporting the hypothesis that *ceteris paribus* neck-and-neck competition, as measured in each industry by the distance between average productivity and the international technological frontier, is associated with greater innovation performance and a more negative relationship between patents and the industry's mark-up.

Cross-country evidence on competition and innovation or productivity growth is limited and often confined to bivariate correlations (Koedijk and Kremers, 1996), case studies (Havrylyshyn, 1990), or the inclusion of a tariff rate or import restriction variable in cross-country growth regressions (Lee, 1993). Some authors also provide indirect evidence on the association of import penetration with innovation and growth, although import penetration may also proxy international technological spillovers and not only the level of competitive pressure (Coe and Helpman, 1995).

There are a number of reasons why cross-country evidence is scarce. Commonly used indicators of competition (such as mark-ups or concentration indexes) are endogenous to innovation and, as typical in empirical studies of growth, it is often difficult to find suitable instruments. Analysis based on panel data with a long time dimension can somewhat alleviate this problem by exploiting the lag structure. However long time series are often not available on a cross-country basis. An additional problem, which also concerns studies conducted on panel data, is that measures such as concentration indexes (e.g. n-firm concentration ratios and the Herfindahl index) or the Lerner index are not likely to be monotone with respect to common notions of competition (see Boone, 2000*a*, 2001*a*). Finally, these indexes fail to provide a direct link to the policy or regulation.

---

[1] See also Cohen (1995) for a survey of earlier studies.

Given that the degree of product market competition cannot be easily gauged from direct observation, an alternative route consists of focusing into its policy determinants. In particular, we will use a set of cross-country quantitative indicators of product market regulation (PMR) and regulatory reform developed by the OECD.[2] These indicators measure the pro-competitive stance of regulation on the basis of a large set of regulatory provisions in OECD countries.[3] Letting aside political economy considerations (see e.g. Duso and Röller, 2001), indicators of regulatory stance can be considered less endogenous to performance variables than mark-ups or concentration indexes. Moreover, their relationship with common notions of competition is, in principle, less ambiguous. Nevertheless, given that these indicators take into account only legal regulatory provisions, they might fall short of capturing all relevant factors determining actual competitive pressure.

Before presenting the econometric analysis, it is instructive to have a graphical look at the cross-country aggregate evidence concerning the links between MFP growth, indicators of innovation performance, and PMR indicators. We start with a quick glance at the empirical relationship between innovative activity and growth. The evidence is generally supportive of a positive and strong relationship between innovation performance and output or productivity growth, especially when the analysis is conducted at the sectoral or firm levels.[4] In aggregate cross-country regressions, it is somewhat more difficult to establish a clear link between an indicator of R&D effort and productivity

---

[2] We use different indicators of the stringency of regulations in the product and labour markets. The overall index of the stringency of PMR is a static indicator (referring to conditions in 1998), composed of three elements: (1) direct *state control* of economic activities, through state shareholdings or other types of intervention in the decisions of business sector enterprises and the use of command and control regulations; (2) *barriers to private entrepreneurial activity*, through legal limitations on access to markets, or administrative burdens and opacities hampering the creation of businesses; and (3) regulatory *barriers to international trade and investment*, through explicit legal and tariff provisions or regulatory and administrative obstacles. In order to further characterize the regulatory settings in the R&D equation, this overall indicator is further split into *outward-oriented* regulations (e.g. tariff and non-tariff barriers) and *inward-oriented* regulations. The latter have also been split into *economic* regulations (state control, legal barriers to entry, etc.) and *administrative* regulations (administrative burdens on start-ups, features of the licensing and permit system, etc.). The indicators of *employment protection legislation* (EPL) focus on both regular and temporary contracts. They are available for two periods (late 1980s and 1998) and in the econometric analysis the shift in regime has been defined on the basis of information about the timing of major EPL reforms (concerning both temporary and regular workers) in OECD countries. See Nicoletti *et al.* (1999) for more details.

[3] The aim of the OECD indicators is to measure to what extent competition and firm choices are restricted in industries and areas where there is no a priori reason to expect the government to interfere or where regulatory goals could be achieved by less coercive means. They have no ambition to measure the quality and the effectiveness of existing regulatory environments (see Nicoletti *et al.*, 1999).

[4] As summarized by Nadiri (1993), the output elasticities of R&D at the firm level tend to be around 0.1–0.3 and the rates of return around 20–30%.

growth, unless control for other factors influencing MFP is included.[5] A simple way to control for these other factors is to work with first-difference series instead of level series as in Fig. 5.1. It shows a significant correlation between *changes* in business expenditure in R&D (BERD) intensity and acceleration in MFP growth between the 1980s and the 1990s.

Furthermore, Fig. 5.2 presents evidence of a negative bivariate correlation between patent performance (another possible proxy for innovation)[6] and the OECD summary indicator of PMR that includes aspects of inward- and outward- economic and administrative regulation (see Nicoletti *et al.*, 1999). The correlation is robust to the elimination of single outliers (such as Turkey), although its significance depends considerably on a small group of countries with significantly lower patent performance (Portugal, Greece, the Czech Republic, Poland, and Turkey), whose elimination makes the correlation coefficient insignificant at the standard statistical level. Similar correlations are found with R&D intensity, another proxy for innovation activity.

Regulation on Intellectual Property Rights (IPRs) is excluded from Fig. 5.3. As stressed above, the fact that some degree of protection of IPRs is likely to have positive impact on innovation is relatively uncontroversial in the literature, while the policy debate focuses now on the optimal degree of protection

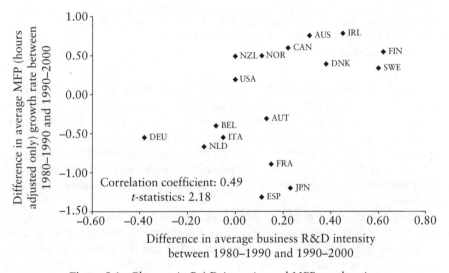

Figure 5.1. *Changes in R&D intensity and MFP acceleration*

Source: Authors' calculations.

---

[5] See among others Cameron, 1998, Frantzen, 2000, and Scarpetta and Tressel, 2002.

[6] We thank Dominique Guellec for the help provided as regard to these data.

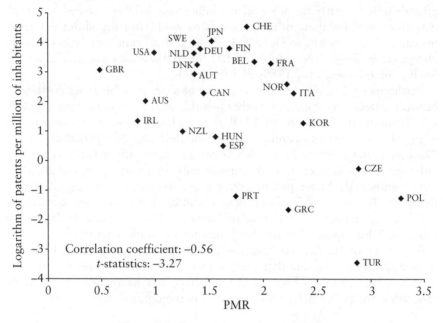

Figure 5.2. *Patents per capita and PMR*

The OECD summary index of PMR is from Nicoletti *et al.* (1999). Patents are defined as consolidated family of patent at the European Patent Office, The United States Patent Office, and the Japanese Patent Office by country of invention and priority year 1993.

Source: Authors' calculations.

(see e.g. Scotchmer, 1991 and David, 2001). Figure 5.3 shows indeed a robust positive correlation between innovation performance and an indicator of protection of IPRs developed by Ginarte and Park (1997). The direction of causality in Fig. 5.3 is however far from being obvious. Indeed, the indicator of protection of IPRs has been found to be endogenous to R&D expenditure (Ginarte and Park, 1997). Thus, care must be taken in evaluating the impact of IPR protection in this type of correlations as well as in the following regression analysis.

Figure 5.4 shows a negative correlation between the acceleration of MFP, the change in anti-competitive PMR, (Fig. 5.4(a)) and the change in regulation concerning IPRs (Fig. 5.4(b)) between the 1980s and the 1990s. Correlations are in both cases significant at the 10 per cent level. Furthermore, in Fig. 5.4(a) Ireland appears to be a clear outlier, whose elimination from the sample makes the correlation become significant at the 1 per cent level. The same occurs upon elimination of Spain in Fig. 5.4(b).

Pooling together these simple relationships in a simple regression we find that changes in anti-competitive PMR and IPRs protection explain 37 per cent of the variance of the acceleration of MFP growth. As suggested by Fig. 5.5 that plots the acceleration of MFP growth against the predicted values from

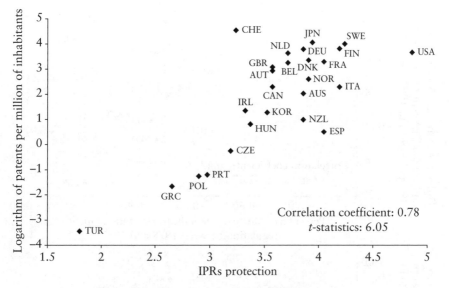

Figure 5.3. *Patents per capita and IPR protection*

The summary index of IPR protection was kindly supplied by Walter Park (see Ginarte and Park, 1997). Patents are defined as consolidated family of patent at EPO, USPTO, and JPO by country of invention and priority year 1993.

Source: Authors' calculations.

this simple regression, the relatively poor performance of these indicators is again due to Ireland (and to a lesser extent Spain) being an outlier. Indeed without Ireland the two regulatory variables become significant at the 5 per cent level and explain more 55 per cent of total variance (that climbs up to 60 per cent with elimination of Spain).

5.2.2. *Labour market institutions, innovation, and adoption*

It can be argued that labour market policies and institutions affect both the size of innovation and technology adoption rents, through their impact on the cost of pursuing innovation and adoption, and the scope for the firm to appropriate these rents rather than sharing them with workers or other firms (see notably Boyer, 1988 and Hall and Soskice, 2001). This occurs in spite of the fact that policy-makers usually do not set labour market policies to accomplish the goal of enhancing innovation or fostering adoption. Three main aspects of policy and institutional settings seem to be more closely related to innovation and adoption, although the links are complex (see Box 5.1 for more details): (1) the system of industrial relations; (2) the costs of hiring and firing (proxied by the stringency of Employment Protection Legislation, EPL); and (3) the possible interactions between industry-specific characteristics of the technology and EPL, which lead to different human resource strategies.

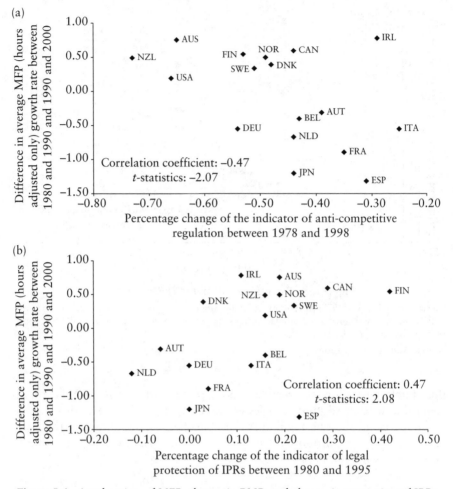

Figure 5.4. *Acceleration of MFP, change in PMR and change in protection of IPRs.
(a) Product market regulation and MFP growth*[a]; *(b) regulation on IPRs and MFP
growth*[b]

[a] The indicator of anti-competitive PMR used in this figure is based on historical data on the
regulatory stance in seven non-manufacturing industries (gas, electricity, post, telecommunications, passenger air transport, railways, and road freight). Depending on the industry, the
following dimensions have been considered: barriers to entry, public ownership, market
structure, vertical integration, and price controls (see Nicoletti *et al.*, 2001*b* for a complete
description).

[b] The indicator of legal protection of IPRs used in this figure is based on the following dimensions:
range of patentable items (coverage), membership in international agreements, risk of loss of
protection, enforcement provisions, and duration of protection (see Ginarte and Park, 1997 for a
complete description).

Source: Authors' calculations.

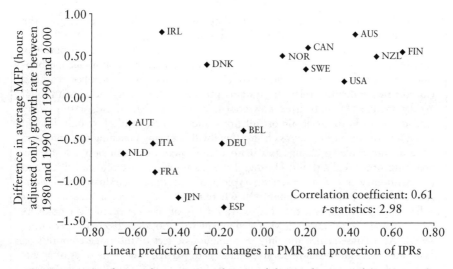

Figure 5.5. *Regulatory changes as predictors of the acceleration of MFP growth*
Source: Authors' calculations.

Box 5.1. *Labour market institutions, regulations, and performance*

Labour market institutions[1] can affect the firms' performance by influencing innovation rents associated with innovation and adoption of new technologies. In decentralized wage-bargaining systems workers can appropriate a large part of the rents generated by successful innovations, thereby reducing incentives to innovate in the first place. The risk of hold-up can be partly mitigated when bargaining occurs at the national level (or at the industry level but with economy-wide coordination) and pins down a general frame for the wage schedule. In such a case, the reservation wage is fixed for all lower level bargaining units and is adjusted mainly in response to aggregate shocks. As a consequence, the firm's incentive to undertake innovative investment no longer depends on the bargaining power of its own workers (Teulings and Hartog, 1998).

The industrial relations systems also play a prominent role on the accumulation of competencies and human capital required for developing and implementing innovations. In centralized/coordinated industrial relations systems wages are typically compressed over the skill dimension.[2] Furthermore, in these systems the possibility for the most efficient firms to attract more skilled people by offering higher wages is limited.[3] Hence it could be argued that coordinated industrial relations systems, by leading to lower expected earnings for the upper range of skills (with respect to unskilled labour), may reduce the workers' willingness to pay for the accumulation of generic human capital, thereby leading to lower innovation performance because of lower supply of skilled labour. Nevertheless, firms too invest in general training (see Booth and Snower, 1996 and Acemoglu and Pischke, 1999*a,b* for surveys), and have greater incentive to pay for training the larger the compression of wages over the skill dimension, because they can reap the greater difference between the marginal productivity of skilled workers and their earnings.

Wage compression is not, however, a sufficient condition to induce a firm to pay for the accumulation of generic competencies when there is no economic mechanism at work to prevent other firms from poaching on its pool of skilled workers. Coordinated industrial relations systems provide at least two such institutional arrangements: (1) centralized and coordinated wage-bargaining settings may extend contracts to cover almost all firms and workers and allow only limited variability of wage offers across firms, thereby dampening poaching since workers have no incentive to change job if no better wage offer can be made by the poaching firm (Teulings and Hartog, 1998; Acemoglu and Pischke, 1999a) and (2) customary interfirm practices, typical of coordinated industrial relations regimes, may enforce an equilibrium wherein poaching is considered as unfair behaviour.[4] Furthermore, the cost of training is often shared among employers when business associations have a prominent role (Soskice, 1997; Casper et al., 1999). As a consequence the only unambiguous effect of the wage compression associated with industrial relations regimes is to partially swap the roles of agents as regard to paying for training. Indeed, Lynch (1994), Blinder and Krueger (1996), Acemoglu and Pischke (1999b), and OECD (1993, 2000) report scattered evidence of more firm-sponsored training in more coordinated countries.

Hiring and firing restrictions may raise the cost of labour adjustment, which is often needed after innovations have been introduced (see e.g. Cappelli, 2000). The effects of these restrictions on productivity and innovation are, however, likely to be mediated by industrial relations regimes. In coordinated countries, firms are less sensitive to the adjustment costs imposed by firing restrictions, because they tend to reallocate labour internally. Likewise, in these countries, statutory or contractual employment protection may also help in solving the moral hazard problem that arise when the process of accumulation of firm-specific competencies (as well as the associated worker's effort) cannot be fully monitored, as is often the case when competencies are acquired on the job. Coordination between employers and trade unions may favour the achievement of a cooperative equilibrium through the establishment of an environment of mutual trust and loyalty. In this case, employment protection complements these arrangements by introducing a commitment mechanism that enforces an otherwise time-inconsistent implicit contract, since the incentive to increase one's own generic human capital (at the expense of a firm-specific one) is smaller the greater the credibility of the career prospects within the same firm.

Industry-specific characteristics of technological change and associated competence requirements are also likely to influence innovation and their effect may depend on industrial relations regimes. In mature and low-tech industries, firms undertake little in-house R&D activity and mostly adopt technology developed elsewhere. The scope for expanding production is often limited and innovation frequently leads to downsizing. In these contexts, strict EPL may have significant repercussions on productivity and adoption of new technologies, especially if competencies required to implement innovations are not available inside the firm.[5] In high-tech industries, two regimes can be distinguished on the basis of their innovation patterns: *Schumpeter Mark I* and *Schumpeter Mark II* (Kamien and Schwarz, 1982, Nelson and Winter, 1982, Malerba and Orsenigo, 1995, Breschi *et al.*, 2000). In *Schumpeter Mark I* industries (e.g. precision instruments, standardized software, and household appliances), firms often undertake sequences of short-lived projects on the basis of the same general knowledge but different specific realizations (e.g. as a consequence of short life cycles of products and rapid capital depreciation). In this process, they rely on a one-shot match of human and physical capital requiring (or at least not being impaired by) a quick turnover of workers (or even firms themselves). Conversely, in *Schumpeter Mark II* industries (e.g. electronic components, aircrafts, and spacecrafts), firms undertake incremental innovations along an existing technological trajectory and competencies for this type of innovations are often found inside the firm. This also implies that the loss of a few staff members may involve significant costs for firms operating in these industries.

---

[1] This box draws heavily on joint work of one of us with Ekkehard Ernst (Bassanini and Ernst, 2002*a*). We are most grateful to him for letting us use part of that material here.

[2] An industrial relations system can be said to be coordinated when: (1) the wage bargain occurs in a centralized way or coordination among employers and/or trade unions sets a uniform band of wages; (2) employers and trade unions cooperate as regard to decision-making inside the firm; and (3) business associations have an active role in solving free-riding problems across firms (Carlin and Soskice, 1990).

[3] Indeed, there is empirical evidence that there are no wage gains to switching jobs in Germany (Zimmermann, 1998) but these gains are substantial in the United States (McCue, 1996).

[4] For instance, Blinder and Krueger (1996) report that interfirm job mobility is virtually non-existent in Japan due to the firms' customary practice of refusing to employ people already working for other firms. Similarly Casper *et al.* (1999) report about legal provisions in Germany that reduce the workers' mobility after training.

[5] For a discussion about the role of strict regulation on the patterns of technological specialization of countries, see Hall and Soskice (2001) and Saint-Paul (2002).

The industrial relations regime prevailing in a country is likely to influence the human resource strategy of an innovating firm. Broadly speaking, in countries where wage negotiations are decentralized and where there is little coordination amongst employers, firms tend to adjust their workforce while innovating by hiring adequately skilled workers on the labour market. Conversely, in centralized or sectoral wage bargaining systems, wages are more compressed and firms, despite finding more difficult to attract high skilled workers on the external market, gain from training their own workers (as there is a greater wedge between productivity and wages at high skill levels). In addition, countries that have centralized or sectoral wage bargaining systems also tend to have comparatively high hiring and firing costs. The combination of wage compression and high labour adjustment costs tend to favour a process of competence accumulation based on firm-supported training and on-the-job learning. Wage compression may not, however, be a sufficient condition for firms to rely on the internal labour market to adapt its workforce and, ultimately, for the decision to innovate and/or adopt a new technology. Another feature of industrial relations system plays a crucial role: the degree of coordination amongst employers. Coordination is implicit in highly centralized wage setting systems but also exists in some countries with predominantly sectoral bargaining systems (e.g. Germany). In coordinated countries, there is only a limited variability of wage offers across firms, thereby reducing the scope for poaching. Likewise, coordination often leads to close interfirm practices where poaching is considered as unfair behaviour.

The potential effects of bargaining regimes and EPL on the incentives to innovate and adopt new technologies may also depend on the technological characteristics of the sector in which firms operate. While in low-tech industries strict EPL is always likely to lead to higher adjustment costs with possible negative effects on innovation and adoption, in high-tech industries the effects of EPL may depend on the technological trajectory of the sector. When technological progress is cumulative (i.e. further innovations along the same trajectory), then investing in the internal labour force may be effective, and firms in these industries are likely to have a better innovation performance when labour market institutions enhance a thorough exploitation of the internal labour market. This is less so if technological progress leads to frequent shifts in the type of physical and human capital required in the production process. In this latter case firms have to rely on the external labour market, which may be costly when EPL is very strict. Empirical evidence indeed suggests countries with coordinated industrial relations systems and relatively stringent employment protection (e.g. Germany and Austria) have stronger technological comparative advantage in industries characterized by cumulative technological progress than countries with decentralized wage bargaining, no coordination, and low EPL (e.g. United States, and also United Kingdom and New Zealand) (see Bassanini and Ernst, 2002*a*).

5.3. THE EMPIRICAL EVIDENCE ON THE LINKS BETWEEN POLICY, INSTITUTIONS, AND PERFORMANCE

Our empirical analysis focuses on the determinants of productivity and innovation (proxied by R&D) in OECD manufacturing, on the basis of country/industry and time-series data. This sectoral analysis allows to consider a set of specific regulatory aspects and to seek possible interactions between them and institutional, policy, and technological factors characterizing each manufacturing industry. At the same time, however, given our results in Chapter 2 (i.e. the fact that most of the productivity growth in manufacturing is explained by within-industry performance), this sectoral analysis may also offer economy-wide indications as to the role of policy and institutions for performance. Our empirical approach starts with the productivity equation and, insofar as R&D is a driving force of productivity, then moves to analyse the determinants of industry R&D intensity. This allows assessment of the direct effect of policy and regulations on productivity and the indirect effects via their impact on innovation activity.

5.3.1. *Policy and institutions and productivity*

The MFP equation is derived from a production function in which technological progress is a function of country/industry specific factors as well as a catch-up term that measures the distance from the technological frontier in each industry (see Scarpetta and Tressel, 2002 for more details). Within each industry, the production possibility set is influenced by technological transfer from the leader country to other countries. In this context, MFP for a given industry j of country i (MFP_{ijt}) can be modelled as follows:

$$\ln \text{MFP}_{ijt} = \beta_1 \ln \text{MFP}_{ijt-1} + \beta_2 \ln \text{MFP}_{Fjt} + \beta_3 \ln \text{MFP}_{Fjt-1}$$

$$+ \sum_k \gamma_k V_{kijt-1} + f_i + g_j + d_t + \varepsilon_{ijt} \tag{1}$$

where MFP_{Fjt} is the productivity level of the frontier country, V_{ijt} is a vector of covariates (e.g. product and market labour regulations, human capital, or R&D) affecting the level of MFP, and f_i, g_j, and d_t are respectively country, industry, and year fixed effects. ε is an *iid* shock.

Equation (1) can be rearranged under a simplifying hypothesis (e.g. $1 - \beta_1 = \beta_2 + \beta_3$) to yield a convergence equation:

$$\Delta \ln \text{MFP}_{ijt} = \beta_2 \Delta \ln \text{MFP}_{Fjt} - (1 - \beta_1) \text{RMFP}_{ijt-1} + \sum_k \gamma_k V_{kijt-1}$$

$$+ f_i + g_j + d_t + \varepsilon_{ijt} \tag{2}$$

where $\text{RMFP}_{ijt} = \ln(\text{MFP}_{ijt}) - \ln(\text{MFP}_{Fjt})$ is the technological gap between country i and the leading country F. MFP_{ijt} is measured as the Hicks neutral productivity parameter, according to a standard neoclassical production technology under constant returns to scale.[7]

The empirical analysis covers seventeen manufacturing industries in eighteen OECD countries over the period 1984–1998 (see Box 5.2 for details on the data).[8]

Table 5.1 presents a set of policy and institutional augmented MFP regressions.[9] We start (column 1) with the simplest specification in which MFP growth is only a function of the growth in the country leader ($\text{MFP}_{\text{leader}}$) and the technology gap (RTFP). We then include R&D to the RHS (column 2) and

---

[7] Scarpetta and Tressel (2002) use the following index as a measure of the MFP level:

$$\text{MFP}_{ijt} = \frac{Y_{ijt}}{\overline{Y}_{jt}} \cdot \left(\frac{\overline{L}_{jt}}{L_{ijt}}\right)^{\alpha_{ijt}} \cdot \left(\frac{\overline{K}_{jt}}{K_{ijt}}\right)^{1-\alpha_{ijt}}$$

where a *bar* denotes a geometric average over all the countries for a given industry j and year t. It is based on sectoral Purchasing Power Parities (PPPs) to convert underlying data into common currency.

[8] The countries are: Australia, Austria, Belgium, Canada, Denmark, Spain, Finland, France, (western) Germany, Greece, Italy, Japan, Netherlands, Norway, Portugal, Sweden, United Kingdom, and United States.

[9] These are the preferred specifications obtained by a model selection process that is discussed in Scarpetta and Tressel (2002). All equations control for the presence of outlier observations in the original sample and for heteroscedasticity. Moreover, specifications including product and labour market regulations correct for cluster effects owing to the fact that indicators of regulations do not vary across industries but only across countries.

Box 5.2. *Data used in the productivity and R&D regressions*

The main data source is the 2001 OECD STAN database that provides information on value added, capital stock, employment, and labour compensation. Data on R&D intensity (R&D expenditure divided by industry value added) is from the OECD ANBERD dataset. It measures both public and privately funded R&D performed by businesses. Data on sectoral occupational skills have been assembled from various sources. The classification of countries as regard to the degree of centralization and coordination of their industrial relations system is based on the OECD indicator of the level of coordination of the wage-bargaining (see Elmeskov *et al.*, 1998), which classifies countries into three groups (low, intermediate, and high coordination). In the productivity and R&D equations, we take countries with an intermediate level of centralization or regression coordination as a benchmark, and include dummies for low and high coordination countries. Indicators of product and labour market regulations are from Nicoletti *et al.* (1999) and those on labour market institutions are from Elmeskov *et al.* (1998).

Import penetration is defined as the ratio of total imports to apparent demand. Data on imports are from OECD Foreign Trade Statistics. Consistent with the computation of R&D intensity, the data on output used in the computation of apparent demand are the result of the harmonization of different sources (OECD STAN Database—edition 2000, OECD Annual National Accounts Database, OECD Industrial Structure Statistics—ISIS).

Data on firm size are from the OECD SME Database. The measure used in the R&D regressions is the ratio of total employment of firms with fifty or more employees to total employment of all firms in the sample (excluding those with fewer than ten employees).

Data on trade barriers are from the OECD Indicators of Tariff and Non-tariff Trade Barriers and refer to 1996. Tariffs are defined as the simple average of *ad valorem* tariff rates applied to the most favoured nation. The indicator of non-tariff barriers is a frequency ratio: it corresponds to the proportion of tariff lines to which anti-competitive non-tariff barriers apply. To avoid tariff measures being non-representative, observations in which the frequency ratio of non-*ad valorem* tariffs is greater than 20 per cent (coke, refined petroleum, and nuclear fuel—ISIC 23—in Japan; other non-metallic mineral products—ISIC 26, and telecommunication equipment—ISIC 32—in Norway) are dropped from the sample.

The indicator of protection of IPRs has been developed by Ginarte and Park (1997). It varies between 0 and 5 from least to most stringent. The data used in this chapter refer to 1995 and have been kindly supplied by Walter Park. All other regulatory indicators (administrative regulation, anti-competitive inward-oriented economic regulation) are from Nicoletti *et al.* (1999). They vary between 0 and 6 from least to most restrictive and refer to 1998.

Two alternative indicators of human capital are used in the R&D regressions: the share of the working-age population that completed at least upper secondary education (OECD, 2000*b*) and the average years of education (Bassanini and Scarpetta, 2002*b*).

Table 5.1. *Productivity regressions: the role of R&D, market structure, and regulatory settings—Manufacturing*

	1	2	3	4	5	6	7
Constant	−0.030*	0.018	0.029*	−0.182***	0.002	−0.009	0.005
	(0.017)	(0.015)	(0.016)	(0.059)	(0.019)	(0.019)	(0.022)
$\Delta TFP_{leader\,jt}$	−0.007	−0.007	−0.007	−0.012	−0.013	−0.013	−0.012
	(0.008)	(0.009)	(0.009)	(0.009)	(0.009)	(0.009)	(0.009)
$RTFP_{ijt-1}$	−0.029***	−0.029***	−0.019**	−0.029***	−0.025***	−0.046***	−0.041***
	(0.003)	(0.005)	(0.009)	(0.005)	(0.005)	(0.012)	(0.011)
$R\&D_{ijt-1}$		0.006***	0.009***	0.006***	0.006***	0.006***	0.005***
		(0.002)	(0.003)	(0.002)	(0.002)	(0.002)	(0.002)
$(R\&D * RTFP)_{ijt-1}$			0.003				
			(0.003)				
Human capital$_{ijt-1}$				0.344***	0.300*	0.319**	0.513***
				(0.116)	(0.156)	(0.155)	(0.169)
PMR					−0.006*	0.004	0.008
					(0.003)	(0.005)	(0.006)
PMR * RTFP$_{ijt-1}$						0.014**	0.010*
						(0.007)	(0.006)
High corporatism							−0.003
							(0.004)
Low corporatism							−0.003
							(0.004)

Table 5.1. (*Continued*)

	1	2	3	4	5	6	7
EPL (high corporatism)							0.005
							(0.004)
EPL (medium corporatism)							−0.016***
							(0.004)
EPL (low corporatism)							−0.003
							(0.003)
Industry dummies	Yes	Yes	Yes	Yes	Yes	Yes	Yes
Country dummies	Yes	Yes	Yes	Yes	No	No	No
Year dummies	Yes	Yes	Yes	Yes	Yes	Yes	Yes
Reset[a]	0.79	1.57	2.34*	0.57	1.08	0.97	1.06
Observations	2,569	2,063	2,063	2022	2,022	2,022	2,022

In all equations with (time invariant) product market regulatory indicators, standard errors are adjusted for cluster level effects. Robust standard errors are in brackets. * significant at 10% level; ** at 5% level; *** at 1% level.

[a] Ramsey's omitted variable test: *F*-test on the joint significance of the additional terms in a model augmented by including the second, third, and fourth powers of the predicted values of the original model.

Source: Scarpetta and Tressel (2002).

test whether its effect also works through the technology gap (column 3, R&D*RTFP). This would be consistent with the idea that R&D is also important for technology transfer and plays a role in developing the 'absorptive capacity' (see Griffith *et al.*, 2000). In column 4, we extend the model to include an industry-level measure of human capital based on information on skill composition of the workforce and relative wages by skill. We then explore (columns 5 to 7) the impact on productivity of PMR—which is assumed to have a direct effect on productivity as well as an indirect effect via the adoption process—and EPL—whose coefficient is allowed to vary depending on the bargaining regime prevailing in each country.

The results suggest a productivity convergence in manufacturing while the short-term pass through (i.e. the coefficient of the MFP growth of the leader country) is generally not statistically significant. As expected both R&D intensity and human capital have a positive effect on productivity. The result on human capital, while fairly standard in aggregate analyses, is rather new in industry-level regressions where we can control for industry-specific factors. The results shown in column 3 do not give support to an indirect effect of R&D to productivity: that is, there is no evidence in our data of R&D boosting productivity via its impact on the ability of firms to learn about advances in the leading edge ('absorptive capacity').

Scarpetta and Tressel (2002) further decompose the effect of R&D on productivity by considering different technology regimes (see Box 5.1). They found that R&D has a strong positive effect in Mark II manufacturing industries, that is, those characterized by 'creative accumulation', with the prevalence of large, established firms and the presence of barriers for new innovators. By contrast, R&D does not have a significant impact on productivity in Mark I industries characterized by 'creative destruction' with technological ease of entry and a major role played by new firms in innovative activities. In the latter cases, returns on R&D may not be long lasting and are likely to be driven by the need to engage in (perceived) product differentiation to acquire/maintain market shares. Moreover, Scarpetta and Tressel (2002) found greater returns from R&D of leading firms compared with followers in Mark II industries but not in Mark I industries. Indeed, in these industries there are high appropriability conditions and knowledge and technological progress is strongly cumulative, which gives the technological leader an advantage in the introduction of innovations.

Moving to policy and institutions, our results point to a statistically insignificant direct effect of product market regulation on productivity (column 5, Table 5.1), but a significant indirect effect via the process of adoption of existing technologies (column 6). In other words, the further an industry/country is from the frontier, the stronger the cumulative negative effect of strict regulations on productivity. These regulations discourage innovation, but also slow down the adoption of existing technologies, possibly by creating artificial barriers to the entry (or expansion) of 'imitating' firms and/or by reducing the scope for international spillovers. We also find inconclusive results as to the possible impact of industrial relations regimes on productivity, proxied by the dummies on the degree of corporatism (the sum of coordination and centralization in wage bargaining).[10] However, differences in these regimes seem to affect significantly the estimated impact of EPL on MFP. If allowed to vary across the different industrial relations regimes (column 7), the negative impact of strict EPL on productivity is stronger and statistically significant only in countries with an intermediate degree of centralization/coordination— that is, where sectoral wage bargaining is predominant without coordination. As discussed above, innovation and adoption require a continuous process of technological change, and the latter is often associated with a skill upgrade of the workforce. In this context, strict EPL raises the costs of adjusting the workforce, and this may have a particularly detrimental effect on innovation and technology adoption if, in addition, the lack of coordination does not offer a firm the required institutional device to guarantee a high return on internal training, because other firms can poach on its skilled workforce by offering higher wages.

5.3.2. *Policy, institutions, and innovation*

The above results clearly point to a significant role of R&D activity on productivity, even if the effect varies significantly depending on the technological regime in which firms operate. Thus, we explore whether policy and institutions also have an impact on R&D activity and, via R&D, on productivity. Following a large theoretical and empirical literature,[11] the simplest possible model of the determinants of innovative effort relates the latter to expected profit differential—that is, the expected difference between profits that the firm can earn once it has successfully innovated and profits that would be earned otherwise. In turn, the expected profit differential depends on the degree of competition (and regulation) in the product market and other factors. Taking the ratio of business-performed R&D expenditure to sales (R&D intensity hereafter) as the indicator of innovative activity, we can write the following reduced form equation (see Bassanini and Ernst, 2002*a*, for details):

$$R\&D = f(\textbf{PMR, OTHER}) \tag{3}$$

where R&D stands for R&D intensity, **PMR** for a vector of indicators of product market regulation, and **OTHER** for a vector of other controls.

In the following, eq. (3) is implemented empirically on a cross-section of eighteen manufacturing industries and eighteen OECD countries. The choice

---

[10] The table reports the coefficients of intermediate and highly centralized countries, with decentralized countries as the reference group.

[11] See, for example, Aghion *et al.* (2001*a,b*), Boone (2000*b*), and Geroski (1990).

of a cross-section—rather than a panel data, as in the case of productivity equation—is justified by the need to include a set of control variables for which time dimension is lacking, including detailed aspects of product market regulations. As indicators of product market regulation we use measures of inward-oriented economic regulation (state control, legal barriers to entry, price controls, etc.), administrative regulation (administrative barriers on start-ups, feature of the licensing and permit system, etc.), indicators of tariff and non-tariff barriers, plus an indicator of global protection of IPRs. Furthermore, we use import penetration as a proxy for competitive pressures not captured by the regulatory indicators. Finally, most of the other factors can be controlled for either by industry dummies (technological opportunity, returns to scale, dynamics of the industry's world demand, etc.) or by country dummies (aggregate demand, supply of human capital, etc.). However, other factors (such as physical and human capital intensity and the dynamics of the industry's domestic demand), being co-determined in equilibrium, are not included in the reduced form, since, in a cross-section, it is impossible to find valid instruments for these variables. A control for the average size of firms represents an exception. In fact, this control captures the bias in R&D intensity across industries and countries owing to different accounting practices between large and small firms and has been proved to play an important role in the literature (e.g. see Griliches, 1990 and Geroski, 1990). Choosing a log-linear form for convenience, eq. (3) can be therefore rewritten as:

$$\log \text{R\&D}_{ij} = \alpha + \sum_h \gamma_h \text{PMR}_{ij}^h + \phi \text{IMP}_{ij} + \delta \text{SIZE}_{ij} + \mu_i + \chi_j + \varepsilon_{ij} \qquad (4)$$

where IMP and SIZE denote import penetration and average size, μ stands for the country dummy, χ stands for the industry dummy, and ε is the standard error term, while h, i, and j index product market regulatory indicators, countries, and industries, respectively.

With the exception of indicators of tariff and non-tariff barriers and inward-oriented economic regulation, all other regulatory indicators refer to economy-wide regulation and institutions that are by definition identical across industries in each country and therefore cannot be identified in the presence of country dummies. Moreover, the same applies to the indicator of inward-oriented economic regulation for which no sector breakdown is available for manufacturing industries, leading us to proxy it with an economy-wide indicator. Therefore, to gather some evidence on the absolute impact of economy-wide product market regulations on R&D intensity we need to complement eq. (4) with a specification of the determinants of the country fixed effect, that is:

$$\mu_i = a + \sum_h c_h \text{PMR}_i^h + \sum_m d_m \text{CNTRL}_i^m \qquad (5)$$

where CNTRL stands for a number of other economy-wide control variables that are indexed by m. As typical in growth regressions, these control variables can be, however, introduced only in a limited number to avoid problems of multi-collinearity. As a consequence, the reader needs to be cautious in interpreting the results presented below that should only be considered as suggestive of the relationship between regulation and innovation. In particular, we consider the degree of coordination of industrial relations systems, in order to distinguish between fully decentralized and uncoordinated regimes, coordinated regimes, and mixed ones, and the overall domestic supply of human capital, proxied either by the share of the population that completed upper secondary education or by the average years of education in the population. By plugging eq. (5) into eq. (4) we obtain the general specification of our R&D equation.[12]

The sample used for the R&D equation includes two-digits manufacturing industries.[13] If not differently specified, all variables have been averaged across 1993–1997, excluding years in which observations were missing for most of the industries. Data on R&D intensity are the same as those described in Box 5.2, that is, the ratio of the industry's BERD to the industry's total output. In a sensitivity analysis, we also use the ratio of government-financed BERD to total output.[14] As we do not always have data on the ratio of government-financed BERD to total BERD for the same years for which we have data for R&D intensity, we construct an estimate of government-financed BERD to total output as the product of the average ratio of government-financed BERD to total BERD[15] by the average ratio of BERD to output. We make here an implicit assumption that these two ratios do not vary over time. This assumption can be justified on the basis of the limited variation over time (with respect to variation cross-country and cross-industry) of both ratios. Data on the ratio of government-financed BERD to total BERD are from the OECD R&D database.

---

[12] As in the case of the productivity equations, we control for the presence of outliers in the sample and correct standard errors for the presence of cluster effects.

[13] The industry *manufacturing not elsewhere classified* (ISIC 36 and 37), being a residual sector, is excluded, while *food, beverages, and tobacco* (ISIC 15 and 16) and *textiles* leader and clothing (ISIC 17, 18 and 19) have been aggregated owing to lack of data availability. Countries considered are Austria, Belgium, Canada, Germany, Denmark, Finland, France, Greece, Ireland, Italy, Japan, Netherlands, Norway, Portugal, Spain, Sweden, United Kingdom, and United States.

[14] The advantage of using R&D intensity data is that they are available for many countries on a comparative basis. Nevertheless, these data suffer from important limitations (for a general discussion, see Griliches, 1990). R&D intensity is an indicator of input in the innovative process rather than output. Consequently improvements in the efficiency of the innovation process (greater output with less input) can be mistakenly interpreted as a reduction of the innovative effort. Moreover, R&D intensity conveys only information about formal innovation expenditure. In many industries informal innovation is a sizeable component of overall innovation activity. Also, reported data tend to overestimate R&D intensity of large incumbents relative to small firms and new entrants.

[15] As in the case of other variables, the ratio of government-financed BERD to total BERD is an average across 1993–1997, excluding years in which observations were missing for most of the industries. In the case of the United Kingdom, however, the ratio of government-financed BERD to total BERD refers to 1989 (last available year).

The first specification in Table 5.2 only includes basic controls for R&D intensity, including country-specific effects.[16] The other specifications try to account for these country-specific effects by including different aspects of the regulatory and institutional environment, as discussed above. Columns 2–5 consider the indicators of inward-oriented administrative and economic regulation separately, while a simple average of these indicators is included in columns 6–7. In both these two groups of specifications non-significant variables are sequentially eliminated.[17]

The estimated coefficients of the human capital variables are positive and significant, as expected. This points to the critical role of the supply of human capital—and thereby education policy—in fostering conditions for innovation. Indeed, taking these results at face value, one additional year of education in the population is associated with 6–9 per cent greater R&D intensity. The share of the population that completed at least upper secondary education seems less significant than average years of education (compare column 2 with column 3); therefore the latter is retained in all the other specifications (columns 4–7).

The insignificant coefficient estimate for tariffs might be due to controlling for import penetration (which captures some aspects of competitive pressure) and the lack of variability of the indicator resulting from the fact that trade barriers are the same across all EU countries (although this statement is true also for non-tariff barriers). Nonetheless, as discussed in Chapter 4, there might be good theoretical reasons for a less negative impact of tariffs (rather than of non-tariff barriers) on innovation. Under Cournot competition in partial equilibrium, conditional to the level of knowledge spillovers, tariffs have a positive impact on profits (because they add to foreign competitors' costs) without changing the incentive to reduce the domestic firms' own costs via innovation. However, in general equilibrium, tariffs interact negatively with imports and might then have a negative overall impact due to their indirect effect on knowledge spillovers. This effect is stronger for non-tariff barriers that have a greater impact on the diffusion of products and, eventually, the possibility of imitation and reverse engineering by domestic firms. Moreover high non-tariff barriers can be thought to directly

[16] One of the purposes of presenting results from a specification including country dummies (column 1) is that it allows assessment of the quality of the estimates obtained with the other specifications. Indeed, if the estimates of those variables that are included in all the specifications changed significantly upon substitution of proxies of the country fixed effects, this may indicate a serious omitted variable problem. It is reassuring that, across all specifications, the point estimate of the coefficients of industry-varying variables fall into the boundaries of the 5% confidence intervals and that the Reset test statistics are always insignificant at standard statistical levels.

[17] Estimates from specifications not including tariff barriers are not shown for brevity. In any case, the exclusion of tariff barriers does not change the estimated coefficients of other variables.

Table 5.2. *The R&D equation: main results*

Dependent variable Logarithm of R&D intensity	1	2	3	4	5	6	7
Employment share of large firms	0.019***	0.027**	0.023**	0.022*	0.022*	0.022*	0.023*
	(0.006)	(0.010)	(0.011)	(0.011)	(0.012)	(0.012)	(0.013)
Import penetration	0.004*	0.005**	0.004*	0.004**	0.004*	0.004*	0.004**
	(0.002)	(0.002)	(0.002)	(0.002)	(0.002)	(0.002)	(0.002)
Non-tariff barriers	−0.014***	−0.018***	−0.023***	−0.023***	−0.023***	−0.023***	−0.023***
	(0.005)	(0.004)	(0.005)	(0.005)	(0.005)	(0.004)	(0.004)
Tariff barriers	0.025	0.002	−0.003	−0.005	−0.007	−0.012	−0.010
	(0.019)	(0.062)	(0.025)	(0.025)	(0.027)	(0.031)	(0.031)
Administrative regulation		0.148	0.134	0.125			
		(0.131)	(0.147)	(0.130)			
Inward-oriented economic regulation		−0.438***	−0.446**	−0.435***	−0.393***		
		(0.135)	(0.162)	(0.134)	(0.122)		
Overall inward-oriented regulation						−0.430**	−0.435**
						(0.176)	(0.181)
Protection of IPRs		0.708***	0.674***	0.660***	0.758***	0.824***	0.856***
		(0.166)	(0.176)	(0.163)	(0.152)	(0.217)	(0.166)
Low coordination dummy		−0.599***	−0.559***	−0.596***	−0.730***	−0.913***	−0.863***
		(0.262)	(0.181)	(0.169)	(0.198)	(0.230)	(0.243)

	(1)	(2)	(3)	(4)	(5)	(6)
High coordination dummy	0.216	0.058				−0.093
	(0.176)	(0.203)				(0.188)
Upper secondary education share	0.020*					
	(0.011)					
Average years of education		0.061**	0.067**	0.066**	0.086***	0.076***
		(0.024)	(0.027)	(0.026)	(0.026)	(0.026)
Industry dummies	Yes	Yes	Yes	Yes	Yes	Yes
Country dummies	Yes	No	No	No	No	No
Reset[a]	2.45*	1.87	1.92	1.94	2.28*	2.00*
R-squared	0.88	0.85	0.85	0.84	0.84	0.84
Observations	254	254	254	254	254	254

All equations include a constant. *, **, and *** denote significance at the 10, 5, and 1% level, respectively. Standard errors adjusted for heteroscedasticity of unknown form and cluster effects on countries in parentheses. The sample is adjusted by excluding influential observations identified by the DFITS cut-off combined with the Covratio cut-off. Excluded observations are food, beverages, and tobacco (ISIC 15–16) in Norway, computers (ISIC 30), telecommunication equipment (ISIC 32), and wood (ISIC 20) in Ireland, other transport (ISIC 35) in Greece, coke, petroleum, and nuclear fuel (ISIC 23) in the United Kingdom, printing and publishing (ISIC 22) and motor vehicles (ISIC 34) in Belgium, printing and publishing (ISIC 22) in France, other transport (ISIC 35) in Italy, and electrical machinery (ISIC 31) in the Netherlands.

[a] Ramsey's omitted variable test: F-test on the joint significance of the additional terms in a model augmented by including the second, third and fourth powers of the predicted values of the original model.

Source: Scarpetta and Thenel (2002).

affect the elasticity of substitution between imported and domestically produced products, thereby inducing low incentives to innovate when domestic
and foreign firms have similar levels of competitiveness (the case of 'neck-
and-neck' competition).

The degree of protection of IPRs appears to be positively and significantly
associated with R&D intensity in all specifications. Nevertheless, results
concerning protection of IPRs must be taken with additional care as the
coefficient of this variable is likely to be overestimated due to the endogeneity of the indicator to the level of R&D expenditure. Inward-oriented economic regulation also appears to be negatively associated with R&D intensity
in all specifications, while the estimated coefficient for administrative regulation is not significantly different from zero. In other words, restrictions to
competition enforced through administrative barriers to entry do not seem to
have a negative effect on innovation performance. This might be due to the
fact that administrative regulation, by discouraging entry, may contribute to
increasing *ex post* innovation rents and improving appropriability conditions,
reinforcing the effect of IPRs protection. Obviously, this positive effect is
stronger for incumbents, and is likely to be overestimated in equations using
R&D data. Nevertheless, several other explanations are possible: (1) by
reducing competitive pressures, high administrative barriers may also reduce
competitive selection and, hence, overall industry efficiency (Vickers, 1995;
Nickell, 1996), including efficiency in turning R&D into innovation (in this
case R&D is less productive and the recorded R&D intensity higher, without
implying that firms are innovating more); (2) tight administrative regulation
may generate rents and wage premia, pushing towards more capital-intensive
and higher-technology production processes (e.g. see Chennels and van
Reenen, 1998 and Acemoglu and Shimer, 2000); and (3) the stringency of
administrative regulation may proxy for size, compensating for possible
errors in the measurement of this variable. The bottom line is that these
regression results do not authorize us to conclude that the level of administrative regulation is irrelevant for innovation. As a partial confirmation of
this no-conclusion, the estimated coefficient of overall inward-oriented regulation in columns 6–7 is strongly significant and virtually identical to that of
economic regulation in columns 2–5.

It could be argued that in small country samples, one individual country
could significantly affect the estimated parameters. In the R&D equation this
problem might be particularly relevant since the results concerning industry-
invariant variables are based essentially on cross-country information, that is,
18 data points. A sensitivity analysis was thus performed on our preferred
specification (corresponding to column 5 of Table 5.2) in order to assess the
robustness of the results to variation of country coverage, by eliminating one
country at a time and re-running the estimation procedure. Figure 5.6 reports
the results of this sensitivity analysis for the coefficients of the regulation and
competition variables (excluding tariffs). Coefficient estimates are relatively

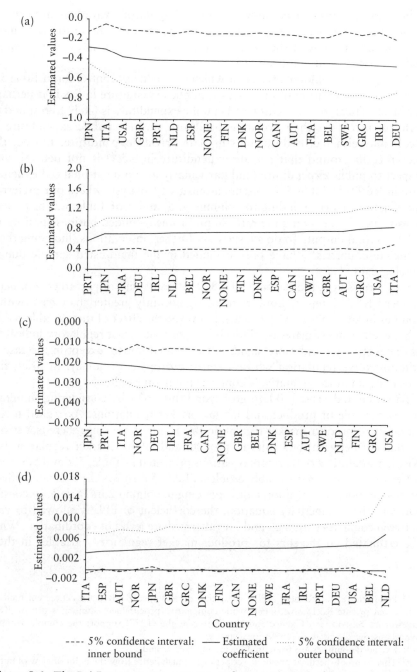

Figure 5.6. *The R&D equation: sensitivity analysis—variation of country coverage. (a) Inward-oriented economic regulation; (b) protection of IPRs; (c) non-tariff barriers; (d) import penetration*

The figure shows central estimates and confidence intervals obtained by re-estimating the preferred specification (cf. Table 5.2, column 5) after excluding one country at a time from the sample. None identifies the preferred specification for the purpose of comparison.

robust to variation of country coverage. Regulatory variables are always significant at the 5 per cent level. Conversely, import penetration is in most cases significant only at the 10 per cent level, but its central estimate is quite stable across the different samples.

Among the possible covariates for which we could not control for in Table 5.2 owing to the limitation of our dataset, public expenditure in R&D is perhaps the most critical for two reasons: (1) public expenditure is likely to respond to different incentives than private expenditure; and (2) public expenditure in R&D may either crowd-out or stimulate private expenditure. Indeed, the literature has found that private expenditure in R&D is not neutral with respect to public expenditure (and particularly government-financed expenditure in R&D).[18] Table 5.3 presents a sensitivity analysis where our preferred specifications (corresponding to columns 4, 5, and 7 of Table 5.2) have been re-estimated by including the ratio of government-funded business-performed R&D to total output. To do so, sixty-six further observations (including three complete countries[19]) have been excluded in the unadjusted sample due to missing data.[20]

Not surprisingly, the elasticity of R&D intensity with respect to government-financed R&D intensity appears to be significantly greater than zero (with a point estimate of about 21 per cent). However, the effect of this variable on the other coefficient estimates is relatively modest, with most regulatory indicators having a stronger and more significant estimated impact except in the case of administrative regulation whose t-statistic drops enormously. In brief, this sensitivity analysis qualitatively confirms the main results.

Bassanini and Ernst (2002b) go beyond this point by considering simultaneously the role of product and labour market regulations. As regard to the estimates of product market regulation this is important since there is a strong correlation between indicators of product and labour market regulation (see Nicoletti *et al.*, 1999), therefore equations presented in Tables 5.2 and 5.3 might suffer from an omitted variable problem. Table 5.4 shows the estimated effects of this extended specification (corresponding to column 2 in Table 5.3): consistent with the productivity equation, the coefficient of EPL is allowed to vary between countries with high and low/intermediate levels of coordination. While the estimated coefficients for product market regulatory variables in these

---

[18] For instance, Lichtenberg (1988) finds that non-competitive R&D procurement tends to crowd out private R&D investment, while competitive procurement stimulates private R&D investment. By contrast, Guellec and Van Pottelsberghe (1997) support the complementarity hypothesis. See David *et al.* (1999) for a survey.

[19] Excluded countries are Belgium, Greece, and Netherlands.

[20] This group of specifications however performs much better from the point of view of outlier control. After adjusting for influential observations the difference between this sample and the sample of Table 5.2 amounts to fifty-nine observations.

Table 5.3. *The R&D equation: sensitivity analysis—controlling for public expenditure in R&D*

Dependent variable Logarithm of R&D intensity	1	2	3
Employment share of large firms	0.015	0.014	0.015
	(0.010)	(0.011)	(0.013)
Import penetration	0.010**	0.010**	0.010**
	(0.004)	(0.004)	(0.004)
Non-tariff barriers	−0.031***	−0.031***	−0.031***
	(0.005)	(0.005)	(0.006)
Tariff barriers	0.000	−0.001	−0.005
	(0.003)	(0.003)	(0.004)
Government-financed R&D intensity[a]	0.216***	0.217***	0.208***
	(0.048)	(0.048)	(0.055)
Administrative regulation	0.040		
	(0.140)		
Inward-oriented economic regulation	−0.499***	−0.498***	
	(0.149)	(0.146)	
Overall inward-oriented regulation			−0.649**
			(0.222)
Protection of IPRs	0.733***	0.766***	0.916***
	(0.175)	(0.145)	(0.180)
Low coordination dummy	−0.899***	−0.950***	−1.111***
	(0.208)	(0.248)	(0.298)
Average years of education	0.052**	0.052**	0.071**
	(0.025)	(0.024)	(0.026)
Industry dummies	Yes	Yes	Yes
Country dummies	No	No	No
Reset[b]	2.98**	2.99**	2.45*
R-squared	0.89	0.89	0.88
F-test on industry dummies	203.43**	371.21***	126.80***
Observations	195	195	195
Industries	18	18	18
Countries	15	15	15

All equations include a constant. *, **, and *** denote significance at the 10, 5, and 1% level, respectively. Standard errors adjusted for heteroscedasticity of unknown form and cluster effects on countries in parentheses. The sample is adjusted by excluding influential observations identified by the DFITS cut-off combined with the Covratio cut-off. Excluded observations are computers (ISIC 30), telecommunication equipment (ISIC 32), and wood (ISIC 20) in Ireland and other transport (ISIC 35) in Japan.

[a] Logarithm of the ratio of government-financed BERD to output.

[b] Ramsey's omitted variable test: F-test on the joint significance of the additional terms in a model augmented by including the second, third, and fourth powers of the predicted values of the original model.

Table 5.4. *Estimated effect of employment protection on R&D intensity*

Logarithm of R&D intensity	Type of industrial relations system	
	Low/intermediate coordination	High coordination
Dependent variable		
Industry type		
Low-tech industries	−0.16	−0.46**
	(0.20)	(0.19)
Mark I industries	−0.38*	−0.11
	(0.21)	(0.26)
Mark II industries	−0.37*	0.69**
	(0.21)	(0.30)

*, **, and *** denote significance at the 10, 5, and 1% level, respectively. Standard errors are in parentheses. The coefficient follows from the estimation of the specification corresponding to column 2 of Table 5.2 augmented by labour market regulation.

Source: Bassanini and Ernst, 2002*b*.

extended specifications are virtually identical to those shown in Table 5.3 (and are not shown for brevity), complex patterns emerge as regard to the effect of the stringency of labour market regulation.

In particular, the effect of employment protection adds to the negative effect of product market regulation in uncoordinated countries,[21] with a degree of magnitude equivalent to that of inward-oriented economic regulation.[22] Conversely, in co-ordinated countries the stringency of employment protection seems to be negatively associated with R&D intensity in low technology industries, but positively associated in Mark II industries.[23] These results are consistent with the theoretical discussion of the role of the interplay between labour market institutions and industry characteristics in shaping incentives for different human resource strategies and thereby innovation patterns.[24] Indeed, these results seem to reflect the fact that hiring and firing restrictions depress the incentive to innovate the greater the need of downsizing and/or reshuffling one's own workforce after having successfully innovated. These negative effects are, however, smaller the larger the scope for internal labour markets. In the context of a cumulative and specific knowledge base, stringent

---

[21] The estimated coefficient of EPL in low-tech industries is not significantly different from zero. However, these industries account on average for only 20% of total R&D expenditure in manufacturing.

[22] The standard deviation of the indicator of employment protection is similar to that of the indicator of inward-oriented economic regulation in our sample.

[23] The estimated coefficient for Mark I industries is approximately equal to zero.

[24] See, for example, Saint-Paul (2002).

employment protection and coordinated systems of industrial relations, by aligning workers' and firms' objectives, enhancing the accumulation of firm-specific competencies and encouraging firm-sponsored training, may allow firms fully to exploit the potential of the internal labour market.

5.4. CONCLUDING REMARKS

The empirical evidence reported in this chapter seems to suggest that stringent regulatory settings in the product and labour markets contribute to explain cross-country differences in efficiency–enhancing efforts of firms, as well as in the pace of innovation and adoption of leading technologies, thus providing an interpretation for the growth patterns discussed in the previous chapters of this study.

It also appears that the impact on performance of regulations and institutions depends on certain market and technology conditions, as well as on specific firm characteristics. In particular, the burden of strict product market regulations on productivity seems to be greater the further away a given country/industry is from the technology frontier. That is, strict regulation hinders the adoption of existing technologies, possibly because it reduces competitive pressures or technology spillovers, and restricts the entry of new high-tech firms. In addition, strict product market regulations have a negative impact on the process of innovation itself. Thus, given the strong impact of R&D on productivity, there is also an indirect channel whereby strict product market regulations may reduce the scope for productivity enhancement.

We have also provided some evidence that high hiring and firing costs (proxied by employment legislation, EPL) are correlated with weaker productivity performance. However, this occurs almost exclusively when wages and/or internal training do not offset these higher costs, thereby inducing sub-optimal adjustments of the workforce to technology changes. The link between EPL and innovation activity is also complex. Our analysis suggests that different joint configurations of EPL and wage bargaining regimes may lead to high innovative activity, though in different sectors of the economy. In particular, strict EPL adds to the negative effects on innovation of strict product market regulations in countries where employers are not well coordinated in countries lacking coordination among employers, adjusting the workforce to the needs of new technologies via internal training—a reasonable strategy where firing costs are high—may not be fully viable because there is always the risk that other firms may poach on the retained workforce. Conversely, in coordinated countries high firing costs tilts the pattern of specialization of innovative activities towards stable and cumulative technological paradigms and away from the activities characterized by large turnover of technologies. To the extent to which important domains of the ICT industry are dominated by the frequent changes in the leading technology (e.g. in software industry), these results may help to explain why continental European countries, while enjoying leading positions in more industries with cumulative technologies (e.g. motor vehicles) are slow in moving into the ICT industry. On the one hand, our results suggests that the combination of strict EPL and intermediate bargaining regimes (i.e. lacking coordination), as in many continental European countries, is likely to lead to lower innovation activity and weaker incentives to adopt leading technologies. On the other hand, countries with a coordinated bargaining system but a high level of anti-competitive product market regulation (*in primis* Italy but to some extent also Japan and Germany among G-7 countries), while being able to keep up with innovations in cumulative industries, have weak incentives in adopting and innovating in ICT technologies. Indeed, product market reforms are perhaps the most important item in an ideal policy agenda in these countries.

Appendix

In this appendix we provide the detailed tables that lie behind either the figures or the analyses discussed in the main body of the chapter. Tables A.1a and A.1b list summary statistics by STAN industry codes. Tables A.2a through A.3b list the results underlying the Figs 3.1 through 3.3. Table A.4a through A.5b list the results underlying Figs 3.4 through 3.6.

Table A.1a. US: means by STAN industry (weighted by sample weights)

STAN industry	Age	Number of establishments	Employment	Skill	Internet access	Investment per worker	Computer investment per worker	Labour productivity per worker	Log payroll per worker
Aircraft and spacecraft	9.8	242	731.7	0.376	0.378	4.954	0.552	4.576	3.753
Basic metals	9.4	1,282	234.9	0.223	0.183	8.741	0.338	4.395	3.526
Shipbuilding	8.5	119	353.7	0.153	0.137	1.887	0.251	4.004	3.439
Chemicals	9.3	2,211	135.3	0.384	0.352	23.362	0.782	4.949	3.694
Petroleum and other fuels	10.4	163	219.8	0.400	0.450	29.010	0.772	5.570	3.965
Electrical machinery	9.6	930	201.9	0.359	0.339	5.626	0.821	4.383	3.545
Fabricated metal	9.7	3,547	84.5	0.244	0.156	4.712	0.300	4.256	3.503
Food and beverages	9.7	2,788	192.1	0.292	0.139	9.106	0.289	4.545	3.358
Machinery and equipment not-elsewhere classified	9.0	3,584	113.4	0.303	0.240	5.642	0.722	4.340	3.623
Manufacturing n.e.c.	9.2	2,035	90.3	0.277	0.168	3.992	0.239	4.042	3.341
Medical and optical instruments	9.3	933	172.8	0.456	0.437	4.505	0.867	4.439	3.605
Motor vehicles	9.3	973	368.1	0.230	0.172	6.459	0.302	4.373	3.527
Computer and office equipment	8.2	155	350.7	0.551	0.632	7.154	1.995	4.623	3.750
Non-metallic minerals	9.2	2,080	73.3	0.228	0.131	16.896	0.236	4.546	3.495
Pulp, paper, and publishing	9.7	3,028	100.9	0.288	0.275	7.276	0.559	4.296	3.538
Radio and telecommunications equipment	8.9	655	240.6	0.338	0.362	10.259	0.750	4.371	3.545
Rubber and plastics	9.3	2,251	120.4	0.222	0.163	7.515	0.263	4.218	3.373
Textiles, leather, and footwear	9.2	1,656	148.0	0.206	0.128	3.816	0.263	3.880	3.125
Wood products	9.2	1,539	87.1	0.177	0.089	6.773	0.327	4.054	3.281

Table A.1b. *Germany: means by STAN industry (weighted by sample weights)*

STAN industry	Age	Number of establishments	Employment	Skill	Internet access	Investment	Computer investment per worker	Labour productivity	Log payroll per worker
Base metals	9.6	548	59.7	0.211	2.606	10.072	0.631	3.688	3.044
Coke, refined petroleum products, nuclear fuel, chemicals, chemical products	9.6	497	73.3	0.526	2.319	10.1	1.806	4.288	3.192
Fabricated metal products	10	965	24	0.208	3.116	9.447	0.478	3.742	3.105
Food, beverage, and tobacco	10.2	858	17.4	0.319	3.061	5.572	0.334	3.281	2.645
Machinery and equipment/not elsewhere classified	8.8	991	42	0.39	2.757	12.389	1.418	3.921	3.155
Manufacturing not elsewhere classified/recycling	9.5	454	15.3	0.186	2.704	5.885	0.462	3.311	2.669
Medical, precision, and optical instruments	9.6	448	13.5	0.444	2.621	2.993	0.594	3.591	2.95
Motor vehicles, trailers, and Semitrailers	8.5	362	161.1	0.208	3.099	8.753	0.546	3.725	2.95
Office, act, comp machinery; electrical machinery and apparatuses /not elsewhere classified; radio and telecommunications equipment	9.1	602	47.1	0.402	2.338	5.174	1.443	3.839	3.135
Other non-metallic mineral products	9.5	453	20.6	0.354	3.101	9.405	0.958	3.635	2.815
Other transport	10.2	169	46	0.21	2.687	8.067	1.064	3.87	2.957
Pulp, paper, printing, and publishing	9.8	470	26.8	0.49	2.468	7.831	1.86	3.801	3.144
Rubber and plastics products	9.8	425	48.7	0.192	2.393	6.784	0.721	3.703	3.069
Textiles, leather, and footwear	10.2	307	19	0.353	3.56	2.616	0.419	3.504	2.656
Wood products	9.9	505	12.6	0.146	2.876	4.33	0.262	3.482	2.773

Table A.2a. US: means by establishment age (weighted by sample weights)

	Age (years)											
	0	1	2	3	4	5	6	7	8	9	10	11
Number of establishments	843	1,297	751	588	561	547	518	520	629	620	634	23,694
Employment	86.9	80.6	80.5	84.4	89.8	88.3	113.5	99.2	88.8	111.5	102.6	157.2
Skill (proportion of non-production workers)	0.24	0.27	0.26	0.26	0.28	0.25	0.24	0.30	0.28	0.28	0.27	0.28
Employee Internet access (percentage)	NA	0.26	0.21	0.19	0.22	0.21	0.23	0.26	0.24	0.22	0.23	0.21
Total equipment investment ($1000)	1162.3	845.3	1242.8	890.2	948.0	846.2	952.2	647.2	641.7	819.7	910.0	1400.6
Total computer investment ($1000)	55.4	44.6	48.2	62.9	47.0	63.3	52.9	55.2	45.9	68.5	64.9	85.8
Total equipment investment per worker ($1000)	36.47	15.38	17.12	11.60	7.19	7.78	9.07	9.70	9.43	6.40	7.03	6.52
Total computer investment per worker ($1000)	0.85	0.61	0.64	1.02	0.37	0.48	0.41	0.44	0.41	0.38	0.58	0.42
Log labour productivity: VA per worker ($1000)	4.34	4.29	4.37	4.33	4.35	4.26	4.12	4.27	4.17	4.25	4.30	4.35
Log payroll per worker ($1000)	3.38	3.32	3.34	3.37	3.38	3.35	3.37	3.45	3.42	3.37	3.38	3.52

Source: Authors' calculations from 1999 CNUS and 2000 ASM, Centre for Economic Studies.

Table A.2b. *Germany: means by establishment age (weighted by sample weights)*

	Age (years)											
	1	2	3	4	5	6	7	8	9	10	11	12
Number of establishments	92	197	250	231	250	292	337	447	581	621	2465	2256
Employment	20.34	22.5	18.35	18.79	15.27	18.45	15.65	15.91	22.02	21.64	32.78	35.65
Skill (proportion of non-production workers)	0.23	0.32	0.26	0.38	0.25	0.31	0.38	0.34	0.31	0.34	0.32	0.33
Employee Internet access (1–5 categories)	2.96	2.85	2.43	2.32	3.16	2.55	2.73	2.54	2.46	2.91	3.12	2.88
Total equipment investment ($1000)	694.18	350.38	394.06	293.31	117.16	309.89	148.39	159.64	190.73	225.97	283.23	375.33
Total computer investment ($1000)	32.23	28.02	93.06	69.79	14.4	20.56	15.96	16.81	17.46	17.94	37.63	35.82
Total equipment investment per worker ($1000)	17.09	8.23	15.01	6.93	7.07	5.45	10.47	7.27	5.52	13.53	6.21	5.78
Total computer investment per worker ($1000)	1.09	0.65	0.56	0.89	0.46	1.21	1.43	1.27	0.51	0.67	0.84	0.59
Log labour productivity: VA per worker ($1000)	3.3	3.36	3.42	3.47	3.77	3.55	3.77	3.77	3.58	3.48	3.66	3.65
Log payroll per worker ($1000)	2.82	2.72	2.66	2.62	2.82	2.83	2.95	2.92	2.87	2.74	2.92	3.03

Source: Authors' calculations from the 2000 and 2001 waves of the IAB Establishment panel.

Table A.3a. US: *standard deviations by establishment age (weighted by sample weights)*

	Age (years)											
	0	1	2	3	4	5	6	7	8	9	10	11
Number of establishments	843	1297	751	588	561	547	518	520	629	620	634	23,694
Employment	277.7	140.4	176.0	140.3	203.7	172.0	400.4	624.8	366.3	304.6	199.7	432.5
Skill (proportion of non-production workers)	0.20	0.21	0.20	0.20	0.22	0.18	0.19	0.24	0.22	0.20	0.20	0.18
Employee Internet access (percentage)	NA	0.29	0.29	0.26	0.27	0.26	0.28	0.33	0.29	0.27	0.28	0.26
Total equipment investment ($1000)	5588.0	4732.8	9679.5	6101.5	9335.6	3961.5	5615.5	3437.5	3129.8	3783.8	4213.9	11588.7
Total computer investment ($1000)	469.8	269.2	327.3	448.4	284.5	416.4	346.3	686.7	484.5	656.2	442.2	1054.7
Total equipment investment per worker ($1000)	151.8	72.80	85.28	26.77	31.89	18.38	49.29	88.11	80.50	15.81	18.70	27.16
Total computer investment per worker ($1000)	4.16	3.18	4.40	3.67	1.31	1.47	2.66	1.16	2.10	1.76	1.97	5.75
Log labour productivity: VA per worker ($1000)	0.94	0.89	0.84	0.88	0.85	0.73	1.18	0.78	0.80	0.79	0.72	0.72
Log payroll per worker ($1000)	0.50	0.51	0.48	0.46	0.46	0.37	0.44	0.47	0.38	0.39	0.41	0.38

Source: Authors' calculations from 1999 CNUS and 2000 ASM, Centre for Economic Studies.

Table A.3b. *Germany: standard deviations by establishment age (weighted by sample weights)*

	Age (years)											
	1	2	3	4	5	6	7	8	9	10	11	12
Number of establishments	92	197	250	231	250	292	337	447	581	621	2465	2256
Employment	99.73	148.08	117.03	178.06	71.54	100.07	49.46	46.71	59.25	67.83	237.12	309.48
Skill (proportion of non-production workers)	0.25	0.36	0.33	0.40	0.34	0.36	0.41	0.39	0.34	0.38	0.32	0.34
Employee Internet access (1–5 categories)	1.83	1.81	1.68	1.65	1.70	1.66	1.64	1.53	1.65	1.63	1.71	1.70
Total equipment investment ($1000)	21635.97	3438.17	6559.35	8679.07	764.23	13690.35	1024.23	954.70	1600.43	2047.34	3231.78	21851.71
Total computer investment ($1000)	321.10	314.09	5481.75	3320.81	130.09	203.26	129.86	78.15	166.20	144.88	785.03	1017.27
Total equipment investment per worker ($1000)	33.64	25.94	48.15	14.70	18.72	11.57	34.03	17.65	13.11	54.68	18.64	19.37
Total computer investment per worker ($1000)	3.19	1.39	5.24	3.86	1.75	3.10	4.46	2.57	1.40	1.60	3.05	1.60
Log labour productivity: VA per worker ($1000)	0.67	0.83	0.83	1.03	0.98	0.76	0.83	0.97	0.83	0.82	0.91	0.90
Log payroll per worker ($1000)	0.53	0.78	0.70	0.74	0.67	0.65	0.58	0.62	0.57	0.56	0.62	0.59

Source: Authors' calculations from the 2000 and 2001 waves of the IAB Establishment panel.

Table A.4a. *US: means by IT and total equipment investment categories (weighted by sample weights)*

			Equipment/IT investment class				
	0/0	Low/0	High/0	Low/Low	Low/High	High/Low	High/High
Number of establishments	40	9047	2872	10,163	4401	2284	2395
Age	9.54	9.41	8.84	9.71	9.53	9.51	8.78
Employment	34.4	101.0	136.7	148.7	149.9	209.1	228.0
Skill (proportion of non-production workers)	0.20	0.25	0.24	0.27	0.37	0.25	0.33
Employee Internet access (fraction)	0.07	0.16	0.21	0.19	0.34	0.22	0.34
Total equipment investment ($1000)	0	282.6	4332.6	396.1	604.5	4322.6	6586.7
Total computer investment ($1000)	0	0	0	22.29	195.17	38.81	668.30
Total equipment investment per worker ($1000)	0	2.47	33.32	2.23	3.44	22.34	36.58
Total computer investment per worker ($1000)	0	0	0	0.16	1.44	0.20	3.04
Log labour productivity: VA per worker ($1000)	3.94	4.19	4.73	4.19	4.42	4.65	4.83
Log payroll per worker ($1000)	3.33	3.39	3.56	3.43	3.62	3.60	3.73

High category is defined as investment exceeding the 75th percentile.

Source: Authors' calculations from 1999 CNUS and 2000 ASM, Centre for Economic Studies.

Table A.4b. *Germany: means by IT and total equipment investment categories (weighted by sample weights)*

	Equipment/IT investment class						
	0/0	Low/0	High/0	Low/Low	Low/High	High/Low	High/High
Number of establishments	1579	793	450	1727	1057	524	1543
Employment	9.15	14.45	16.54	44.43	34.05	76.33	58.5
Skill (proportion of non-production workers)	0.34	0.25	0.24	0.25	0.4	0.26	0.39
Employee Internet access (1–5 categories)	3.23	2.94	3.03	2.71	2.2	2.2	2.44
Total equipment investment ($1000)	0	36.16	420.16	112.54	119.43	962.77	1467.63
Total computer investment ($1000)	0	0	0	12.27	47.35	25.59	209.36
Total equipment investment per worker ($1000)	0	2.69	32.91	2.11	3.1	13.05	25.45
Total computer investment per worker ($1000)	0	0	0	0.29	1.66	0.35	4.15
Establishment age	9.94	9.53	8.49	9.96	9.85	10.23	9.25
Log labour productivity: VA per worker ($1000)	3.45	3.46	3.73	3.57	3.81	3.75	4.03
Log payroll per worker ($1000)	2.77	2.74	2.93	3.05	3.09	3.13	3.13

High category is defined as investment exceeding the 75th percentile.

Source: Authors' calculations from the 2000 and 2001 waves of the IAB Establishment panel.

Table A.5a. US: standard deviations by IT and total equipment investment categories (weighted by sample weights)

	Equipment/IT investment class						
	0/0	Low/0	High/0	Low/Low	Low/High	High/Low	High/High
Number of establishments	40	9047	2872	10,163	4401	2284	2395
Establishment age	2.935	3.023	3.522	2.781	2.933	2.978	3.561
Employment	33.66	291.45	422.19	396.27	457.50	422.18	669.98
Skill (proportion of non-production workers)	0.109	0.179	0.190	0.178	0.213	0.159	0.213
Employee Internet access (fraction)	0.153	0.223	0.281	0.235	0.313	0.264	0.321
Total equipment investment per worker ($1000)	0	2.181	103.60	2.065	2.143	64.612	96.252
Total computer investment per worker ($1000)	0	0	0	0.117	12.679	0.125	6.656
Log labour productivity: VA per worker ($1000)	0.572	0.744	0.922	0.606	0.652	0.891	0.944
Log payroll per worker ($1000)	0.239	0.405	0.441	0.356	0.380	0.361	0.414

High category is defined as investment exceeding the 75th percentile.

Source: Authors' calculations from 1999 CNUS and 2000 ASM, Centre for Economic Studies.

Table A.5b. *German standard deviations by IT and total equipment investment categories (weighted by sample weights)*

	Equipment/IT investment class						
	0/0	Low/0	High/0	Low/Low	Low/High	High/Low	High/High
Number of establishments	1579	793	450	1727	1057	524	1543
Employment	28.07	39.56	81.64	169.32	118.44	313.96	409.87
Skill (proportion of non-production workers)	0.38	0.31	0.33	0.25	0.34	0.28	0.34
Employee Internet access (1–5 categories)	1.81	1.72	1.7	1.54	1.44	1.34	1.54
Total equipment investment ($1000)	0	141.99	1963.85	588.83	573.66	4841.08	34957.82
Total computer investment ($1000)	0	0	0	45.41	278.73	101.55	3735.69
Total equipment investment per worker ($1000)	0	1.7	60.61	1.67	1.6	9.94	37.35
Total computer investment per worker ($1000)	0	0	0	0.17	1.1	0.14	6.46
Establishment age	2.77	3.04	3.71	2.9	2.79	2.7	3.27
Log labour productivity: VA per worker ($1000)	0.93	0.8	0.85	0.84	0.8	0.66	0.94
Log payroll per worker ($1000)	0.64	0.66	0.55	0.52	0.65	0.49	0.56

High category is defined as investment exceeding the 75th percentile.

Source: Authors' calculations from the 2000 and 2001 waves of the IAB Establishment panel.

Table A.6a. US: *standard deviations of predicted values and residuals by IT and total equipment investment categories (based on regression in Table 3.3)*

	Equipment/IT investment class						
	0/0	Low/0	High/0	Low/Low	Low/High	High/Low	High/High
Standard deviation of predicted values	0.210	0.267	0.321	0.250	0.253	0.298	0.325
Standard deviation of residuals	0.448	0.682	0.783	0.555	0.607	0.780	0.750

High category is defined as investment exceeding the 75th percentile.

Source: Authors' calculations from 1999 CNUS and 2000 ASM, Centre for Economic Studies.

Table A.6b. Germany: *standard deviations of predicted values and residuals by IT and total equipment investment categories (based on regression in Table 3.3)*

	Equipment/IT investment class						
	0/0	Low/0	High/0	Low/Low	Low/High	High/Low	High/High
Standard deviation of predicted values	0.285	0.277	0.309	0.325	0.351	0.293	0.341
Standard deviation of residuals	0.856	0.751	0.641	0.804	0.704	0.651	0.818

High category is defined as investment exceeding the 75th percentile.

Source: Authors' calculations from the 2001 wave of the IAB Establishment panel.

Comments

ROBERT J. GORDON

Any comparison of European and US performance regarding the interplay of information and communication technology (ICT) investment and productivity growth is sensitive to the evolution of the data and its interpretation. The apex of American performance was reached in the data for 1995–2000 available in early 2001; at that time it appeared that the rate of post-1995 productivity growth had reached 2.9 per cent, fully double the rate achieved from 1972 to 1995. That measure of the post-1995 productivity growth revival was ample to make room for several explanations, including not only the production and use of ICT investment but also an overall revolution in multifactor productivity (MFP) growth not directly related to hi-tech investment.

But time has changed that verdict. First, extension of the post-1995 interval from an end-date of 2000 to an end-date of 2001 substantially reduced the size of the revival, since productivity growth for the year 2001 was close to zero, and the post-1995 revival was further reduced in magnitude by substantial downward revisions of output growth in the national income accounts announced in mid-2001 and again in mid-2002. In a later interpretation, post-1995 productivity growth through 2001 was not 2.9 per cent but rather 2.25 per cent, and in the work of Steven Oliner and Daniel Sichel (2002) the revival is sufficiently modest in size to be fully explained, indeed over-explained, by the production and use of ICT equipment.

But this conclusion raises a deep puzzle that is not adequately addressed in Part I by Bartelsman *et al.* Since Europe is using the same computer hardware and software, why has Europe not enjoyed the same productivity revival as the United States? The chapters point out that part of the puzzle is resolved by a simple adjustment of time intervals; when the decade of the 1990s is viewed as a whole, rather than only its second half, Europe does much better, both because Europe's relative performance was better during 1990–1995 and because that of the United States was so abysmal.

Part of the European puzzle is resolved when we recognize that heterogeneity among European countries is more pronounced than the difference between the European Union and the United States. This paper and others have shown a relatively strong positive correlation between MFP growth and measures of ICT intensity, for example, the ratio of ICT expenditure to gross domestic product (GDP) or the change in personal computers (PCs) intensity per 100 inhabitants over the 1990s. In such comparisons, numerous countries achieve higher MFP growth rates than the United States over the 1990s, including

Ireland, Finland, Sweden, Denmark, Norway, Canada, and Australia. Some, but not all, of these countries surpass the United States in PC intensity and/or in the share of ICT expenditure. What differs most between Europe and the United States is the low level of PC adoption and ICT expenditure in the 'olive belt' ranging from Portugal and Spain in the west to Italy and Greece in the east. The contrast between the Nordic and olive-belt countries suggests irreverent comments about how Scandinavians in their dark winters find PCs more appealing than do olive-belt residents cavorting on their sunny beaches.

Contrasts within Europe also suggest that perhaps we could try to disaggregate the United States to provide a more appropriate comparison with Europe. Silicon Valley could be compared to Ireland and Finland, New England could be compared to Denmark and Sweden, Texas to Australia, and the midwestern heartland to France and Germany. What stands out in this suggestion is the absence of any US equivalent for the European olive-belt countries. Political borders are a product of history, and perhaps the United States would look more like Europe, which includes the olive belt, if we were to aggregate US data with those for the tequila belt, that is, Mexico.

Going beyond issues of time interval and aggregation, we can make progress in understanding Europe's problems by examining several possible reasons why the Oliner–Sichel methodology may overstate the contribution of the *use* of ICT investment to the productivity revival through the channel of capital deepening, that is, an increase in the growth rate of the ratio of ICT capital input to labour input. If ICT investment played a smaller role in the post-1995 US productivity revival, then this would make room for other explanations involving factors which, unlike ICT investment, Europe could not duplicate simply by buying Intel hardware and Microsoft software.

First, the Oliner–Sichel technique, as with most of the literature in this area, requires that the full productivity pay-off from the use of computers occurs at the exact moment that the computer is produced. Leaving aside any delay between production and installation, the computer produces its ultimate productivity benefit on the first day of use. Numerous observers argue instead that there is a substantial time delay in reorganizing firms to take advantage of new hardware and software. If there is a substantial delay in the real world that is not taken into account by the Oliner–Sichel method, then they exaggerate the contribution of ICT capital deepening to the post-1995 revival and understate the importance of a residual acceleration in MFP growth that could be owing to non-ICT-related factors.

A second qualification relates to the robust productivity revival recorded in the retail sector in the US data on output by industry. An important study (Foster *et al.*, 2002) based on data for a large set of individual retail establishments shows that *all* of retail productivity growth in the entire decade of the 1990s (not just the revival but the entire measured amount of productivity growth) can be attributed to more productive entering (new) establishments that displaced much less productive existing establishments. The average establishment that continued in business exhibited zero productivity growth, and this despite the massive investment of the retail industry in ICT equipment that presumably went to both old and new establishments. In the Foster *et al.* results, productivity growth reflects the greater efficiency of newly opened stores, and most of these highly efficient new stores were large discount operations, the proverbial 'big boxes' like Wal-Mart, Home Depot, Best Buy, Circuit City, and new large supermarkets.

The Foster *et al.* findings seem to conflict with the Oliner–Sichel implication that all of the productivity revival in retailing was achieved by purchasing new computers, software, and communications equipment. All retailers, whether new estabilishments of the 1990s or older establishments of the 1980s or prior decades, have adopted ICT technology. Bar-code readers have become universal in new and old stores. The check-out process at Home Depot involves laser bar-code readers that operate identically to the bar-code readers in the ancient hardware store in my own town of Evanston, Illinois. It is likely that the productivity revival in retailing associated with newly built 'big box' stores involves far more than the use of computers, including large size, economies of scale, efficient design to allow large-volume unloading from delivery trucks, stacking of merchandise on tall racks with fork-lift trucks, and large-scale purchases taken by customers to vehicles in large adjacent parking lots.

And this is where Europe comes in. A study by van Ark *et al.* (2002) allows us to trace the location of productivity growth accelerations and decelerations to particular industrial sectors, divided into ICT-producing, ICT-using, and non-ICT industries. Surprisingly, ICT-producing industries exhibited both higher productivity growth and a greater acceleration in the late 1990s in Europe than the United States. The core of the US success story appears to have been in *ICT-using* industries, where literally *all* of the productivity growth differential of the United States over Europe in the late 1990s came from three industries, with retail contributing about 55 per cent of the differential, wholesale 24 per cent, and securities trade 20 per cent.

Just as we argued earlier that the US retailing sector has achieved efficiency gains for reasons not directly related to computers, including physical investments in a new type of 'big box' organization, so we can suggest in parallel that Europe has fallen back because European firms are much less free to develop the 'big box' retail formats. This interpretation is entirely consistent with the Bartelsman *et al.* findings albeit more focused on the retail sector than theirs. Impediments to productivity growth in European retailing include land use regulations that prevent the carving out of new 'greenfield' sites for 'big box' stores in suburban and exurban locations, shop-closing regulations that restrict the revenue potential of new investments, congestion in central city locations that are near the nodes of Europe's extensive urban public transit systems, and restrictive labour rules that limit flexibility in organizing the workplace and make it expensive to hire and fire workers with the near-total freedom to which US firms are accustomed.

Just as European performance was heterogeneous, with the European average disguising outstanding performance in some countries and an abysmal outcome in others, so the performance of the US economy differs across states. In another important new paper, Francesco Daveri and Andrea Mascotto (2002) create data on productivity by state and conclude that all of the post-1995 productivity growth revival occurred in states that were intensive in ICT production, non-ICT durable goods production, or both, while there was no evidence of *any* acceleration in productivity growth in states that specialized in the *use* of ICT equipment. This again suggests that the role of ICT *use* is exaggerated in the standard decompositions such as those of Oliner–Sichel.

What do these decompositions miss? As suggested above, they miss the delay in obtaining the benefits of ICT installation. But perhaps more important, there is ample anecdotal evidence that much US ICT investment in the late 1990s produced a zero or even negative return (in contrast to the competitive rate of return assumed in the standard decomposition). Most obviously, the US telecom equipment industry built a vast amount of overcapacity in fibre-optic cable, and much equipment and software was sold to e-commerce 'dot.com' firms that were unable to make a profit and promptly went out of business. Yet the standard decomposition mechanically attributes the same contribution of 'capital deepening' no matter whether the equipment and software were used fruitfully or totally wasted.

Bartelsman *et al.* emphasize the American advantage in 'experimentation'. Indeed, US developments in ICT production (as well as in biotech firms) have been fostered by American leadership in higher education, especially the private research universities (e.g. Stanford, Harvard, and MIT) that account for the location of much of the innovative activity in the United States. Similarly, the venture capital industry had the capacity to explode in size to finance the hi-tech boom of the late 1990s and the flexibility almost to disappear when the hi-tech stock market bubble began its collapse in mid-2000. Finally, compared to some European countries, the United States has a patent system that provides better protection for the fruits of innovative ideas.

Overall, the Daveri–Mascotto results support Bartelsman *et al.* in their emphasis on the location of ICT production in regional locations where experimentation and innovative activity is geographically specialized, while the Foster *et al.* results lead us to focus on the unique set of circumstances that have created a productivity 'take-off' in American retailing. As Krueger emphasizes in his accompanying comment, it is very difficult to draw policy implications from these disparate findings, as 'American exceptionalism' has many aspects, including for Krueger the scale of the market, an entrepreneurial culture, a welcoming environment for immigrants, a possible role for inequality in fostering innovation and efficiency, and the role of venture capital and more generally equity funding. Putting it all together, Europe faces a more complex task of 'catch-up' than can be achieved by getting rid of all its labour and product market regulations, as if that were remotely within the realm of political possibility.

ALAN B. KRUEGER

Nearly a decade ago, John Haltiwanger discussed one of my papers at the Brookings Institution and began his discussion by saying, 'There's something in this paper for everyone'. I have been waiting a while to return the compliment, but I finally have a chance. There is indeed something in the chapter by Eric Bartelsman, Andrea Bassanini, John Haltiwanger, Ron Jarmin, Stefano Scarpetta, and Thorsten Schenk for everyone. The chapters cover national growth accounting; industry comparisons of MFP growth; decompositions of firm-level productivity growth; employment flows; macro and microeconomics; industrial organization and labour economics; and policy advice and fundamental research. Who could ask for anything more?

Part I, being so long, it is easy to lose sight of the bottom line, and the bottom line here is worth repeating. The authors conclude that (1) information and computer technology has helped the United States develop a 'new economy'—a phrase that is used less frequently and more cautiously these days—beginning in the early 1980s; (2) Europe lags slightly behind the United States in this regard; and (3) experimentation is the key to growth in this technological environment.

I have little quarrel with the first conclusion. I would also praise the way the authors account for the business cycle in their productivity analysis. Their finding that the productivity acceleration in the United States between the 1980s and 1990s was not particularly great is potentially very important and contrary to the conventional wisdom. Indeed, if they are correct, the Solow paradox (i.e. computers are everywhere except in the productivity statistics) was never a paradox, because MFP growth was strong all along. And the authors' cross-country analysis of the relationship between information and computer technology and productivity acceleration is also intriguing. I would like to see this taken even more seriously; for example, how robust is the relationship to controlling for institutional, skill, and other differences among countries? Also, how much of the greater acceleration in the United States does the relationship predict?

The authors' hypothesis that US start-ups experiment more because the labour and product markets there are less rigid is also provocative. Nevertheless, I believe it remains to be proved that the 'best' survive. By most accounts, for example, Sony betamax was a technologically superior product, but lost out to VHS. In any event, I think this analysis should be done in terms of profit, not productivity growth.

There are also some competing explanations for the United States' comparatively stronger productivity acceleration that are not adequately addressed. First, the scale of the market may well be relevant, and the United States represents a large, high-income market for many products. Second, the United States has an entrepreneurial culture, as exemplified by the high status and high demand for business schools. As an illustration, I note that in my state it is common for elementary school students to make a class trip to Thomas Alva

Edison's laboratory in West Orange, New Jersey, and learn that he not only invented the light bulb, phonograph, and motion picture, but also marketed them and developed the entire electrical power generation industry to support them. This kind of a climate could encourage innovation and experimentation. Third, the United States has a work force with a wide variance in skills. At the top end—for example, the top 10 per cent of individuals on standardized tests—the United States performs as well as or better than the top 10 per cent in other countries. The top of the distribution, rather than the average, probably matters for innovation. Moreover, the United States has provided a relatively welcoming environment for highly skilled immigrants. Fourth, the United States is more heterogeneous in terms of labour input and wage levels than most countries, which facilitates a wider range of capital-to-labour ratios. Fifth, the United States may have advantages in terms of capital markets (e.g. thriving venture capital funds), which increase financing to risky startups. To varying extents, these factors could be much more important than labour and product market flexibility.

Let me next make five more general points that pertain to many aspects of the study.

1. The combination of micro and macro analysis in these chapters is a great strength and a real advance. I would have liked to have been assured, however, that the macro relationships that are found in the national income statistics are also found in the micro data sets that are studied here, when those data sets were aggregated to the national level. Along these lines, I would have thought it would be more natural to weight the individual observations by establishment size if the goal was to try to link the micro-level analysis to the macro-level analysis.
2. I realize that researchers are often restricted to manufacturing data, but I am concerned that the chapters overemphasize the manufacturing sector. Manufacturing is an increasingly smaller share of the economy, so I worry if results for manufacturing generalize to the entire economy, especially insofar as productivity is concerned.
3. Some of the regressions that are estimated with micro establishment data (e.g. wage regressions) are more appropriately estimated with worker-level data, which afford more precise controls for worker skills.
4. One advantage of using the firm or establishment as the unit of observation is that one could model human resource practices. Ichniowski and Shaw (2003), for example, argue that human resource practices are very important for productivity growth.
5. I am somewhat concerned about using wages as a proxy for skill, because the returns to skills—for example, as measured by the educational wage gradient—increased dramatically in the 1980s and 1990s.

I found the policy recommendations the weakest part of the chapters. This is in part because policy analysis is inherently difficult, and in part because

I thought more could be done to explore whether alternative forces and policies were at work. For example, I would be very concerned that a bivariate scatter diagram of the relationship between patents per capita and intellectual property rights protections reflect a tendency for companies in countries with many patents to lobby for stronger intellectual property rights protection. The authors, however, interpret the direction of causality as running in the opposite direction, from protection to patents, which may also be the case. Moreover, the fact that many studies have found that measures of employment protection legislation has little affect on employment growth (e.g. OECD, 1999), and that such variables only seem to matter for productivity when they are interacted with corporatism indices, makes me wonder if the role of labour market protection is over-rated in these chapters. Indeed, one can think of good reasons why job security might lead to more innovation: workers who feel secure in their job will be more likely to offer suggestions to improve productivity, and to implement and adapt new technology when it is available. These quibbles aside, these chapters are a *tour de force* of modern micro and macroeconometric analysis. The results deserve to be carefully considered and debated by academics and policy-makers alike.

References

Ark, Bart Van (2001), 'The Renewal of the Old Economy: Europe in an Internationally Comparative Perspective', *STI Working Paper 2001/2*, forthcoming.

Bassanini, A. and S. Scarpetta (2002a), 'Growth, Technological Change and ICT Diffusion: Recent Evidence from OECD Countries', *Oxford Review of Economic Policy*, 18(3), 324–44.

Berry, S.T. and J. Waldfogel (1999), 'Free Entry and Social Inefficiency in Radio Broadcasting', *RAND-Journal-of-Economics*. Autumn; 30(3): 397–420.

Bresnahan, T.F. and P.C. Reiss (1987), 'Do Entry Conditions Vary across Markets? Brookings-Papers-on-Economic-Activity, 3(0): 833–71.

Bresnahan, T.F. and M. Trajtenberg (1996), '*General Purpose Technologies: "Engines of Growth"?*' Journal of Econometrics v65, n1 (January 1995): 83–108.

Caballero, R.J. and M.L. Hammour (1998), 'Jobless Growth: Appropriability, Factor Substitution and Unemployment', *Carnegie-Rochester Conference Series on Public Policy* 48, North-Holland.

Council of Economic Advisors (2001), *Economic Report of the President*, United States Government Printing Office.

Daveri, F. (2002), '*The new economy in Europe (1992–2001)*,' Working Papers 213, IGIER (Innocenzo Gasparini Institute for Economic Research), Bocconi University.

Daveri, Francesco and Andrea Mascotto (2002), 'The IT Revolution Across the U.S. States,' University of Parma, November.

Davis, Steve J. and John Haltiwanger (1991), 'Wage Dispersion Between and Within U.S. Manufacturing Plants, 1963–1986', *Brookings Papers on Economic Activity: Microeconomics*, 115–200.

Dunne, T.L., Foster, J. Haltiwanger and K. R. Troske (2002), 'Wage and Productivity Dispersion in U.S. Manufacturing: The Role of Computer Investment', *IZA Discussion Paper No. 563*.

Feenstra, R.C. (2000), 'World Trade Flows 1980–1997': Institute of Governmental Affairs, University of California Davis.

Forsman, Pentti (2000), 'The Electronic Equipment Industry and Finland's Transformation into a High-Tech Economy', *Bank of Finland Bulletin*, Vol. 74, No. 3, pp. 11–16.

Foster, Lucia, John Haltiwanger, and C.J. Krizan (2002), 'The Link Between Aggregate and Micro Productivity Growth: Evidence from Retail Trade', NBER Working Paper no. 9120, August.

Grossman, G.M. and E. Helpman (1991), 'Quality Ladders in the Theory of Growth' *Review-of-Economic-Studies*. January; 58(1): 43–61.

Hamel, J. (1999), 'Bringing Silicon Valley inside', *Harvard Business Review*, Boston, Sep/Oct.

Ichniowski, Bernard and Kathryn Shaw (2003), 'Beyond Incentive Pay: Insiders' Estimates of the Value of Complementary Human Resource Management Practices', *Journal of Economic Perspectives*, 17(1), Winter 2003, 155–80.

Jones, C.I. and J.C. Williams (1998), 'Measuring the Social Return to R&D', *Quarterly-Journal-of-Economics*. November; 113(4): 1119–35.

Moscarini, G. and S. Lones (2001), 'The Optimal Level of Experimentation', *Econometrica-*. November; 69(6): 1629–44.

OECD (Organization for Economic Cooperation and Development) (1999), *OECD Employment Outlook*, Paris: OECD.

Oliner, Stephen D. and Daniel E. Sichel (2002), 'Information Technology and Productivity: Where are we Now and Where are we Going?' *Atlanta Federal Reserve Bank Review*, Finance and Economics Discussion Series 2002–29/Board of Governors of the Federal Reserve System (US).

OECD (2000a), 'Measuring the ICT Sector', Paris, OECD.

Solow, R.M. (1960), 'Investment and Technical Progress', in K. Arrow *et al.* (eds.), *Mathematical Methods in the Social Science*, Stanford, Ca.: Stanford University Press.

Shapiro, C. and H.R. Varian (1998), 'Information Rules', Harvard Business School Press.

van Ark, Bart, R. Inklaar, and Robert H. McGuckin (2002), 'Changing Gear: Productivity, ICT, and Service Industries: Europe and the United States', Paper presented at Brookings Workshop on Services Industry Productivity, 17 May.

Yoo, K.Y. (2000), 'The Role of IT Industry in Korean Economy', Korean Ministry of Finance and Economy, Seoul, mimeo.

References

Abowd, J.M., J. Haltiwanger, J. Lane, and K. Sandusky (2001), 'Within and Between Firm Changes in Human Capital, Technology, and Productivity', mimeo, Maryland University.

Acemoglu, D. and S. Pischke (1999a), 'The Structure of Wages and Investment in General Training', *Journal of Political Economy*, 107, 539–72.

——(1999b), 'Beyond Becker: Training in Imperfect Labor Markets', *Economic Journal*, 109, F112–42.

Acemoglu, D. and R. Shimer (2000), 'Wage and Technology Dispersion', *Review of Economic Studies*, 67, 585–607.

Aghion, P. and P. Howitt (1992), 'A Model of Growth through Creative Destruction', *Econometrica*, 60, 323–51.

——(1998), *Endogenous Growth Theory*, Cambridge, MA: MIT Press.

——, M. Dewatripont, and P. Rey (1999), 'Competition, Financial Discipline and Growth', *Review of Economic Studies*, 66, 825–52.

——, C. Harris, P. Howitt, and J. Vickers (2001a), 'Competition, Imitation and Growth with Step-by-Step Innovation', *Review of Economic Studies*, 68, 467–92.

——, N. Bloom, R. Blundell, R. Griffith, and P. Howitt (2002), 'Empirical Estimates of Product Market Competition and Innovation', mimeo, University College London.

Ahn., S. (2001), 'Firm Dynamics and Productivity Growth: A Review of Micro Evidence for the OECD Countries', OECD Economics Department Working Paper no. 297.

Arrow, K. (1962), 'Economic Welfare and the Allocation of Resources for Inventions', in R. Nelson (ed.), *The Rate and Direction of Inventive Activity*, Princeton: Princeton University Press.

Audretsch, D.B. (1995a), 'Innovation and Industry Evolution', Cambridge, MA: MIT Press.

——(1995b), 'Innovation, Survival and Growth', *International Journal of Industrial Organization*, 13, 441–57.

Aw, B.Y., X. Chen, and M.J. Roberts (1997), 'Firm-level evidence on productivity differentials, turnover, and exports in Taiwanese manufacturing', NBER Working Paper Series no. 6235.

Baily, M.N. (2002), 'The New Economy in Europe and the United States', Paper prepared for the conference Transatlantic Perspectives on the US and European Economies: Convergence, Conflict and Cooperation, J.F. Kennedy School of Government, April.

—— and H. Gersbach (1995), 'Efficiency in Manufacturing and the Need for Global Competition', *Brooking Papers on Economic Activity: Microeconomics*, '95 Microeconomics 307–48.

Barnes, M., J. Haskel, and M. Maliranta (2002), 'The Sources of Productivity Growth: Micro-Level Evidence for the OECD', mimeo.

Bartelsman, E.J. and J. Hinloopen (2002), 'Unleashing Animal Spirits: Investment in ICT and Economic Growth', Amsterdam University.

——, S. Scarpetta, and F. Schivardi (2003), 'Comparative Analysis of Firm Demographics and Survival: Micro-level Evidence for the OECD Countries', OECD Economics Department Working Papers, no. 348 Paris.

Bassanini, A. and E. Ernst (2002*a*), 'Labour Market Regulation, Industrial Relations, and Technological Regimes: A Tale of Comparative Advantage', *Industrial and Corporate Change*, 11(3), 391–426.

——(2002*b*), 'Labour Market Institutions, Product Market Regulation, and Innovation: Cross-country Evidence', OECD Economics Department Working Paper no. 316.

——and S. Scarpetta (2002*c*), 'Does Human Capital Matter for Growth in OECD Countries? A Pooled-Mean-Group Approach', *Economics Letters*, 74(3), 399–405.

——, S. Scarpetta, and I. Visco (2000), 'Knowledge, Technology and Growth: Recent Evidence from OECD Countries', National Bank of Belgium Working Paper no. 6.

Bender, S., A. Haas, and C. Klose (2000), 'IAB Employment Subsample 1975–1995', IZA-Discussion Paper no. 117, Bonn.

Bernard, A. and C.I. Jones (1996*a*), 'Comparing Apples to Oranges: Productivity Convergence and Measurement Across Industries and Countries', *The American Economic Review*, 86(5), 1216–38.

——(1996*b*), 'Productivity Across Industries and Countries: Time-series Theory and Evidence', *The Review of Economics and Statistics*, Vol. 78, no. 1, 135–46.

——(1996*c*), 'Productivity and Convergence across U.S. States and Industries', *Empirical Economics*, 21, 113–35.

Black, S.E. and L.M. Lynch (2001), 'How to Compete: The Impact of Workplace Practices and Information Technology on Productivity', *Review of Economics and Statistics*, Vol. 83, no. 3, August.

——(2002), 'Measuring Organizational Capital in the New Economy', mimeo.

Blanchflower, D. and S. Machin (1996), 'Product Market Competition, Wages and Productivity: International Evidence from Establishment-level Data', Centre for Economic Performance Discussion Paper no. 286, April.

Blinder, A. and A. Krueger (1996), 'Labor Turnover in the USA and Japan: A Tale of Two Countries', *Pacific Economic Review*, 1, 27–57.

Blundell, R., R. Griffith, and J. Van Reenen (1995), 'Dynamic Count Data Models of Technological Innovation', *Economic Journal*, 105, 333–44.

——(1999), 'Market Share, Market Value and Innovation in a Panel of British Manufacturing Firms', *Review of Economic Studies*, 66, 529–54.

Boone, J. (2000*a*), 'Competition', Tilburg University Center Discussion Paper no. 2000–104.

——(2000*b*), 'Competitive Pressure: The Effects on Investments in Product and Process Innovation', *RAND Journal of Economics*, 31(3), 549–69.

——(2001*a*), 'Intensity of Competition and the Incentive to Innovate', *International Journal of Industrial Organisation*, 19(5), 705–26.

——(2001*b*), 'Measuring Competition: How are Cost Differentials Mapped into Profit Differentials?', CPB Working Paper no. 131.

Booth, A. and D. Snower (eds.) (1996), *Acquiring Skills*, Cambridge: Cambridge University Press.

Boyer, R. (1988), 'Technical Change and the Theory of Regulation', in G. Dosi, C. Freeman, R. Nelson, G. Silverberg, and L. Soete (eds.), *Technical Change and Economic Theory*, London: Pinter.

Breschi, S., F. Malerba and L. Orsenigo (2000), 'Technological Regimes and Schumpeterian Patterns of Innovation', *Economic Journal*, 110, 388–410.

Bresnahan, T.F., E. Brynjolfsson, and L.M. Hitt (2002), 'Information Technology, Workplace Organization, and the Demand for Skilled Labor: Firm-level Evidence', *The Quarterly Journal of Economics*, February, 339–76.

Caballero, R.J. and M.L. Hammour (1994), 'The Cleansing Effect of Creative Destruction', *American Economic Review*, 84(5), 1350–68.

—— (1996), 'On the Timing and Efficiency of Creative Destruction', *Quarterly Journal of Economics*, 111, 1350–68.

Cameron, G. (1998), 'Innovation and Growth: A Survey of the Empirical Evidence', mimeo, University of Oxford.

Cappelli, P. (2000), 'Examining the Incidence of Downsizing and Its Effect on Establishment Performance', in D. Neumark (ed.), *On the Job*, New York: Russell Sage Foundation, 463–516.

Carlin, W. and D. Soskice (1990), *Macroeconomics and the Wage Bargain*, Oxford: Oxford University Press.

Casper, S., Lehrer, M., and D. Soskice (1999), 'Can High-technology Industries Prosper in Germany? Institutional Frameworks and the Evolution of the German Software and Biotechnology Industries', *Industry and Innovation*, 6(1), 5–24.

Caves, R.E. (1998), 'Industrial Organization and New Findings on the Turnover and Mobility of Firms', *Journal of Economic Literature*, 36(4), 1947–82.

—— and Barton (1990), *Efficiency in US Manufacturing Industries*. Cambridge, MA: MIT Press.

Caves, D., L. Christensen, and E. Diewert (1982), 'Multilateral Comparisons of Output, Input, and Productivity using Superlative Index Numbers', *Economic Journal*, 92.

Chennels, L. and J. Van Reenen (1998), 'Establishment Level Earnings, Technology and the Growth of Inequality', *Economics of Innovation and the New Technology*, 5, 139–64.

Cheung, Y.W. and A. Garcia Pascual (2001), 'Market Structure, Technology Spillovers, and Persistence in Productivity Differentials', CESifo Working Paper Series no. 517.

Coe, D.T. and E. Helpman (1995), 'International R&D Spillovers', *European Economic Review*, 39, 859–87.

Cohen, W. (1995), 'Empirical Studies of Innovative Activity' in P. Stoneman (ed.), *Handbook of the Economics of Innovation and Technological Change*, Oxford: Blackwell.

Colecchia. A. and P. Schreyer (2002), 'ICT Investment and Economic Growth in the 1990s: Is the United States a Unique Case? A Comparative Study of Nine OECD Countries', *OECD Economic Studies*, 33.

David, P.A. (2001), 'The Digital Technology Boomerang: New Intellectual Property Rights Threaten Global "Open Science"', mimeo, University of Oxford.

——, B.H. Hall, and A.A. Toole (1999), 'Is Public R&D a Complement or Substitute for Private R&D? A Review of the Econometric Evidence', *Research Policy*, 29(4–5), 497–530.

Davis, S. and J. Haltiwanger (1991), 'Wage Dispersion Between and Within U.S. Manufacturing Plants, 1963–1986', Microeconomic Brookings Papers on Economic Activity, pp. 115–200.

Dean, E.R. (1999), 'The Accuracy of the BLS Productivity Measures', *Monthly Labor Review*, February, 24–34.

DiNardo, J. and J. Pischke (1997), 'The Returns to Computer Use Revisited: Have Pencils Changed the Wage Structure Too?', *Quarterly Journal of Economics*, 112(1), 291–304.

Disney, R., J. Haskel, and Y. Heden (2000), 'Restructuring and Productivity Growth in UK Manufacturing', CEPR Discussion Paper Series no. 2463, May.

Dollar, D. and E. Wolff (1994), 'Capital Intensity and TFP Convergence by Industry in Manufacturing, 196385', in Baumol, W.R. Nelson, and E. Wolff (eds.), *Convergence of Productivity: Cross-national Studies and Historical Evidence*, Oxford University Press, 197–224.

Doms, M., T. Dunne, and K. Troske (1997), 'Workers, Wages and Technology', *Quarterly Journal of Economics*, 112(1), 253–90.

——, R. Jarmin, and S. Klimek (2002), 'IT Investment and Firm Performance in U.S. Retail Trade', Center for Economic Studies, CES-WP-2002-14.

Dunne, T. (1994), 'Patterns of Technology Usage in U.S. Manufacturing Plants', *RAND Journal of Economics*, 25(3), 488–99.

——, L. Foster, J. Haltiwanger, and K. Troske (2001), 'Wages and Productivity Dispersion in U.S. Manufacturing: The Role of Computer Investment', *Journal of Labor Economics*, mimeo, University of Maryland.

Duso, T. and L.H. Röller (2001), 'Towards a Political Economy of Industrial Organization: Empirical Regularities from Deregulation', WZB Discussion Paper, FS IV 01-03.

Duysters, G. and J. Hagedoorn (2000), 'Learning in Dynamic Inter-firm Networks— the Efficacy of Multiple Contacts', MERIT Research Memoranda 009.

Eaton, B. Curtis, and R.G. Lipsey (1989), 'Product differentiation', in R. Schmalensee and R. Willig (eds.), *Handbook of Industrial Organization*, Vol. 1, Amsterdam: North-Holland.

Elmeskov, J., J. Martin, and S. Scarpetta (1998), 'Key Lessons for Labour Market Reforms: Evidence from OECD Countries' Experiences', *Swedish Economic Policy Review*, 5, 205–52.

Ericson, R. and A. Pakes (1995), 'Markov Perfect Industry Dynamics: A Framework for Empirical Analysis', *Review of Economic Studies*, 62(1), 53–82.

Eurostat (1995), 'Recommendation Manual: Business Register', Doc.Eurostat/D3/REP/2rev8.

Evans, D. and R. Schmalensee (2001), 'Some Economic Aspects of Antitrust Analysis in Dynamically Competitive Industries', NBER Working Paper Series no. 8268.

Fisher, F.M. (1965), 'Embodied Technical Change and the Existence of an Aggregate Capital Stock', *Review of Economic Studies*, 32, 263–88.

Foster, L., J.C. Haltiwanger, and C.J. Krizan (1998), 'Aggregate Productivity Growth: Lessons from Microeconomic Evidence', NBER Working Paper no. 6803.

Frantzen, D. (2000), 'Innovation, International Technological Diffusion and the Changing Influence of R&D on Productivity', *Cambridge Journal of Economics*, 24, 193–210.

Geroski, P.A. (1990), 'Innovation, Technological Opportunity, and Market Structure', *Oxford Economic Papers*, 42, 586–602.

——(1995), 'What Do we Know about Entry?', *International Journal of Industrial Organization*, 13, 421–40.

Gilbert, R. and D. Newbery (1982), 'Pre-emptive Patenting and the Persistence of Monopoly', *American Economic Review*, 72, 514–26.

Ginarte, J. and W. Park (1997), 'Determinants of Patent Rights: A Cross-national Study', *Research Policy*, 26, 283–301.

Gordon, R.J. (2000), 'Does the "New Economy" Measure up to the Great Inventions of the Past?', *Journal of Economic Perspectives*, 14(Fall), 19–65.

—— (2002), 'Technology and Economic Performance in the American Economy', CEPR Discussion Paper Series no. 3213, February.

Gottschalk, P. and T. Smeeding (1997), 'Cross National Comparisons of Earnings and Income Inequality', *Journal of Economic Literature*, 35, 633–87.

Green, A. and D.G. Mayes (1991), 'Technical Efficiency in Manufacturing Industries' *Economic Journal*, 101, 523–38.

Griffith R., S. Redding, and J. Van Reenen (2000), 'Mapping the Two Faces of R&D: Productivity Growth in a Panel of OECD Industries', IFS Working Paper W00/02.

Griliches, Z. (1990), 'Patent Statistics as Economic Indicators: A Survey', *Journal of Economic Literature*, 28, 1661–797.

—— and H. Regev (1995), 'Firm Productivity in Israeli Industry, 1979–1988', *Journal of Econometrics*, 65, 175–203.

Guellec, D. and B. Van Pottelsberghe (1997), 'Does Government Support Stimulate Private R&D?' *OECD Economic Studies*, 29, 95–122.

—— (2001), 'R&D and Productivity Growth: Panel Data Analysis of 16 OECD Countries', *OECD Economic Studies*, 33(2), 103–26.

Hall, P. and D. Soskice (2001), *Varieties of Capitalism*, Oxford: Oxford University Press.

Hamel, G. (1998), 'Bringing Silicon Valley Inside', *Harvard Business Review*, September/October.

Haskel, J. and A. Sanchis (1995), 'Privatisation and X-inefficiency: A Bargaining Approach', *The Journal of Industrial Economics*, 43(3), 301–21.

Havrylyshyn, O. (1990), 'Trade Policy and Productivity Gains in Developing Countries: A Survey of the Literature', *World Bank Research Observer*, 5, 1–24.

Hax, A.C. and D.L. Wilde (1999), 'The Delta Model: Adaptive management for a Changing World', *Sloan Management Review*, Winter.

Hempell, T. (2002), 'Does Experience Matter? Productivity Effects of ICT in the German Service Sector', Centre for European Economic Research, February.

Hodrick, R. and E. Prescott (1997), 'Post-war US Business Cycles: An Empirical Investigation', *Journal of Money, Credit and Banking*, 29, 1–16.

Holmström, B. (1982), 'Moral Hazard in Teams', *Bell Journal of Economics*, 13, 324–40.

Jarmin, R. and J. Miranda (2002), 'The Longitudinal Business Database', Center for Economic Studies, CES-WP-2002-17.

Jorgenson, D.W. (1966), 'The Embodiment Hypothesis', *Journal of Political Economy*, 74(1), 1–17.

—— and K.J. Stiroh (2000), 'Raising the Speed Limit: U.S. Economic Growth in the Information Age', *Brookings Papers on Economic Activity*, 1, 125–211.

Jovanovic, B. (1982), 'Selection and the Evolution of Industry', *Econometrica*, 50(3), 649–70.

—— and Y. Nyarko (1996), 'Learning by Doing and the Choice of Technology', *Econometrica*, 64, 1299–310.

Kamien, M. and N. Schwartz (1982), *Market Structure and Innovation*, Cambridge: Cambridge University Press.

Klette, T.J. and Z. Griliches (2000), 'Empirical Patterns of Firm Growth and R&D Investment: A Quality Ladder Model Interpretation', *Economic Journal*, 110, 363–87.

—— and S. Kortum (2002), 'Innovating Firms and Aggregate Innovation', NBER Working Paper no. w8819.

Koedijk, K. and J. Kremers (1996), 'Market Opening, Regulation and Growth in Europe', *Economic Policy*, 23(October), 445–67.

Kölling, A. (2000), 'The IAB-Establishment Panel. Schmollers Jahrbuch', *Journal of Applied Social Science Studies*, 120(2), 291–300.

Lazear, E.P. and S. Rosend (1981), 'Rank-order Tournaments as Optimum Labor Contracts'. *Journal of Political Economy*, 89, 841–64.

Lee, J.W. (1993), 'International Trade, Distortions, and Long-run Economic Growth', *IMF Staff Papers*, 40, 299–328.

Levin, R. (1978), 'Technical Change, Barriers to Entry and Market Structure', *Economica*, 45, 347–61.

Lichtenberg, F.R. (1988), 'The Private R&D Investment Response to Federal Design and Technical Competitions', *American Economic Review*, 78, 550–9.

Lynch, L. (ed.) (1994), *Training and the Private Sector: International Comparisons*, Chicago: University of Chicago Press for the NBER.

MacDonald, J.M. (1994), 'Does Import Competition Force Efficient Production?', *Review of Economics and Statistics*, 76(4), 721–7.

Malerba, F. and L. Orsenigo (1995), 'Schumpeterian Patterns of Innovation', *Cambridge Journal of Economics*, 19, 47–65.

——(1997), 'Technological Regimes and Sectoral Patterns of Innovative Activities', *Industrial and Corporate Change*, 6, 83–117.

McCue, K. (1996), 'Promotions and Wage Growth', *Journal of Labor Economics*, 14, 175–209.

McKinsey Global Institute (1997), *Removing Barriers to Growth and Employment in France and Germany*, McKinsey.

Meyer, M. and J. Vickers (1997), 'Performance Comparisons and Dynamic Incentives', *Journal of Political Economy*, 105(3), 547–81.

Milgrom, P. and J. Roberts (1995). 'Complementarities and Fit: Strategy, Structure and Organizational Change in Manufacturing', *Journal of Accounting and Economics*, 19, 179–208.

Moulton, B.R. (1986), 'Random Group Effects and the Precision of Regression Estimates', *Journal of Econometrics*, 32, 385–97.

Nadiri, M.I. (1993), 'Innovations and Technological Spillovers', NBER Working Paper no. 4423.

Nalebuff, B. and J. Stiglitz (1983), 'Information, Competition and Markets', *American Economic Revue, Papers and Proceedings*, 73, 278–93.

Nelson, R. and S. Winter (1982), *An Evolutionary Theory of Economic Change*, Cambridge, MA: The Belknap Press of Harvard University Press.

Nickell, S. (1996), 'Competition and Corporate Performance', *Journal of Political Economy*, 104, 724–46.

——, D. Nicolitsas, and N. Dryden (1997), 'What Makes Firms Perform Well?', *European Economic Review*, 41, 3–5, 783–96.

Nicoletti, G., S. Scarpetta, and O. Boyland (1999), 'Summary Indicators of Product Market Regulation with an Extension to Employment Protection Legislation', OECD Economics Department Working Papers no. 226.

——, R.C., G. Haffner, S. Nickell, S. Scarpetta, and G. Zoega (2001*a*), 'European integration, Liberalisation and Labour Market Performance', in G. Bertola, T. Boeri, and G. Nicoletti (eds.), *Welfare and Employment in a United Europe*, Cambridge, MA: MIT Press.

Nicoletti, G., A. Bassanini, E. Ernst, S. Jean, P. Santiago, and P. Swaim (2001*b*), 'Product and Labour Market Interactions in OECD Countries', OECD Economics Department Working Papers no. 312.

OECD (1993), *Education at a Glance*, Paris: OECD.

——(1996), *Industry Productivity—International Comparison and Measurement Issues*, Paris: OECD.

——(1997), *The OECD Report on Regulatory Reform*, Paris: OECD.

——(1998*a*), *Technology, Productivity and Job Creation—Best Policy Practices*, Paris: OECD.

——(1998*b*), *Science, Technology and Industry Outlook 1998*, Paris: OECD.

——(1999), *The OECD Jobs Strategy: Assessing Performance and Policy*, Paris: OECD.

——(2000*a*), *A New Economy? The Changing Role of Innovation and Information Technology in Growth*, Paris: OECD.

——(2000*b*), *Education at a Glance*, Paris: OECD.

——(2001*a*), *The New Economy Beyond the Hype: The OECD Growth Project*, Paris: OECD.

——(2001*b*), *OECD Economic Studies*, 32, Special issue on Regulatory Reform, Paris: OECD.

——(2003), *The Sources of Economic Growth in the OECD Countries*, Paris: OECD.

Oliner, S.D. and D.E. Sichel (2000), 'The Resurgence of Growth in the Late 1990s: Is Information Technology the Story?' *The Journal of Economic Perspectives*, 14(4), 3–22.

Pakes, A. and R. Ericson (1995), 'Markov Perfect Industry Dynamics: A Framework for Empirical Work', *Review of Economic Studies*, 62(1), 53–82.

——(1998), 'Empirical Implications of Alternative Models of Firm Dynamics', *Journal or Economic Theory*, 79(1), 1–45.

Pavitt, K. (1998), 'Technologies, Products and Organization in the Innovating Firm: What Adam Smith Tells us and Joseph Schumpeter Doesn't', *Industrial and Corporate Change*, 7(3), 433–52.

Perez, C. and L. Soete (1988), 'Catching up in Technology: Entry Barriers and Windows of Opportunity', in G. Dosi, C. Freeman, R. Nelson, G. Silverberg, and L. Soete (eds.), *Technical Change and Economic Theory*, London: Pinter.

Pilat, D. and F. C. Lee (2001), 'Productivity Growth in ICT-Producing and ICT-Using Industries: A Source of Growth Differentials in the OECD?', OECD STI Working Papers 2001/4.

Porter, M. (1990), *The Competitive Advantage of Nations*, London: MacMillan Press.

Reinganum, J. (1983), 'Uncertain Innovation and the Persistence of Monopoly', *American Economic Review*, 73, 61–6.

Saint-Paul, J. (2002), 'Employment Protection, International Specialisation and Innovation', *European Economic Review*, 46(2), 375–95.

Scarpetta, S. and T. Tressel (2002), 'Productivity and Convergence in a Panel of OECD Industries: Do Regulations and Institutions Matter?', OECD Economics Department Working Papers no. 342.

——, A. Bassanini, D. Pilat, and P. Schreyer (2000), 'Economic Growth in the OECD Area: Recent Trends at the Aggregate and Sectoral Level', OECD Economics Department Working Papers no. 248.

Scharfstein, D. (1988), 'Product Market Competition and Managerial Slack', *Rand Journal of Economics*, 19, 147–55.

Schreyer, P. (2000), 'The Impact of Information and Communication Technology on Output Growth', OECD STI Working Paper 2000/2.

Scotchmer, S. (1991), 'Standing on the Shoulders of Giants: Cumulative Research and the Patent Law', *Journal of Economic Perspectives*, 5(1), 29–41.

Solow, R.M. (1957), 'Technical Change and the Aggregate Production Function', *Review of Economics and Statistics*, 39, 312–20.

Soskice, D. (1997), 'German Technology Policy, Innovation, and National Institutional Frameworks', *Industry and Innovation*, 4, 75–96.

Stolarick, K. (1999a), 'Are some firms better at IT? Differing relationships between productivity and IT spending,' Center for Economic Studies, CES-WP-99-13.

—— (1999b), 'IT spending and firm productivity: Additional evidence from the manufacturing sector,' Center for Economic Studies, CES-WP-99-10.

Teulings, C. and J. Hartog (1998), *Corporatism or Competition? Labour Contracts, Institutions and Wage Structures in International Comparison*, Cambridge: Cambridge University Press.

Thomke, S., Von Hippel, E., and R. Franke (1998), 'Modes of Experimentation: An Innovation Process—and Competitive—Variable', *Research Policy*, 27(3), 315–32.

Van Wijnbergen, S. and A.J. Venables (1993), 'Trade Liberalization, Productivity, and Competition: The Mexican Experience', mimeo, Centre for Economic Performance, London School of Economics.

Vickers, J. (1995), 'Entry and Competitive Selection', mimeo.

Wieland, V. (2000), 'Learning by Doing and the Value of Optimal Experimentation', *Journal of Economic Dynamics and Control*, 24(4), 501–34.

Winston, C. (1993), 'Economic deregulation: Days of reckoning for microeconomists', *Journal of Economic Literature*, XXX1(September) 1263–89.

Winter, S. (1971), 'Satisficing, Selection and the Innovating Remnant', *Quarterly Journal of Economics*, 85, 237–61.

Zimmermann, K. (1998), 'German Job Mobility and Wages', in I. Ohashi and T. Tachibanaki (eds.), *Internal Labour Markets, Incentives and Employment*, London: MacMillan, 300–32.

PART II

INTERNET: THE ELUSIVE QUEST OF A FRICTIONLESS ECONOMY

Edited by Daniel Cohen

with

Bruno Amable, Philippe Askenazy, Andrea Goldstein, and David O'Connor

Introduction and Overview

Despite the demise of many a dot.com at the dawn of the twenty-first century, there is little doubt that the ICT revolution is having an important impact on business organization, productivity, and trade flows in the Organization for Economic Cooperation and Development (OECD) countries. Conveying thorough, reliable, timely, and rich information has always been integral to the organization and conduct of economic activity, and this function has undoubtedly been improved by the revolution in information and communication technology (ICT)—including network technologies such as cell phones, fax machines, electronic data interchange (EDI[1]), and the Internet, as well as others such as personal computers and laser scanners. In historical perspective, the Internet has diffused at a far faster rate than earlier generations of communications technology: from 1990 to August 2001, the estimated number of Internet users grew more than twelvefold to more than 500 million.[2] In the United States, the number of Internet users surged 26 per cent in 2001, with the result that for the first time more than half the population is now online. Internet diffusion is even more rapid, from a far smaller base, in some other parts of the world.

The naïve approach to the Internet views it as a means to make the world perfectly competitive. In particular, by making information cheap and readily available, e-commerce would allow consumers to raise competitive pressure on firms, helping them in turn to exert pressures on suppliers. As far as poor countries are concerned, the story goes, Internet would lower the barriers to entry on rich countries' markets for both intermediate (business-to-business, B2B) and final (business-to-consumers B2C) products, thus fostering the inclusion of their firms into world markets. As explained in this report, not all is false in the 'naïve' story of the Internet as the great equalizer.

Yet, the idea that this revolution in communication will deliver a frictionless world may fail to grasp the core of the Internet story. First, it is worth emphasizing that not everyone has access to Internet, no more than everyone could read a book in Gutenberg's time. In rich countries Internet penetration remains low in poor neighborhoods and poor regions—and so it does in poor countries in

---

[1] EDI systems are proprietary networks that enable firms to send data between remote establishments or to link with other firms and conduct business transactions.

[2] According to NUA Ltd.

general. Beyond this dimension, however, there are a number of critical features of the Internet itself that makes the naïve model of the frictionless world irrelevant. One first aspect of the 'frictionless world' fallacy regarding the Internet is that *information is quite often not a digitizable commodity.* A wide number of transactions require face-to-face (F2F) interaction. You do not buy a car without trying it, not to mention a house without visiting it. This may explain why Internet does not appear to have taken a major bite out of most B2C markets. An OECD publication predicted in 1999 that up to perhaps 10–20 per cent of cars would be purchased online within the next 5 years. The numbers today remain *tiny.* Internet may have a massive impact on the productivity of the F2F match, but rarely suppress it. For most goods, the routine procedure today is to gather price information online and close the deal eye to eye. From this perspective, Internet may have much to do with the telephone. As interpreted by Leamer and Storper (2001), the telephone has allowed a new *mix* of voice communication and F2F encounters, where the former can solve trivial problems and the latter can easily be organized whenever needed. In their interpretation, the invention of the telephone has raised the equilibrium size of big cities rather than the size of small ones.[3] This (simple) constraint appears to have a major impact on the ability of poor countries to take over business of Northern intermediaries. As we shall see when analyzing the market for cut flowers, an apparently inefficient process such as the one that obliges South African exporters to air freight their flowers to Amsterdam only to auction them before resending them somewhere else in the world, could not be streamlined by the Internet because of what we shall call the *F2F constraint.*

A second, perhaps more fundamental reason why Internet is not the vector of an equalization of opportunities, has to do with the idea that ICT makes the sale and purchase of merchandise easier. In fact, as we shall repeatedly find in this report, *Internet quite often raises the complexity* of a given transaction. Consider the case of buying a book. The casual buyer goes to the bookshop, pays for instance in cash and leaves the shop carrying his book. Buying online is more complex. The transaction now depends on a number of intermediate products, which involves logistics, security of transaction, security of delivery, and so on. An Internet book carries with it a wider number of intermediate products that raise the diversity of the products that can be delivered. As most empirical studies that we shall examine demonstrate, it is then no surprise that one should observe a wider dispersion of prices on the Internet than in traditional bricks-and-mortar business. Beyond this effect, this pattern of increased complexity explains why poor countries find it extremely difficult to get rid of powerful intermediaries whose role may turn out to be increased, not reduced, by the use of the Internet. The analysis of the clothing industry will strongly point to that tendency.

---

[3] In fact, if one follows the results known as Zipf law, the big cities remain stable in their relative size to one another.

Beyond this aspect, the complexity of the task involved, as well as the anonymity of the medium and the newness of the players, raises the need for branding and reputation of the suppliers of the good. While Internet may be thought of as a means to lower the barriers to entry for outsiders, the forces that increase the need for higher standards in reputation tend to restore them. Far from creating a frictionless world, the new medium may instead result in a world with *endogenous entry barriers* and frictions of its own kind. As John Sutton has demonstrated in a couple of books, the benefits of lower barriers may be more than offset if new costs arise endogenously. The case of digital television (TV) provides a telling example. When it was launched, the new technology was expected to lower the barriers to entry and open the spectrum of choices available to the consumer. The outcome, however, has been very different. Digital TV may allow very small specialized broadcasts such as all-opera or all-weather channels to reach the consumer, but major channels have kept their share. In France for instance, the first channel (TF1) still commands one-third of the market, the second channel (France 2), one-third of the remaining market (21 per cent of the overall market), the third channel, one-third of what remains, and so on. The explanation can be found in the soaring costs for purchasing the rights of soccer championships and other major events that the consumer cherishes. So, if the digital TV precedent holds true, Internet may help tiny players in small market segments but pose no challenge to big firms.

Our evidence supports this hypothesis. For Internet-based intermediaries branding is an important aspect of marketing,[4] and branded B2C retailers can charge a premium over cheaper unbranded retailers. Marketing, advertising, or any other type of reputation-building expenditures are likely to be high because to a large extent they will determine market shares. Again, this *branding/reputation constraint* appears to play a critical role in the case of poor countries. The example of coffee producers will demonstrate the power of this effect. Beyond the logistics constraints that are in themselves import- ant (small producers who wish they could sell a few lots by the Net soon find that this is not possible), coffee producers from poor countries have a hard time taking the job of Starbucks and other brands that control for quality (at least in the rich countries' markets).

These reputation concerns are especially important in the B2B world, which accounts for most of today's Internet transactions. If firms are using Internet widely to outsource non-essential activities along their supply chain, firms which resort to online suppliers of intermediate products typically require them to undertake an (expensive) *certification* process to check for the quality of the good they supply. The role of this certification process would appear to

---

[4] A consumer survey on the use of Internet conducted in January/February 2000 in Austria showed that the most important criterion for consumer choice was the brand name of the B2C company followed by the trade mark of the good purchased (Latzer and Schmitz, [2001]).

play a critical role in our understanding of how the firms subcontract their activities. In the one success story that we shall document in the poor countries, the software industry in India, the entry cost of certification would appear to be essential. This could well be just a one-time entry cost, but this could also well play a role akin to the endogenous sunk cost mechanism described by Sutton: as more entrants apply, the certification process will also endogenously become more difficult as the standards may themselves be rising over time.

This takes us to the third naïveté of the Internet apologist, namely interpreting it as a means to kill *distance*. To start with, economic geographers do not support the naïve idea that location becomes irrelevant as the cost of distance is reduced. Instead, when investigating the impact of the first communication revolution in the nineteenth century, they point to quite opposite trends. Rather than fostering the 'dispersion' of economic activity across territories, railways, telegraph, and telephone produced extraordinary concentration—centripetal forces proved much more powerful than centrifugal ones. The intuition behind that outcome is obvious in retrospect: railways allowed producers to reorganize their organization, concentrating in one (or few) sites, exploiting economies of scale, and sending the goods into the whole territory. It is the small villages, hamlets, and so on, spread out over the entire territory that are destroyed. Here we get a somehow different story from the one that we told with television: it is the tiny niches that are destroyed. The fact that the *forces of agglomeration* are as important in the Internet world as they appear to be in the past is easily demonstrated by the Silicon Valley syndrome, of which Bangalore, India, is a revealing developing country offshoot. But there is more to it in the case of Internet than the issue of increasing returns that is usually mentioned. One of the most important features of business organization has been the so-called *flexible/lean production*. One implication is that, according to a common rule of thumb, suppliers need to be within a 24-h truck journey from the client—in the car industry case the trend is indeed for suppliers to co-locate with the assemblers. Although new technologies may make it possible to achieve 'just-in-time' practices over longer physical distances, and therefore to relocate far from traditional industrial centres, there are also important advantages in clustering similar companies. Agglomeration economies are not only the consequence of 'physical' transportation costs, but also the result of less material positive external effects.

This leads us to the fourth naïve expectation concerning the links between economic geography and the *development* process. Following the previous discussion, some observers have argued that, by 'killing distance', the Internet is an unstoppable driver of relocation to low-wage areas. While in a few cases—notably Indian software and information technology (IT)-enabled services—IT diffusion has opened up new opportunities for developing country entrepreneurs and workers, in more traditional sectors like agricultural commodities, the new technologies have had a less dramatic impact, with powerful industry incumbents (e.g. the big trading houses and auctioneers) resistant to the dissipation of their rents and in a relatively strong position to use the technologies to their advantage. Other examples that we already alluded to in this introduction include ornamental horticulture, where the bottleneck is the information on quality, and coffee, where it is the ability of producers to create premium products. In travel and tourism, finally, the rising profile of online agencies in industrial countries has no parallel in developing countries, where small-scale operators seem unlikely to by-pass source-country travel agents and online 'info-mediaries'.

In the Bangalore case—the classic success story of the Internet—we argue that this is an example where each of the constraints that we have mentioned so far has been relatively slack. First, software is a perfectly digitizable product: the F2F constraint is not much binding (although, obviously Indian software engineers still often travel to their US customers' premises to observe their operations and learn more intimately about their software needs). Second, the quality is readily identified by the consumer: the reputation constraint is not binding either (too much at least: some certification has been part of its success). Finally, the pool of Indian engineers has allowed the forces of agglomeration to play their positive role. In other (albeit possibly less impressive) success stories such as the data-processing industry in the Philippines, local companies could also build on the weightless nature of the good they supply—in this case the ability to answer phone calls across the time barriers, which allows to have 24-h-a-day response. Whenever the nature of the good becomes more material, however, failure stories are more often the case. In clothing, for instance, design and brand names remain in the hands of rich countries' firms. Producers in developing countries have found it extremely difficult to climb up the ladder of production; middlemen and importers typically extract up to 40 per cent of wholesale prices. Upgrading is not impossible, as demonstrated by the success of some Asian firms, but case studies show that this takes an enormous investment in building reputation, gathering information, and mustering the organizational know-how needed to manage the production chain.

What policy implications can be drawn from our results? From the perspective of reducing income and wealth inequality between rich (OECD) countries and 'the rest' through more intensive trade flows, it should be borne in mind that in the past economic growth has played a much greater role than falling transport costs—which comes a distant third after tariff reductions in explaining North–South trade growth. This suggests that even if the actual governance of global industries and supply chains became more friendly for developing countries, technology-induced lowering of transport and transaction costs would still have a relatively insignificant impact on trade opportunities. Simple claims about the links between equity, well-being, and the unhindered development of ICTs are also not correct, and may in some cases be dangerously wrong. The legal system, the stability of institutional and political conditions, and levels of government distortions are important determinants of ICT diffusion—although our results shed a sceptical light on the role of telecommunication deregulation (proxied by the price of local calls and telephone subscription) when considering fixed effects.

None of this is meant to imply that Internet is not a welcome innovation. The Internet and ICT are often referred to as advanced technologies, the presumption being that only people with advanced education and high levels of skill can make effective use of them. This does not seem plausible, since they are designed to serve a mass market consisting mostly of people with only moderate levels of education. The fact that young school children are often more adept at using computers and the Internet than their doctorate-toting parents should give a pause. In this there is some cause for optimism: the technology itself does not appear to be inherently skill-biased, so modest human capital endowments should not exclude a developing country from enjoying its potential benefits. The diffusion of ICT will thus have potentially significant consequences for productivity improvements—as highlighted in the companion report for this Conference. Internet-based commerce will also set in a significant reshaping of the intermediation sector, with benefits of ICT not limited to the confines of information-intensive activities—what is known as the 'weightless' economy.[5] New technologies also offer new opportunities for managing 'weighted', material goods.

But this reshaping process needs to be carefully examined, on a case by case basis, before sweeping claims can be made about winners and losers. On the down side, neither is the technology as powerful a leveler as some had originally believed, if not hoped. While in many applications using the technologies may not pose insurmountable barriers, apart from the familiar one of affordability of infrastructure and capital equipment, producing the ideas that underlie the major innovations that make up ICT and the Internet is what generates the truly big technological rents; likewise the use of the technologies to support other knowledge production. Moreover, even with widespread Internet access and use, existing market structures and sources of competitive advantage cannot so easily be overturned. There may be welfare changes at the margin, some benefiting developing country entrepreneurs, probably many more benefiting online customers, but if a revolution is in the offing it is at best a gradual one, on the model of previous 'general purpose technologies' whose economic and social impacts have unfolded over decades rather than years.

---

[5] According to Danny Quah, the weightless economy comprises four main elements: (1) ICT, the Internet; and intellectual assets; (2) Electronic libraries and databases; (3) Biotechnology; and (4) Carbon-based libraries and databases, pharmaceuticals.

6

Markets and Consumers

Like all technological revolutions, the diffusion of information and communication technology (ICT) is expected to bring substantial productivity and welfare gains. The 'digitalization' of information combined with the use of efficient information-processing technologies is expected to improve the efficiency of the production process through a dramatic decrease in the costs of transacting, and particularly costs related to routine transactions: payments, processing and transmitting of financial information, maintaining records, and so on. Thus, some information-intensive activities are likely to benefit to a large extent from the diffusion and use of ICT: health care, banking, insurance, or public services, for instance.[1]

The new technologies are expected to substantially increase consumer choice (Litan and Rivlin 2000): consumers would have access to a wider range of products through Internet since they are no longer limited by the product choice that a physical intermediary can propose, but can shop anywhere on the planet, provided that sellers are online. Internet also helps buyers and sellers to find each other much more easily. When the product itself is digitalizable, online distribution cuts costs dramatically: there is no longer a need for physical storing, delivery vehicles, etc. The drop in intermediation costs benefits customers but provides new opportunities for sellers as well. Producers will have access to a much larger market, thanks to the Internet. This market-widening effect should foster competition and favour entry in many industries, ultimately leading to price reductions and welfare improvements.

There is another aspect to the diffusion of Internet commerce. Lower search costs mean that consumers are better informed about prices. This gives new power to customers: they can search, compare, and even bargain more efficiently. A direct consequence is that the position of some intermediaries is threatened and their rent should decrease. The diffusion of ICT and Internet commerce should thus set in a significant reshaping of the intermediation sector. Lower information

---

[1] Danzon and Furukawa (2001) note that the potential for transactions cost savings from transition to the Internet is especially high in the health care sector, because it is large (14% of GDP), information-intensive, and dependent on paper records. For the United States, they estimate that Internet could divide by a factor of 100 the cost of processing claim forms. No more than 50% of doctor's claims are now processed electronically, but a complete shift to web processing would represent a total saving equivalent to 0.2% of the GDP.

costs would lead to the vanishing of some 'traditional' intermediaries in favour not only of direct producer/consumer transactions (Business to Consumer, B2C), but also producer/producer transactions (Business to Business, B2B) and even Consumer to Consumer (C2C), for instance, for second-hand goods, real estate, and so on. This process involves another transformation; face-to-face (F2F) transactions may no longer be as necessary as before since new 'digital' interme- diaries can provide a better service at a lower cost. Not all intermediaries face the same threat however. Those that provide a service that sellers or buyers cannot produce themselves will certainly maintain their market shares. Besides, rather than a process of disintermediation, one may actually see the emergence of new intermediation, where portals will be strategic places. This is probably all the more significant for intercompany transactions.

However, if the benefits brought by the diffusion of ICT and the Internet are potentially very large in theory, there remains to be seen whether they are likely to be that substantial in practice. In spite of its rapid development, B2C e-commerce is still anecdotic. In 2001, it weighted less than 5 per cent of the whole retail trade in the United States and less than 2 per cent in France. According to data concerning the main B2C companies, this share has doubled in 2001 in France, while statistics from the US Department of Commerce suggest that its share has slightly declined over the same period. Despite this mitigated performance, analysts continue to expect high growth rates for online retail commerce. *In this section we try to review the reasons why B2C appears to have been disappointing so far, and see whether this is likely to change in the future.*

6.1. INTERNET MAKES LIFE MORE COMPLEX

Consider the case of buying a book. 'Bricks and mortar' commerce in this instance is a quite simple process. The buyer goes to the bookshop, pays for instance in cash, and leaves the shop carrying his book. Buying online is more complex. Even without problems associated with online payment, the book delivery is dependent on postal or other services, which may fail to bring the book in good condition. Even if correctly delivered at home, the book may still vanish in the absence of the buyer, and so on. Following Latzer and Schmitz (2001), one may say that the utility derived from the purchase of goods through e-commerce depends on the quality attributes of a composite good: that is, not only the purchased product itself, but also several other comple- mentary goods such as consumer and privacy protection, transparency of information, reliability and efficiency of the delivery service, efficiency and security of the payment procedure, and so on. *Contrary to the common belief that Internet commerce is necessarily a disintermediation process, one may state that the number of involved parties actually increases.* Online retail com- panies must face numerous logistic requirements, shipping charges, custom duties, payment, fraud, and so on. Furthermore, the efficiency of the service provided by the B2C e-intermediary is dependent on logistic factors (delivery, etc.) that the intermediary itself may not have full control on.

Security problems are one commonplace example of the complexity involved in B2C, when compared to traditional 'bricks and mortar' commerce. Paying online mostly involves giving one's credit card number to the selling firm. There is also always a risk associated with credit card payment, not only with e-commerce. Paying with a credit card in, say, a shop involves a certain risk: the shop owner may be dishonest and use your credit card number for his own purchases. Less likely is also the possibility that someone breaks into the shop and steals the credit card number used in the shop. These security problems are exacerbated when buying online. Information asymmetry is usually higher between the consumer and the Internet retailer, because Internet retail shopping is still a 'new' activity and transactions take place in an environment of relative anonymity and uncertainty. This is after all one of the positive aspects of Internet commerce, allowing transactions between parties that were previously oblivious to one another. But such anonymity may well increase consumers' reluctance to pay. It is a known fact that buyers are hesitant when they have to use their credit card in a foreign country. Since some of the Internet retailers originate from a different country from that of the buyer, this is an additional source of distrust towards this type of transactions. Paying with credit card online means letting the number travel through an unknown number of channels, where the consumer has no control. Encryption and other solutions exist, but they slow down information processing and do not entirely allay consumers' fears. Besides, hackers may break into the Internet retailer and steal not a few dozens, but probably a few hundreds or thousands of credit card numbers. With such expected high profits, credit card number stealing might become an activity worth entering.

The presence of all these complementary attributes increases the *heterogeneity* within any online market; the same good will be proposed by intermediaries offering different combinations of complementary attributes. Besides, buying under such circumstances involves thus a certain degree of uncertainty, even if the quality of the good itself is perfectly known. Buying online for the first time means making a bet on the quality of the complementary attributes. This type of decision tends to reinforce established market positions. A positive experience with one intermediary will be an incentive to stay with this intermediary. Thus, one of the most important criteria for consumer choice may not be the extent of the range of available goods but rather the reputation of the online seller.

A limitation of e-commerce then concerns the dramatic increase in the availability of information enabled by ICT. The amount of information treated by agents may increase substantially so that information costs do not decrease. For instance, one may not observe large productivity gains in the banking industry because the benefits of lower transaction costs will be offset by the sharp increase in the number of transactions. ICT may thus generate larger information flows, heavier to process. This caveat concerns not only online firms but also the consumers. The larger choice of distributors and products can overload confused consumers. Regarding the efficiency of the price mechanism, the drop in menu costs enabled by Internet may provide incentives for frequent price changes. Therefore price variability may actually increase, making price comparisons more difficult, and robbing the consumers of the expected benefits of lower information costs. In brief, and perhaps somehow paradoxically, for B2C as well as in B2B e-commerce, *information-related costs matter more than in traditional F2F commerce.*

6.1.1. *Product differentiation and price discrimination*

It is well established theoretically and empirically that firms prefer to be differentiated because it softens price competition. Although the prices of books are regulated in France (a bookseller cannot make a discount larger than 5 per cent), a practice of the main online booksellers shows large dispersion in the availability and the delivery time of books. Thus with product differentiation, prices may not converge in equilibrium and could actually diverge. Several authors have found evidence of product differentiation for online markets. In a seminal study of the online travel industry, Clemons *et al.* (2002) find agents responded to identical requests with different time/price pairs. This evidence suggests that online ticket agents engaged in significant product differentiation. Clay *et al.* (2000), using data from April 1999, find indirect evidence that online booksellers were engaging in product differentiation through price, selection, and other non-price attributes. Brynjolfsson and Smith (2000) also find evidence that is consistent with product differentiation for books and compact discs (CDs). This result is supported by Clay *et al.* (2001): online bookstores have succeeded in differentiating themselves even though they are selling a commodity product, by the type of services they propose. These results are also consistent with a low menu cost mechanism. It is straightforward that the dramatically low menu costs on the Internet should lead to high price dispersion. While high menu costs make the prices sticky, the Internet ensures every online store to often change its prices (e.g. for following the demand trend) inducing higher volatility and possibly higher dispersion.

In a seminal work, Lee (1998) compared pricing of used autos in Internet and physical channels and found that prices were higher in the Internet channel![2] Bailey (1998), using matched sets of books, CDs, and software also found higher price levels on the Internet for the 1996–1997 period. In a careful work on books and CDs for 1998–1999, Brynjolfsson and Smith (1999) found that Internet retailers had lower prices, made smaller price adjustments, and had larger or narrower price dispersion than conventional retail trade, depending on whether prices were weighted by proxies for market share. Studies on

---

[2] The authors claim that this finding can result from unobserved heterogeneity.

European cases are still scarce. Friberg *et al.* (2001) provided evidence for the Swedish markets for books and CDs. On an average, the prices of these goods were 15 per cent cheaper on the Internet. However, transport costs would make the purchase of a single item as expensive as purchasing through a conventional retailer. Therefore, Internet purchases are cheaper when the basket is sufficiently large, since transport costs are largely fixed costs.

To sum up, these studies have generally found *large dispersion of prices online.* On the other hand prices online are either modestly lower or actually higher than their offline counterparts. These results are not as supportive of the optimistic theory as most management analysts expect, especially they have not conformed to the standard view of falling search costs. These results can be compared to the studies from the standard search theory on advertising. Comparisons of the prices of goods such as eyeglasses, optometry services, and prescription drugs in states that permitted or did not permit advertising showed that advertising was associated with lower prices and price dispersion (Kwoka, 1984). Recent works confirm these findings in line with the search theory (Sorensen, 2000; Milyo and Waldfogel, 1999[3]).

6.2. CASE STUDIES: THE LASTING ROLE OF F2F

In all the examples that we shall now offer, one will see that F2F always remains a powerful force, although an unequal one. Some commodity such as a home loan or bargaining the sale of a car with a client will appear to be too complex a process to be handled online. In almost all examples, Internet appears to be a good way to raise the productivity of F2F. This is spectacularly the case for the real estate market, which is one example where the matching process between buyers and sellers appears to be significantly improved.

6.2.1. *Banks*

The banking system weights about 5–10 per cent of the workforce in the OECD countries. The Internet—especially e-trading—affects mainly the brokers. Securities and commodity brokers and dealers buy and sell securities and commodity contracts and provide advice to investors. Traditionally, full-service firms bundled the execution of trades and investment advice into one transaction fee, with advice provided by securities, commodities, and financial services sales workers (registered sales representatives) assigned to specific customers. Discount brokers, who existed in the United States before the advent of online sales of securities, permitted customers to place, buy or sell orders, provided less advice, and charged a commission that was discounted from the one charged by full-service brokers, have appeared in continental Europe with the development

---

[3] Sorenson finds that average price–cost margin and price dispersion of drugs across drugstores are lower if the prescription is purchased repeatedly.

of the Internet. Actually, online brokers are an improvement of discount brokers, but are able to offer a vast amount of investment information and advice through their websites and e-mail; these brokers are currently developing the ability to customize their online investment advice.

The consequences of the development of online banking on employment are a priori ambiguous. On the one hand, e-business should dampen employment requirements in this industry. E-trading permits security sales without the need for marketing and sales workers, who are primarily securities, commodities, and financial services sales agents. E-business also permits partial self-service as customers of traditional brokers obtain account, market, and investment information online and then place orders with sales agents (who can handle more customers in this model). E-trading also makes self-service or automates functions of administrative support workers (who help open accounts, provide information to clients, write up orders, and handle account records). More generally, most commercial banks offer free services such as checking the balance of the individual account. For example, in France, according to the Accenture e-banking index (March 2001), 5 million customers regularly check their bank account online, 4 million make bank transfers, and 1.5 million buy or sell assets via the web. Finally, ICTs simplify long-distance services in accountancy, banking, and secretarial services; therefore, a part of the remaining jobs in the banking system should be delocalized in some low-wage high-human capital countries.[4]

On the other hand, to the extent that transactions entail assistance by customer service representatives, employment requirements in this occupation will rise. Moreover, drop in costs of bank intermediation should stimulate the demand and therefore the employment in this sector. In France, the online asset brokers estimates that about half of their customers are new active asset investors; this mechanism should hold particularly in countries with a limited share of individuals already playing on stock markets. However, this miracle is not so obvious for incumbent commercial banks. On a study of thousands of client records of four leading commercial banks in the United States, Frei and Hitt (2002) show that 70–85 per cent of adopters are existing customers. Compared to the regular customers, the ones banking with personal computers (PCs) have a higher rate of adoption of assets. Among the customers holding assets, the value of these assets is 20–100 per cent larger. Similar figures hold for the level of the deposited liabilities, the number of bank products, and the account balance. A part of these differences can result from the heterogeneity of consumers; especially, online adopters have higher income and are younger. Now, correcting for the observed characteristics (income, age, time as customer, marital status, own home), the gap in holding assets and liabilities between regular and PC banking clients remains large and even deeper.

---

[4] This claim is fragile. Indeed, long-distance banking using standard EDI technology is already developed. For instance, the European American express cardholders receive their account positions from the United States.

Demographic differences between the two populations account for very little of the differences in consumption behaviour. The authors have also longitudinal data for consumers from two banks. They not only know their demographic and income characteristics but also their consumer behaviour before and after the adoption of online banking (for those who adopt it). The careful exploitation of these statistics reveals that online customers have statically changed their behaviour. Nevertheless, these changes do not contribute substantially to overall observed differences. For instance, online customer, following adoption acquires at most 0.2 more products than the similar non-online customers while the cross-section estimates are 1.5 products (the average number of products per consumer is between 3 and 4). Therefore, this study on early adopters of online banking suggests that the Internet should only slightly stimulate the activity of historical commercial banks.

However, a part of the banking activities will not be concerned by the Internet. An important case is the home loan. Numerous providers of home loans have appeared with the development of the Internet. Actually, online companies face a considerable amount of applications but the number of real online customers is anecdotic. Overall, this online activity does not seem profitable because of this overload of false clients. The web users exploit the home loan brokers in order to have global information on the market, especially the interest rate. The customers will bargain F2F with a physical sales agent. *A home loan is still too complex a deal.* Because such loan can represent a large part of the income for numerous years, the client wants to have the best combination of the interest rate, the file charges, the caution costs, and the insurance. The financing can also include credits supported by the national or local government, or by the employers. Moreover, for giving the best offer, the bank sellers need to accumulate information on their potential clients. This information is sometimes suggestive; for example, if the customer is young, it should gauge if he or she will be a future profitable client (growing income, trustful, and aims to buy bank products or assets).

Again, we see that the key to understand which activities will be online is not their physical weight but their potential digitalization. Overall, for banking labour, the Internet will mainly extend the previous trend of a reduction of employment in the commercial agencies, such as that done by the development of the Automatic Teller Machines (ATMs).

6.2.2. *Insurance*

In a very stimulating work, Brown and Goolsbee (2000) provide empirical evidence on the impact that the rise of Internet comparison shopping sites has had on the prices of *life insurance* in the 1990s. Contrary to the home loan, *term life insurance is a simple quite homogeneous service good.* Using micro data on individual life insurance policies, they find that, controlling for individual (mortality, etc.) and policy characteristics, a 10 per cent increase in the share of individuals in a group using the Internet reduces average insurance prices for the group by as much as 5 per cent. Moreover, prices did not fall with rising Internet usage for insurance types that were not covered by the comparison websites, nor did they in the period before the insurance sites came online. The results suggest that growth of the Internet has reduced term life prices by 8–15 per cent. Finally, Brown *et al.* (2000) also show that the initial introduction of the Internet search sites is initially associated with an increase in price dispersion within demographic groups, but as the share of people using the technology rises further, dispersion falls.

Actually, industry analyses have emphasized the still conservative character of the offline insurance business and their reluctance to conduct commerce online (e.g. Klauber, 2000). However, by 1996, in the United States, there were a number of insurance-oriented websites that provided consumers with access to online quotes for insurance products. These sites have also multiplied in Europe for the past 3 years. The customer would, essentially, answer the medical questionnaire online including age, gender, personal medical history, and the like and then enter the amount of coverage they sought. The sites would then report numerous companies that would offer such a policy and would give a price quote from each. But with the creation of these sites, the costs of comparing prices for a given set of risk factors, age, gender, and so on became extremely low. Users can get dozens of quotes in a matter of seconds that would previously have taken a great deal of searching. These Internet search sites providing information sources between the consumer and the life insurance company were formerly available only to brokers (see Garven, 2000). Clemmer *et al.* (2000) indicate that by 1999, more than 5 million American households had researched life insurance online.

With these search services a connection to the offline seller remains. Consumers must still take a blood test, for example, to qualify for various policies. Therefore, the consumers generally do not buy the product online directly from the websites. Nevertheless, insurance carriers, agents, or brokers should be concerned by the new intermediation driven by the Internet. Insurance carriers underwrite annuities and insurance policies against various risks, pay benefits, and may also sell their own products. Insurance agents and brokers sell annuities and insurance policies issued by one or more carriers, primarily as independent contractors. Websites of pure e-insurance businesses, as well as those of traditional establishments, permit customers to calculate their insurance needs and design policies, and insurance malls permit customers to fill out just one application, yet receive quotes from a number of companies.

By permitting the sale of routine personal[5] insurance (e.g. auto, homeowner, health, and term life insurance) without the need for insurance sales agents or brokers, online business should dampen employment requirements in this industry. As for banking or car retail trade, e-business also develops partial

---

[5] The online sales also include some routine commercial insurance.

self-service, with customers obtaining product information online and then purchasing those products they wish through a sales agent; here again, this arrangement leads to a situation where these agents can handle more transactions. The efficiency of the sales agents is also increased by Intranets and Extranets that improve the access to information on products provided by companies they represent, offer detailed explanations of procedures, and permit direct downloading of forms. The insurance business is also a long-term relation between the company and the customers; the latter have to update personal information on policies to request changes in coverage, to pay bills, and even to complain. Theoretically, these functions can be handled through a self-service online system. This reduces the requirement for both sales agents and administrative support workers. However, online transactions that require assistance from customer service representatives stimulate employment in that occupation.

6.2.3. *Internet car retailer*

In a study published in 1999, the Organization for Economic Cooperation and Development (OECD) forecasted that by 2002, 10–20 per cent of cars would be purchased online![6] Actually, car selling on Internet is currently still anecdotic. However, a new type of intermediary—the so-called online referral service agencies—has appeared in the car retailer activity, weighing about 3–5 per cent of the GDP in OECD countries. Scott Morton *et al.* (2000) have studied in detail a major US online referral service: Autobytel.com. This type of Internet service is also developed in Europe. Car buyers using an Internet referral service submit a purchase request. They specify the characteristics of the car they want and the time frame in which they expect to make their purchase. In theory (and also in practice), a buyer needs to visit the dealership only to pick up the car. The referral sites have contracts with one or two car dealerships in each geographic area. The online referral company sends the consumer requests to their affiliated dealerships in the consumer's area. In return, the dealerships finance the online site through either an annual fixed fee for referrals or a combination of annual fee and a fee for each referral. The Internet sales person at the dealership then contacts the potential buyer with a non-binding price for the requested car. Referral sites control quality indirectly, using consumer satisfaction surveys and by tracking the number of referrals that result in sales. Dealerships with conversion rates that the referral service deems too low, or who generate large numbers of consumer complaints, may be dropped from the referral network. Emphasizing the conversion rate gives dealerships an incentive to offer an attractive initial price to customers referred by the Internet service. Scott Morton *et al.* (2000) find that the average Autobytel customer pays 2 per cent less for his or her car.

---

[6] OECD, 1999: 44.

According to the authors, about one quarter of this price difference is owing to purchasing at Autobytel affiliated dealerships, which have lower prices than average; and the remainder of the price difference is owing either to the know-how buyers choosing to use Autobytel, or Autobytel improving the bargaining position of standard customers.

For auto retailers, the question of whether the Internet makes it easier for previously naïve buyers to educate themselves, or whether those who have always been savvy car buyers have migrated to the referral services is crucial; the first story would be expected to reduce their profits, while the second would not. The authors restrict the sample to less sophisticated buyers who obtain financing from the dealer and find that the Autobytel price discount remains for buyers referred via the Internet. In addition, the more cars a dealership sold through Autobytel.com, the smaller was the observed spread in the prices consumers paid at that dealership. Again, they conclude that their results suggest that Internet referrals increase buyer information and bargaining power.

Although Internet car buyers pay less for their cars, the authors claim that participating in an Internet referral service can be profitable for individual dealers. Using data from one Midwestern dealership, Scott Morton *et al.* (2000) estimate that the cost of a traditional sale could be as much as US$ 600 higher than the cost of selling to an Internet referral. Given that the average Internet buyer pays only some US$ 500 less for his car, the profitability of a dealership can increase despite the lower purchase price. Consequently, the authors conclude that both consumers and dealers can win through the Internet car retailing. Such study seems an excellent argument for an extension of the Internet car retailing. However, this prediction should be qualified.

A simple criticism of Scott Morton *et al.* (2000) helps to understand the gap between optimistic prediction and a more serious interpretation of statistical study on the one hand, and reality on the other hand. First, as shown by the authors, people using the referral service were less likely to finance their cars through the dealer, to buy insurance through the dealer, or to buy a repair contract from the dealer. Despite the potential selection biases (buyers also tended to live in areas with higher average income) and the restriction of the authors' analysis to the buyers who obtain a financing through the dealer, the profits for the car dealer then seem overall limited. So, why do car dealers cut Internet price? The response is given by Autobytel itself. Far from the idea of improving bargaining for the consumer, the car dealer chooses to cut their price because they have incentive from the manufacturers to increase their results or to sell non-sexy cars. This dealer rebate is the money given back to the dealer by the manufacturer to move certain cars. Dealer incentives are often offered in tandem with other incentives that depend on the regional manager's specific judgement call. They are particularly volatile from one dealer to another.

Autobytel specifies that the buyers should check the date the vehicle you want was actually manufactured. If it has been in the showroom for 6 months or more, some kind of dealer incentive may be placed on it. Dealers pay money to keep cars on their lot (they are financed through a bank) especially after a car has been on that lot for more than 3 months, and they have an increased incentive to sell. In the United States and Continental Europe, European manufacturers also impose a minimum level of sales in a year. For example, in France, Renault or PSA can completely cut the dealer rebate if the dealer does not reach the minimum amount of sold cars. In this case, a dealer can just sell off cars in order to reach the key level.[7] Therefore, the real market for Internet referral service is reduced to a marginal share of total available cars. The own logic of Autobytel suggests that the 2 per cent price reduction would not be the result of a higher competition, but rather a better arrangement between dealer and consumers, who have the chance to want the car that nobody else will buy.

However, *the consequences of Internet can be dramatic for traditional car intermediaries*. The traditional job of a car retailer consists in giving advices and information, price bargaining, and other financial services (loan, insurance, package, etc.), car repair, and maintenance. *On the one hand, the advice task is dramatically affected by the Internet*. Indeed, the main constructors have Internet sites that offer the potential buyers the opportunity to design their car. For instance, on the site of Volkswagen you can choose all the options of your car, can try its colours, and can find the complete constructor information. According to confidential studies of constructors, the time spent with the car retailer by a buyer who has first designed his or her car on the Internet is divided by a factor four; therefore, the labour productivity of the car intermediary can increase twofold. These indirect gains explain that the constructors invest massively on the Internet while the number of cars purchased directly on their sites is virtually null.

On the other hand, the car retailer is still necessary. First, the constructors do not offer discount to the Internet users. The buyers should bargain the price, and eventually the credit and the insurance; the retailer should evaluate the bargain clout of the buyer, determine if this client can be a long-term client, or if he or she should buy a second car, and so on. In France, a buyer can obtain a discount as large as 7 per cent, and for example, the reimbursement of the car registration. Such deal is extremely complex, cannot be performed via the web, and thus still needs F2F.

To sum up, the Internet as a pure information medium should not induce the end of the traditional car retailers but should dramatically improve their productivity and thus should lead to employment reduction in that sector. The previous mechanism should also hold for various commercial activities where the information is crucial and the F2F exchange of standardized information is time consuming.

---

[7] Note that the project of the European Commission to open the car market should destabilize this system. Car manufacturers that weight 15% of the market will have to accept to sell cars via non-affiliated dealers. Therefore, even if this project does not include plans devoted to enhance e-trade, it will have consequences for the development of electronic commerce.

6.3. REAL ESTATE IN PARIS

The real estate market is a stimulating example of the effects of Internet, when analysed as a means to enhance the productivity of F2F transactions. On specialized websites, sellers can write or modify their advertisements themselves, which can also be published on a standard paper journal. The sellers can also add photos or plans of the product. The buyers can fill applications with their requirements (size, view, style, etc.) to the leading online C2C intermediaries; the latter then send alert e-mail including new fitted announces. For example, an individual seller with a nice product at a reasonable price can find a buyer within 3 days on the housing market of central Paris, while it takes at least 2 weeks through professional real estate agents. The cost of the advertisement on the Internet is about €100, which is marginal compared to the size of the potential transaction. Unfortunately, the consequences on prices are hard to measure because of the high heterogeneity of goods. The main question is the sharing of the rent, induced by this disintermediation, between the buyers and the sellers. However, an illustration can be given using a comparison of average sell prices in Paris. We exploit the data of the Parisian notaries who centralize the exhaustive logs of the transactions and the statistics of the leading C2C actor (De Particulier à Particulier, PAP[8]) on the sales of their clients. The total number of apartment transactions is about 40,000 in 2000 and about 38,000 in 2001. PAP contacts its clients when they should renew their advertisement; if they have sold their goods, PAP tries to collect information on the transaction. PAP uses this survey to provide a commercial service of estimation of your apartment; unfortunately, it does not communicate the details of its methodology, especially the number of logs (presumably between 2000 and 4000 per year) but it gives the summary statistics. Most of the transactions on the Paris market are still through intermediaries (real estate professionals, notaries, lawyers, etc.); the standard fee is about 8 per cent for small apartments and about 5 per cent for wider ones.

Table 6.1 reports the estimations for the first three quarters 2001. The comparison for flats with four or more rooms is difficult because the price reported for all transactions in that category includes some exceptional apartments that are not sold through C2C. The fact that the price of the apartment potentially sold by C2C is lower than the average price of transaction is consistent with the idea that the buyers with very high revenue will still use intermediaries. The results for smaller flats suggest that, as expected, the direct bargaining between the seller and the buyer drives to a transaction price between the standard price paid by the buyers and the amount that the seller receives if their transaction holds through an intermediary. Moreover, it seems that the

---

[8] 'From individual to individual'. The advertisements are printed each week, and are available on the Internet and on the French Minitel. During winter 2001, about one million pages have been visited per month on the website of PAP (for the whole of France).

Table 6.1. *Parisian real estate market (apartment only): average price paid by the buyers during the first three quarters 2001 (thousands euro)*

	Studio	1 bedroom	2 bedrooms	3 bedrooms	4+ bedrooms
All transactions	70	116	200	321	634
Growth compared to first 9 months of 2000	+8.3	+12.3	+9.8	+9.6	+2.3
Price minus standard commissions of intermediaries	64	109	190	305	NA
Final price through C2C	65	116	194	296	385
Estimated rent surplus for the seller in %	1.6	6.4	2.1	NA	NA
Estimated rent surplus for the buyer in %	7.1	0	3.0	NA	NA

NA: not available.

Sources: Authors' calculation based on Parisian notaries' statistics; Fourth Quarter 2001, PAP study of the sells.

sharing of the rent is intuitive: the seller captures the rent when her good is relatively scarce (higher price growth) and thus the market is tight.

Despite these potential gains for the seller and the buyer, the number of advertisements posted each week by PAP is not clearly growing much more than the overall number of transactions. For PAP, Internet seems to just offer a media complementary to the French minitel and the hard copy. However, the number of new advertisements has steadily increased. Indeed, Internet should have induced a dramatic decrease of the duration between the first posting of an advertisement and the transaction. We do not have direct evidence for supporting this view; however it is suggesting that this duration has been felt after the implementation of the website (see Fig. 6.1) while the market was not particularly tight. Note that we can estimate that about one-third of the Parisians had access, in summer 1999, to the Internet at home or at work.

Moreover, the introduction of the website does not seem to have changed the price of the goods sold through PAP since the PAP price deflated by the index of whole transactions is basically flat. Therefore, the gains for buyers and sellers are (1) they can split the commissions of the intermediaries as in a standard C2C transaction, and, this is the specific improvement owing to Internet; (2) the matching process of C2C market is dramatically faster; and (3) yet Internet itself seems to have little impact either on prices or on quantities.

6.4. CONCLUSION

That a simple transaction such as buying a book may become a complex transaction in the Internet world is telling of the difficulties of handling transactions

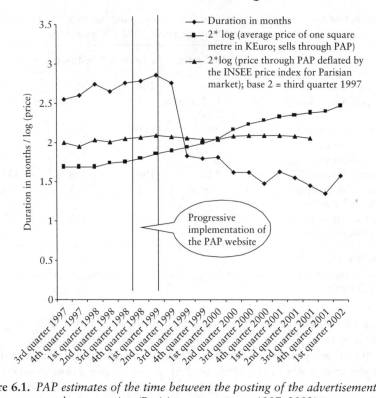

Figure 6.1. *PAP estimates of the time between the posting of the advertisement and the transaction (Parisian appartments, 1997–2002)*

Sources: First quarter 2002 PAP survey of sells; INSEE.

that are complex in the first place, such as a long-term loan for the purchase of a house. As our examples show, many of the informations are actually very difficult (costly) or impossible to codify, and thus to digitalize, and many transactions still require F2F exchange in order to exchange sensitive infor- mation. For some industry goods, a direct contact with the product/seller is necessary before buying so that not all information will be gathered online. For many information-sensitive products (e.g. real estate loans) information asymmetry can only be overcome through F2F contacts, except in the case of perfectly standardized products that the insurance market are sometimes offering. At this stage, then, we can say that Internet quite often fits the same pattern as the telephone: make F2F relationships more productive, which is clearly quite something, yet totally different from making distance irrelevant. We shall return to this F2F constraint when analysing the barriers that poor countries face in making use of the Internet.

7

Firms and Suppliers (B . . . 2B or not 2B?)

Benefits of business to business (B2B) e-commerce have not been unnoticed by large firms. In order not to let intermediaries reap all the benefits enabled by e-commerce, a number of large buying or selling companies have taken ownership stakes in B2B companies. Furthermore, some companies have made alliances in order to create new marketplaces called industry-sponsored marketplaces (ISMs): some major aerospace companies (Boeing, Lockheed Martin, BAE Systems, and Raytheon) have formed an exchange for aerospace parts; in the car industry, DaimlerChrysler, Ford Motor Company, and General Motors have formed a single global B2B supplier exchange (COVISINT), later joined by Renault and Nissan.[1] One may also find examples of exchanges formed by sellers rather than buyers (in the paper industry for instance).[2] The ownership of the exchange is a crucial issue; in general, it is on the side of the market where the greatest concentration of market power is. This indicates that Internet technologies might not only lead to transaction cost decreases and associated productivity gains, but also to changes in the relative distribution of market power within an industry. This again qualifies the optimistic predictions concerning the effects of ICT and web-based technologies on the markets' efficiency.

The development of B2B implies a significant reorganization of industry. Internet and ICTs etc promise to significantly reduce transaction costs (for search, contract, monitoring, etc.) between companies not only if firms implement changes in their purchase and buying functions, but also if they modify their make or buy decisions. It is well-known, at least since Coase (1937), that transaction costs define the frontiers of the firm.[3] By altering the

---

[1] Note that Covisint is still far from its initial objective announced in February 2000. It expected US$ 750bn of annual purchasing. Actually, Covisint's launch was delayed due to technological pitfalls and administrative squabbles. However, its activity is growing. For example, in May 2001, DaimlerChrysler had held an online auction where over 1200 parts changed hands for a total value of €3 bn. Five suppliers have participated in this auction.

[2] Lucking-Reilly and Spulber (2000).

[3] Garricano and Kaplan (2000). See Grossman and Hart (1986) or Grossman and Helpman (2002b) for improved model of integration versus outsourcing decision.

structure of relative transaction costs, the diffusion of Internet commerce will influence the pattern of outsourcing and redefine the boundaries of the large corporation.

In that framework, e-commerce should accentuate the current trend of outsourcing emphasized by recent research. Firms are outsourcing inputs and services that formerly had been produced in-house. For example, in Europe, the business services have taken about 4 points of the gross domestic product (GDP) in the 1980s and 1990s. The increase of outsourcing is both national (see Abraham and Taylor (1996) for evidence of rising outsourcing of business services in US industries) and international (Feenstra, 1998).

7.1. THE KEY ROLE OF QUALITY CERTIFICATION

Transactions between companies through the Internet are subject to the same kind of difficulties like those that we alluded to in the case of B2C, but their implication and their resolution involve substantially different issues from those concerning B2C e-commerce. Purchases of intermediate products have much more significant consequences for the efficiency of the productive process and value chain of the buying company; the issues of quality of the parts bought, the design specifications and the overall reliability of the selling company are crucial. For some industries where the issue of safety is most important (aerospace, airlines, automobile, etc.) purchasing of parts implies a high degree of confidence in the suppliers. This is why direct purchases generally involve long-term relationships and not the type of 'faceless' exchange that e-commerce is supposed to make possible since most business transactions are not anonymous. Some sort of face to face (F2F) exchange would then be involved here too, for basically the same sort of reasons as mentioned earlier: if information and communication technologies (ICTs) decrease the cost of conveying and treating information, they do very little when it comes to decreasing information asymmetries. This is why it is sometimes said that the Internet will be used to deepen already existing business relationships between companies rather than to create new ones.[4]

Indeed, inviting tenders online is complicated and involves fixed costs: it requires standard processes as well as elaborate preparations. Again, specifications other than price matter much and are more difficult to standardize and digitalize. Therefore, Cairncross (2001) argues that the impetus is to work with existing suppliers in new and more sophisticated ways than ordering the cheapest product from the lowest cost producers, which is what Internet commerce is supposed to enable. Internet would then be used to specify requirements with greater precision, track orders, and more generally, exchange information in a cheaper and more accurate way. One may nevertheless expect that electronic data interchange (EDI), and not just the Internet

---

[4] Cairncross (2001).

as such, would have an important role, only because of the sunk cost aspect of these infrastructures. In fact, some estimates on the growth of B2B e-commerce would give EDI as much as a 50 per cent share by 2004.[5]

However, the issue of the quality and reliability of outsourced parts is not specific to e-commerce and can be dealt with in a number of ways that involve different degree certification or quasi-integration. To recall and for simplification matters, one may say that some of the potential benefits that e-commerce should bring stem from the possibility for, say, a buying firm to discover through Net-surfing that there exists a potentially cheaper supplier somewhere on the planet that the firm had never heard of. However, if the buying firm cannot resolve the uncertainty regarding the reliability of this potential supplier, the value of the additional information brought by Internet, that is, the existence of the supplier, is of little value. But such a problem is not specific to e-commerce. In this example, Internet has just been used as an information source for finding new potential suppliers. These suppliers having been found, the decision to include them in the firm's supply chain is taken by the firm according to standard evaluation and testing procedures. But this use of Internet, limited to act as an extensive firms' directory, is far too restrictive. The exploitation of the full benefits of e-commerce implies automating as many steps of the purchasing function as possible. This means that the evaluation of the potential supplier should be itself partially 'automated'.

For complex quality-sensitive goods, the efficient functioning of B2B will necessitate certification of subcontractors by the buying firm. Certification allows alleviation of problems related to information asymmetry. It is all the more important that the subcontractor is not well known by the contractor, is small, does not have a well-established situation in the industry, etc. This, incidentally, is the profile of a firm that would most benefit from having B2B e-commerce, in order to find new contractors and expand its activity towards new areas. Therefore, certification and B2B e-commerce—at least commerce concerning direct parts—should be complementary to each other: the firms that would benefit most from B2B would also benefit most from certification, and certification should be instrumental in generalizing e-commerce between companies. One may further say that certification is a prerequisite for B2B e-commerce.

Certification can be made by third parties or by contractors themselves, in which case the implications for competition differ accordingly. Whereas for business to consumer (B2C), certification is necessarily made by a third party because the individual consumer cannot afford to pay the cost of certification, both possibilities exist for B2B. Which option will be chosen depends on the market. Large contractors certify their own subcontractors: they express minimum quality demands in order for the subcontractor to be allowed to bid

---

[5] Lucking-Reilly and Spulber (2000).

for online tenders. This actually enables the contractor to have more control on the subcontractor, in order to extract more rent. This process also favours the establishment of long-term business relationships through repeated contracts.

A telling example is provided by CISCO Systems: every day, the company posts its requirements on an extranet connecting the headquarters to thirty-two manufacturing plants, none of which it owns. But each manufacturer has been through a lengthy process of certification to ensure that they meet the company's quality standards. This is then a private certification procedure that grants a company the privilege to do business with CISCO. However, this private arrangement does not imply that the contractor and the manufacturers should use a proprietary EDI to commerce with each other. There is no problem doing commerce through an extranet once companies have entered the circle of accepted subcontractors. The improvements brought by exchanges over the Net are considerable. Suppliers respond to requirements within hours not only with a price and a delivery time, but also with a record of their past performance on reliability and product quality. Thus ICT makes quality and reliability controls easier and more efficient and complement the initial certification process. Such a certification process is strictly private; it concerns a specific business relationship between a contractor and a subcontractor.

There also exist more public ways for quality certification. The primary goal of certification is to give public information about a company to other companies, which could consider doing business with the former. Third parties may step in to certify that the company fulfils some previously specified quality demands. Concerning industrial norms, the International Standard Organisation (ISO) fulfils this task; it proposes a set of industrial norms, such as the ISO9000 norm.[6] This norm is meant to be applicable to all firms, irrespective of the industry or the size. Of course, some industries have developed specific norms in order to specify more precisely the quality requirements, but these norms complement the ISO9000 norm rather than substitute it. Obtaining the ISO9000 certificate means fulfilling a set of quality requirements established by the ISO. It is in general a lengthy (12–18 months) and somewhat expensive process.

A complementary face of the consequences of ICT on outsourcing and certification is connected to the information of the customers. Because ICT, especially Internet, induces the consumers to have a more complete information on the product and can simply perform comparisons and benchmarking, the emphasis on quality is more acute in firms. The development of ISO9000 certification has been rapid in most developed countries over the 1990s (Fig. 7.1). The increasing trend is almost universal, but one may notice some persistent international differences, which are most probably related to industrial structures (average size of firms, etc.) as well as differences in the pattern

---

[6] One may also mention the ISO14000 norm that deals with environment aspects.

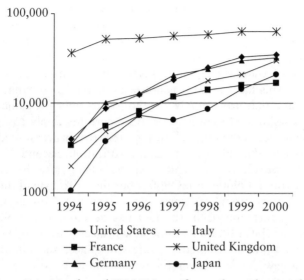

Figure 7.1. *Number of ISO9000 certificates (logarithmic scale)*

of information diffusion. The value chain is ISO certified at each step; that is, for example, the case for Nokia; the world leading manufacturer of mobile phone demands that all its suppliers be compliant with ISO standards, and the main ones should also demand that their suppliers be compliant with those standards, and the main suppliers shall also have Quality Management System certificates.[7]

Certification through industrial norms may not be the only means for communicating information about quality and reliability to prospective business partners or to consumers. A private company may also be assessed through financial and accounting information. In a way, being listed on a stock market is also a means of communicating information about quality, which involves a third party assessment. Although such information communication procedure is not strictly equivalent to obtaining an ISO9000 certificate, it may be more commonplace in some countries to rely on accounting-based information for such matters, presumably countries where accounting and financial information is sufficiently rich and reliable. Therefore, one may expect that ISO certification will not matter as much in the United States as it does in Germany for instance, because 'financial' information is much more important in the former country than in the latter. In most European countries where 'market' information is not as readily available as in North America, ISO certification is bound to be more important and accordingly more present. However, the

---

[7] Information provided by Unto Kuivalainen, Nokia Corporation, Finland.

Anglo-American type of financial control possesses major weaknesses as the hurricane driven by the ENRON embezzlements has shown.[8] One may presume that the aftermath of the scandal should boost the diffusion of a more 'industry-based' certification process, such as ISO, in the United States.

An important facet of the ISO norms is that they seem to act as an *endogenous sunk cost*. This means that it is not just one set up cost that remains the same forever and that firms simply have to pay to enter the game. It is in fact a cost that is rising endogenously, as more entrants apply for entering the game. The sequence is then the following. First, the principal tends to impose on all its suppliers the obligation to gain certification. Second, ISO standards are regularly improved by the quality experts.[9] They raise the technical level of the norm (from ISO9000 to ISO9002) but they also extend the normalization to all activities (from manufacturing to services). Moreover, along with this quality-product approach, the ISO has developed environmental and ecological norms (ISO14000). And the new project is to outline social norms (sexual or racial non-discrimination, safe workplace, and job stability) that can drive to a new divide between the workers in certified firms and workers out of this system.

In any case, certification is deemed crucial for the development of B2B exchanges on the Net. The development of e-commerce should then depend on the diffusion of industry certification. The available evidence does not contradict this alleged importance of industry certification for the development of B2B. Figure 7.2 plots the share of small- and medium-sized enterprises (SMEs) doing B2B in 2000 against an indicator of the diffusion of ISO9000 norms.[10] The limited number of points does not allow for a formal check of the relation between ISO-norms and B2B diffusion across countries. The results are only given as an indication. Certification being a prerequisite for the development of B2B, countries where ISO certification is more common should be countries where B2B e-commerce has the best opportunities to develop. As shown in Fig. 7.2, there is a positive, though fragile, relationship between the initial (1997) level of ISO9000 certification and the diffusion of B2B among SMEs. Therefore, countries where ISO norms were diffused widely are also countries where B2B is more frequent. However, this relationship only hints at the links between certification and B2B. The share of ISO certified firms in the economy would have been a better indicator than the one used here, relative to GDP. It could have split apart countries where the industrial structure rests on a high number of small firms from the others and allowed a finer distinction between Italy and Portugal on the one hand, and Finland on the other. At around

---

[8] The ENRON scandal seems to have far-reaching consequences for the 'certifying' party, Arthur Andersen Consulting, which faces indictment before a US Court.

[9] The so-called 'qualiticians'.

[10] We have used the following indicator: the number of firms with an ISO9000 certification relative to the GDP. (*Sources*: ISO and European Union.)

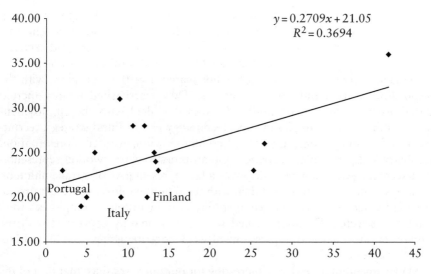

Figure 7.2. *ISO9000 certification and the propensity of SMEs to trade B2B*
Source: Data from Eurostat, computations by the authors.

20 per cent, the share of SMEs active in B2B is the same in these three countries, but Fig. 7.2 makes it clear that the ISO diffusion indicator varies between 4.95 for Portugal and 12.3 for Finland (Italy being the point in the middle of the three along the 20 per cent line). An indicator of ISO diffusion relative to the number of firms would have moved Italy to the left, nearer to the point representing Portugal and nearer to the regression line, most probably improving the fit of the linear relationship.

We can test further the importance of certification for firms and check the correlations between Internet or ICT use and certification procedures for a representative sample of French firms.[11] The second in a series of surveys which began in 1992, REPONSE 1998 (Relations professionnelles et négociations d'entreprises), contains detailed and statistically reliable information on workplace and technology practices in France.[12] The REPONSE 98 Cross Section survey contains data from interviews held with managers and worker representatives, as well as information from a self-completion questionnaire filled by employees in the selected workplace.[13] It has been conducted during

---

[11] Insofar as it mixes European and North American influences, the United Kingdom would be an interesting country for our analysis. Unfortunately, WERS (Workplace Employee Relations Survey 1998, previously known as the Workplace Industrial Relations Survey, WIRS), the main information source on workplace practices, does not provide data on Internet use nor direct statistics on the diffusion of certification.

[12] The REPONSE survey is exploited under a convention with the French minister of Labour.

[13] Actually, the survey includes three sub-surveys: the interview of a manager, the interview of a worker representative, and the interviews of workers.

the first months of 1999 and questions deal with the work organization in 1998. The sample of 2000 observations covered French private establishments with at least twenty employees in manufacturing, construction, and services. The survey also includes a panel from 1992 to 1998 (600 establishments).

Managers were usually the most senior manager at the workplace with the responsibility for employment relations. They were asked mainly factual questions covering a wide range of issues that deal with the employment relationship. Some examples include: technology use, business strategy, recruitment and training, consultation and communication, worker representation, flexibility and performance, change, and attitudes to work. Worker representatives were interviewed where there was a lay representative of a trade union or, if there was no trade union member, with the senior employee representative of any joint consultative committee operating at the workplace. Employees were randomly selected. Questions asked were predominantly concerned with the employees' attitudes and impressions of work covering issues such as satisfaction and commitment.

Management interviews are interesting for our purposes since that part of the survey contains more complete information on the technology and certification process and because managers should have a more accurate view of the global workplace organization. In 1998, managers were questioned about:

(1) the proportion of workers who are connected to Internet;
(2) the use of total quality management processes and among them the involvement in ISO certification (ISO9000 or ISO14000);
(3) the development of outsourcing during the three previous years;
(4) the just-in-time organization with suppliers or customers.

Numerous other questions or administrative information can be used as controls: industry, status (mono-establishments or affiliated to a corporate group), union representation, share of workers using a computer, composition of the workforce, employment, evolution of the activity (decreasing, stable, or increasing), expectability of the demand, boundary of the market (local, regional, national, European, or international), share of the main client, and so on. The complete set of controls is given in Appendix 3.

Our main hypothesis is that certification is a requirement for making e-commerce. Unfortunately, REPONSE does not provide information on the implication of the establishment on B2B or B2C trade. Actually, in 1998, especially in France, Internet was still a new 'revolutionary' technology. Therefore, we can assume that early investment on Internet (meaning here connection of some workers to the Net) is a correct proxy for the reality (for the pioneers) and the wish of the establishment to conduct business via Internet. Therefore, we will test the correlation between the involvement in ISO norm and Internet use. Table 7.1 reports the estimations, derived from a standard logistic model, of this relation for the whole sample of French establishments and for the sample restricted to manufacturing or services. These results confirm a strong

Table 7.1. *Internet and ISO certification in French business (1998)—logistic estimations (odds ratio)*

	Dependant variable: connection to Internet					
	Whole sample (1)	Whole sample (2)	Manufacturing (3)	Manufacturing (4)	Services (5)	Services (6)
ISO norm	1.58***	1.52***	1.91***	1.76***	1.39**	1.38**
	(0.19)	(0.18)	(0.37)	(0.32)	(0.23)	(0.22)
Whole set of controls[a]	Yes		Yes		Yes	
Groups of significant controls[b]		Yes		Yes		Yes
N	2183	2294	871	906	1296	1369
Pseudo R^2	0.21	0.20	0.22	0.19	0.17	0.17
Log likelihood	−1175	−1247	−404	−434	−744	−790

Standard errors in parentheses.
Coverage: French establishments with twenty or more workers in 1998.
[a]See Appendix 1 for details. Note that owing to missing values for some questions, the sample is different for the even and odd columns; we have nevertheless verified that the results are not altered for odd columns if the sample is restricted to the observations used for even tests.
***1% significant; **5% significant; *10% significant.
Source: Authors' calculation using REPONSE 1998.

and significant correlation between the involvement in ISO certification and the connection to Internet for the private French establishment with twenty workers or more.[14] The coefficient for the ISO variable is strongly significant everywhere. The correlation is higher in the manufacturing sector but is still statistically significant in tertiary activities.

One may however question the relevance of such results. A certain number of papers have proposed improvements of the estimation methods. These methods, introduced by Heckman, are commonly used in labour economics (Heckman *et al.*, 1999). They are also introduced in the economics of innovation and technical change. Their aim is to correct for a possible selection bias in the estimation driven by the heterogeneity across the sample. Actually, the logit estimation is biased when the dependant variable has different effects according to the characteristics of the firms. We have here two types of firms, those certified with ISO norms, and those which are not certified. We want to estimate the impact of certification on the adoption of Internet. Correlations such as those of the table above could be interpreted as a causal relationship

---

[14] Lesne and Mairesse (2001) investigated the reasons for small firms (under twenty employees) to connect to Internet and their findings complement ours. Although not specifically concerned by the relationship between certification and B2B, their results emphasize that the small French firms that decided to be connected to Internet were in general more innovative, had a more computer-intensive production process, a high-skilled work force, and were ISO certified.

Table 7.2. *Impact of certification on the adoption of Internet*

	Full set of controls	Clean set of controls
Estimator	6.25	7.53*
	(4.51)	(4.35)
Estimator divided by the observed percentage of establishments using Internet	11	13
Number of observations	2180	2006

Weighted estimation in %.
Standard errors in parentheses.
Coverage: French establishments with twenty or more workers in 1998.
*10% significant.

Source: Authors' calculation using REPONSE 1998.

between certification and the use of Internet. There is however a potential selection bias. Certain firm characteristics may affect both the certification policy and the Internet adoption of the firm. If such is the case, we would estimate a parameter that includes not only the effect of certification for certified firms but also the contribution of the difference in average characteristics on the Internet adoption differentials across both certified and non-certified firms.

To correct for such a bias, we implement a 'weighted estimator' developed by Crépon and Iung (1999), inspired by Abowd *et al.* (2001).[15] This estimator W gives the average effect of the treatment: let X denote the theoretical average percentage of establishments using Internet if ISO norms are not applied; then, $X + W$ will be the share of establishments exploiting Internet if ISO norms are fully adopted. Results of the new estimations are given in Table 7.2. The estimator W divided by the observed percentage of establishments using Internet is also given.

The coefficient of the ISO variable in these new estimations turns out to be lower than with the original logit estimation. This result shows that the selection bias on the observable characteristics is large. However, using a clean set of controls, the coefficient is still significant (at a 10 per cent level). This result, that is, obtaining a lower but still significant coefficient when implementing the unbiased estimator, is verified for all the other estimations we made. Therefore, in what follows, we present the results of the latter type of estimation only. Table 7.1 gives the increase in the probability of adopting the Internet brought by certification. Therefore, being ISO9000 certified implied a probability of adopting the Internet augmented by 15 per cent.

---

[15] See Appendix 2 for a more precise description.

It is certainly an exaggeration to consider all firms with an Internet access to be trading online. Though lacking a variable accounting precisely for the extent of B2B e-commerce at the individual level, we can still try to improve our estimations by considering the joint use of Inter- and Intranet. Such a variable is of special interest considering what was said about B2B. As mentioned earlier, B2B associates both the Internet and proprietary EDI, and will continue to do so for the next few years according to most business forecasts. Therefore, firms that are the most likely to do e-commerce certainly make use of both types of access to the Net. We implement estimations of the effect of certification on this new and more complete 'Net' variable. Estimation results are documented in Table 7.3.

Results using the Net variable are improved in terms of fit when compared to the earlier estimations using the Internet variable. The impact of certification also seems to be higher with this new variable, showing that certification has a larger impact on the joint Intra- and Internet use than just on the latter. This is broadly consistent with the fact that firms doing B2B exchanges through the Net most probably use EDI alongside the Internet. Therefore, the estimates of Table 7.3 are certainly closer to the estimation of the effects of certification on actual B2B than those of Table 7.2. Again, these results are consistent with the hypothesis that certification is a prerequisite for making B2B commerce.

The econometric method used does not allow for correction with respect to unobserved variables. One may wonder whether some variables could indeed explain the correlation between Internet and ISO norms. Tighter competition, for instance, might push firms towards both using Internet and being ISO-norms certified, without any causality between the two. To reduce this heterogeneity problem, we tried to include industry dummies at a disaggregate level, in an attempt to take into account industry-specific patterns. The results,

Table 7.3. *Effect of certification on Net adoption*

	Full set of controls	Clean set of controls
Estimator	9.18**	8.61**
	(4.56)	(3.95)
Estimator divided by the observed percentage of establishments using Internet	17	16
Number of observations	2180	2006

Weighted estimation in %.
Standard errors in parentheses.
Coverage: French establishments with twenty or more workers in 1998.
**5% significant.

Source: Authors' calculus using REPONSE 1998.

not reported here, were only marginally altered. In order to take a particular account of the competition problem, we used a proxy for the intensity of competition that each firm faces. The REPONSE survey gives some information in this respect. The following variables were included in the regressions reported in the previous tables: whether the firm's market is local, national, or international, and the share of the firm's main customer. Another variable was not included in the regressions above because it was missing for one-fourth of the firms: the firm's market share. This variable is an indication of the de facto intensity of competition faced by the firm. In spite of the numerous missing observations, we performed regressions with this variable included. The results, not reported here, were only a slight decrease in the main coefficient of interest (the effect of certification on Net adoption). Therefore, controlling as much as possible for the intensity of competition does not change our conclusions.

7.2. E-INTEGRATION AND SPATIAL LOCATION

As argued by Cairncross (2001) and Venables (2001), a large bulk of the transformations set in motion by the diffusion of ICT and Internet will concern the new pattern of location of economic activities. The ease with which it is now possible to separate physical from information flows will open new opportunities for relocation. New technologies dramatically decrease the costs associated with the remote control of many activities:

(1) inventory control; for instance, monitoring the position of electronically tagged containers or checking stock on supermarket shelves;
(2) navigation; electronic maps may be used to pinpoint the location of a lorry, a parcel, or even a letter;
(3) alerting; new technologies help in tracking stolen goods or monitor the state of a patient's health.

Gains are thus not only limited to the conveying of information but also affect the transportation of physical goods. Anything that moves can be connected much more easily and cheaply. The new technologies are then expected to favour new patterns of activity location. They reduce many of the costs associated with distance and allow firms to relocate activities to take better advantage of cost differentials.

These transformations are not happening in a vacuum however. One important item that we now want to highlight is indeed the effect of just-in-time practices and flexible production on outsourcing and on spatial location. As the example of Zara that is presented in Box 7.1 demonstrates, this may be one of the goals of e-business to foster these new management practices. In order to test whether the use of the web has favoured what we may call *e*-reorganization, we need to define a variable that would account for these *flexible reorganizations* since there is no ready-made solution available in the original survey. We need a variable related to the pattern of externalization of the firm's

---

Box 7.1. *The Zara case*

Established in 1988, Zara, part of the Inditex group, is a Spanish apparel manufacturer and retailer that has been able to achieve a sales growth of 20 per cent in consecutive years since 1990. Its profit margin of 10 per cent is the highest among its competitors. In March 2002 it operated 500 shops in five continents, including 220 units in Spain. With sales of US$ 1.6bn, Zara is the largest European apparel retail store, although Gap is about 6 times larger.

The two companies have adopted very different business models. While Gap has a nine-month lead time, operates on four seasons, and refreshes its stock once a month, Zara makes extensive use of sales and demographics data to create new products on a rolling basis, price their products aggressively, and quickly make products obsolete in response to market signals. Demand-based management enables it to introduce new products every week, amounting to 12,000 new products introduced each year.

The company also makes use of a very efficient and flexible design and manufacturing supply chain so that the design to sales cycle can be as short as 20–30 days. Zara has heavily invested in ICT and has appointed an ICT specialist as CEO. Designs are scanned into computer and electronically transmitted to factory computers, including computer-controlled cutting equipment. Store managers carry handheld computers to regularly communicate selling trends, customer comments, store orders, and design suggestions to headquarters. On the other hand, Zara has maintained very low advertising costs (as opposed to competitors such as H&M). It encourages 'impulse buying' by showing to customers that if they like something, they must buy it now, because it will not be in the shops the following week.

Efficient supply chain management is the key. Zara delivers to each store twice a week and while it still holds textile in inventory, this stock is less risky than finished garments. Small-batch production allows planning flexibility. What is of course peculiar is that most textile cutting and apparel manufacturing is made in southern Europe. Capital-intensive functions, such as dying and cutting fabric, are performed in highly automated factories in Spain, whereas responsibilities for labour-intensive steps are subcontracted to 300 SMEs in Spain and Portugal. Zara helps with info/logistics technology. Production in Europe obviously drives labour costs higher, but it also allows to speed up transport to local stores (mainly in France, Spain, and Portugal) by truck. Overseas stores (e.g. in New York) are replenished from Spain using air transport, although Zara plans to start production in Mexico if the US store network grows.

---

activity as well as just-in-time techniques. We define our flexible reorganization variable as the product of two variables available from the answers to the survey: the first variable reports whether the firm has a just-in-time organization with its customers or suppliers; the second variable informs whether the firm has developed outsourcing during the last 3 years. Making use of the information provided in the survey, we take into account firms that have successfully implemented outsourcing only (about 90 per cent of the relevant sample).

We therefore test the impact of the use of the worldwide web on this flexible reorganization process using the 'Net' variable, that is, the connection through Intra- and Internet, as a regressor. Results are reported in Table 7.4. The correlation between the use of the Net and flexible reorganization is even more significantly positive with this variable. The probability of having made a flexible reorganization can be augmented by as much as 50 per cent. Therefore, the correlations between the type of firm reorganization that ICT and web-based technologies are supposed to set in motion and the effective use of the Net can be said to be well established.

This pattern of reorganization through quasi e-integration will have geographical consequences. But just as much as industries differ in this respect, we can argue that countries will have different opportunities too. It is worth emphasizing that Europe and the United States are different with respect to the process of outsourcing set in motion by the diffusion of ICT. The American specificity in this context is its peculiar geography. In order to reap the benefits of externalization and e-integration, relocation of subcontracting activities may not take subcontractors too far from the centre (i.e. contractors) because there are still limits to the productivity gains achieved in the transportation of physical goods. Digitalized information may travel far at great speed and low costs, but most 'physical' goods may not. The limits of flexible reorganization through e-integration may well be set by technical progress in physical transportation.

Considering the patterns of outsourcing of parts and the organization of just-in-time practices (low inventory stocks and immediate adaptation to the consumer demand), the standard in manufacturing seems to be that 1 day of road transport is the acceptable norm. Beyond this distance, the costs related to outsourcing and relocation exceed the benefits, in spite of all the progress made in ICT—as suggested by the experience of Zara (see Box 7.1). The

Table 7.4. *Effect of Net use on flexible reorganization*

	Full set of controls	Clean set of controls
Estimator	3.87***	3.74***
	(1.45)	(1.43)
Estimator divided by the observed percentage of establishments using Internet	51	50
Number of observations	1736	1733

Weighted estimation in %.
Standard errors in parentheses.
Coverage: French establishments with twenty or more workers in 1998.
***1% significant.

Source: Authors' estimations using REPONSE 1998.

consequences for Europe and the United States are immediate in terms of opportunities. The US geography makes it difficult to expand such a relocation/integration process too far outside the country and even too far from the traditional industrial districts. Only two countries (Canada and Mexico) are accessible within 1 day's lorry driving from the most important American industrial centres. Therefore, the range of cost differentials that the US industry can potentially exploit is limited to these two countries as far as going abroad is concerned. Of course, Mexican labour costs are low and the Canadian labour force is highly skilled. But the United States does not have the access to the diversity characteristic of Europe. It is not just that, within the same range of geographical distance as the United States, western European countries may have access to as low labour costs as in Mexico and as highly skilled a work force as in Canada, more importantly, they have access to a cheap and highly skilled labour force, in eastern Europe for instance. Besides, 1 day of road transport from the most important industrial centres opens many opportunities to European firms for exploiting the advantages provided by the existence of significant cost differentials in southern countries, not only Greece, or Portugal, but also the Maghreb, where labour is certainly cheaper as in Mexico.

This emerging organization of the supply chain is illustrated by the geographic localization of ISO certified firms in Europe and closed regions (North Africa and West Asia). Map 7.1 reports the number of certified business per million of inhabitants.[16] It shows that the European Community (and Israel) experienced a large diffusion of ISO norms. But, firms in bordering countries also extensively enter in the ISO process. This figure is clear for 'west eastern' Europeans and the main candidates for joining the European Community: Czech Republic, Slovenia, and Hungary. The intensity of ISO certifications decreases along the east direction to become negligible in Russia, Byelorussia, and Ukraine. This figure is also true in the northern Europe: the Baltic republics (Estonia, Latvia, and Lithuania) close to the highly certified Finland also have numerous ISO firms. Significant geographical connections appear between Italy, Malta, and even Tunisia, between Greece and Cyprus, and between Israel and Jordan.

Note that while the consequences of ICT on the level of outsourcing are straightforward, their effects on the relative localization of outsourcing are ambiguous. Grossman and Helpman (2002) develop a simple model of location of subcontracted activity between the North and the South (in our European perspective from the West to the East). Outsourcing requires search for a partner and relationship-specific investments that are managed by incomplete contracts. The development of international outsourcing depends on the

---

[16] Unfortunately, we do have the number of firms or establishments in most of the European countries. Therefore, we use the overall population to normalize the number of certified firms (labour force ponderation drives to similar figures).

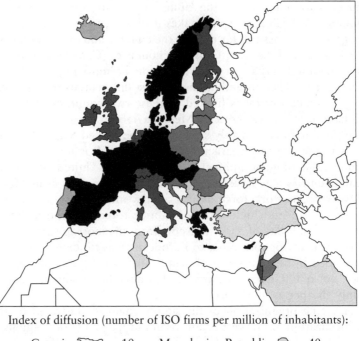

Index of diffusion (number of ISO firms per million of inhabitants):

Georgia	< 10	Macedonian Republic	< 40
Croatia	< 100	Latvia	< 200
Cyprus	< 500	Netherlands	> 500

Map 7.1. *Diffusion of ISO9000 norms in Europe, North Africa, and West Asia (December 2000)*

Source: Authors' calculus using ISO survey 2001.

relative cost of searching in each market, the relative cost of customizing inputs, along with the contracting environment in each country. In that framework, Internet that facilitates B2B matching plays as a technological shock that reduces the cost of search and also the cost of customization. When this improvement is worldwide and homogeneous, the profitability of search rises in the West and in the East. Therefore, final producers will conduct more intensive searches for outsourcing partners, irrespective of the location of this search. Actually, outsourcing activity can shift from the West to the East if and only if the improvement of search or customization technology is larger in the East. Now, more than the Internet, the complementary ISO certification acts as such positive shock on search technology; this shock is disproportionate in the East. Indeed, eastern companies are harder to control, and the regulation does not ensure a reliable protection of the contractor. The certification process guarantees that a priori low-quality eastern firms meet the high standards of normalization.

An index of the diffusion of ISO norms normalized by the GDP shows similar figures (Map 7.2). The geographic connections are also clear. Central European countries—Czech Republic, Slovenia, and Hungary—close to the European Union market are strongly certified. The case of Jordan and Israel is interesting. Israel is heavily certified on both criteria. The relatively high level of certification in Jordan derives from the commercial agreement signed by Israel and Jordan after the peace treaty of 1994 to foster the development of six joint industrial zones and which benefit from free access to the US market and from favourable tax treatment. Since 2001, this free access has been extended to Jordan as a whole; thus, Israel and Jordan have free trade with both the United States and the European Union.

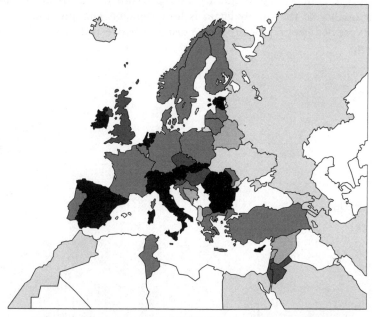

Index of diffusion (number of ISO firms per billion dollar GDP):

Albania	< 2	Georgia	< 5
Luxembourg	< 10	Macedonian Republic	< 20
Cyprus	< 40	Hungary	> 40

Map 7.2. *Diffusion of ISO9000 norms in Europe, North Africa, and West Asia (December 2000)*

Source: Authors' calculus using ISO survey 2001.

Firms can thus outsource and relocate in countries where they can benefit from low labour costs and/or a skilled workforce. This extended range of relocation possibilities suggests that the potential for e-integration may well be much more important for European firms than for their American counterparts. European geography, coupled with the single European market and the various trade agreements established with accessing or neighbouring countries are factors that should incite firms to deeply modify their internal structures. This process should have macroeconomic consequences too. If this process is put in practice deep enough, one may expect significant structural and geographical change to accompany the current diffusion of ICT in Continental Europe. These changes may be facilitated or hindered by other structural factors characteristic of the European economies: labour market features, product market competition, training and education systems, and so on. In order to be effective, e-integration will probably call for transformations in these areas too. Thus, the diffusion of Internet requires a double unity of the supply chain, affecting quality and proximity. Certification ensures that the quality of the supply chain is homogeneous enough, and this unity is also expressed geographically in the distance between different elements of the chain.

8

Supply Chains, Market Access, and the Internet: A View from the South

In principle, the Internet[1] can give poor countries and poor people access to markets, information, and other resources that would otherwise have been inaccessible. It may also allow for the reduction in the number of intermediaries between developing country producers and developed country buyers (whether firms or final consumers), perhaps permitting the former to retain a larger share of total value added. Spirited statements about new opportunities for 'leapfrogging' abound, such as this by one of the world's largest investment banks:

The Internet makes it possible for lower income countries (1) to integrate into the global supply chain and (2) to disseminate knowledge at a greater speed. Greater transparency over the supply chain makes vertical integration less necessary. The world is about to be unbundled, which would create massive new outsourcing opportunities. If a developing country can latch onto this trend, its income growth should surely accelerate.[2]

The new technologies do not, however, negate all pre-existing sources of comparative and competitive advantage. Access to technology may not be enough if the capacity to use it productively demands a certain level of education and skills. Infrastructural bottlenecks in telecommunications, transport, and logistics also remain formidable in many developing countries. Furthermore, underdevelopment is importantly a function of the lack of functioning institutions and non-OECD (Organization for Economic and Cooperation Development) countries are very likely to fall behind in solving those governance issues—pertaining for instance to consumer protection, security of transactions, privacy of records, and intellectual property—that are crucial to achieve e-business readiness. And finally, while new technologies may make it easier and less expensive to trade *information*, it remains to be seen how it may affect the process of *knowledge* creation and diffusion. For all these reasons, there is a risk that a 'digital divide' will simply reinforce existing income and wealth inequalities between countries. The focus here is not on putting in place the preconditions for low-cost Internet

---

[1] The Internet is used here as a shorthand for the full complement of ICTs that are diffusing at varying rates through different economies.

[2] See Morgan Stanley Global Economic Forum, 'Leapfrogging.com', 4 September 2000, at http://www.morganstanley.com/GEFdata/digests/20000904-mon.html#anchor5

access and effective use, but rather on how—assuming these are already in place—developing country entrepreneurs stand to gain (or lose) from the broad diffusion of Internet-based e-commerce in different economic sectors.

It is too early to conduct any *ex post* assessment of the impact on developing countries of the Internet *per se*, though macroeconomic studies of telecommunications point to a significant growth effect (e.g. Pohjola, 2001). Our orientation is decidedly micro, drawing on theoretical analysis of trade and industrial organization, new economic geography, and 'value chain analysis' to inform a series of sector studies of how the Internet is affecting global supply chains and the place therein of developing country entrepreneurs. Inevitably, the analysis remains exploratory at this stage. The sectors studied are coffee, flowers, garments, software development, and tourism services. The first three share two important characteristics, namely that developing countries account for a large and growing share of world production and trade and that, in addition, these products are key sources of income for a significant proportion of the population in such countries. Tourism is also an important source of revenue for certain developing countries, and it is an industry heavily influenced by the advent of the Internet. The software sector employs a much smaller percentage of the workforce, but it produces the quintessential digitizable product for which traditional transport costs are negligible. In each case we attempt to answer the following questions:

1. How has global industrial structure evolved over the past few decades? What role do developing country producers play in the industry?
2. What is happening to prices, profit margins, and the distribution of value added along the supply chain from input suppliers to producers onto customers?
3. What impact has the information and communication technology (ICT) advance, including the Internet, had on global production organization? Has it contributed to greater 'fragmentation' of production and outsourcing of specific processes? If so, to what extent has the technology itself (and the ease of access in different locations) affected the geographic distribution of those processes?
4. What implications has the diffusion of the technology had for the global distribution of revenues and profits along major supply chains, and has this worked in general to the advantage or detriment of developing country entrepreneurs? Are there any general rules or patterns that emerge?

In trying to respond to these questions, we shall find that the constraints that were apparent in the discussion of the rich countries are almost identical for the poorest countries. *The complexity of the e-product, the face-to-face (F2F) constraint, the reputational constraint, the lean production constraint, are all hampering the proper use of Internet in poor countries quest of the rich countries' markets.*

In each of the case studies, we first set out the main features of industry structure and dynamics, before trying to explain in detail how new information technologies are affecting them. We then attempt to assess qualitatively the main opportunities the Internet offers to developing country entrepreneurs in the sector as well as the main conditions for and constraints to seizing those opportunities. Finally, where possible, we bring bare quantitative evidence to shed light on how the various changes described are affecting the distribution of value added along specific supply chains and, in particular, whether developing country entrepreneurs are retaining an expanding or shrinking share. In some—perhaps most—cases, changing value added distribution is attributable to market forces that have until now been only marginally impacted by the Internet. The question we seek to answer is whether, as the Internet diffuses further, it is likely to reinforce or attenuate the underlying trends.

Case studies have been used in varied investigations, particularly in sociological studies, but much less frequently in economics. In our view, this is an ideal methodology when a holistic, in-depth investigation is needed. By taking a system of interrelated activities as the unit of analysis and focusing on one or two issues that are fundamental to understanding the system being examined, case studies permit multi-perspective analyses. We take inspiration from Ronald Dore's comment that 'back in the old Marshallian days [...] economists took their concepts from everyday life rather than trying to take everyday life from their concepts' (Dore, 1987: 170). There is, however, a risk of sample bias—cases must be selected so as to maximize what can be learned in the period of time available for the study—and limitations must be borne in mind—especially that this method is sometimes seen as less rigorous than quantitative analysis insofar as the results are not easily generalizable. We think that the descriptive theory presented above provides an appropriate framework for the cases and allows us to derive certain analytical generalizations, some of which would no doubt benefit from further empirical testing as quantitative data becomes available (Yin, 1994).

8.1. SOFTWARE DEVELOPMENT

Unlike many areas of electronic equipment and component manufacturing, software development—at least in the case of customized software—is not subject to significant scale economies. This provides opportunities for prospective small-scale entrants. A schematic representation of software development (known as the Waterfall Model) divides the process into five sequential steps: high-level design, low-level design, coding, testing, and post-production support. Not only do skill requirements vary across steps, but so also do other determinants of competitiveness like the need for 'relational capital', since the front-end processes can involve the sharing of commercially sensitive information that assumes a relationship of trust between software designers and customer. The fact that software products and services can be delivered electronically means that, given an acceptable electricity supply and international data link, location is not a significant entry barrier, at least into certain stages of the development cycle.

Different segments of the software market are not all equally contestable. By far the least contestable is that for packaged software (notably operating systems but also standard applications like word processing, spreadsheets, and database managers) for personal computers (PCs). The economies of scale in this product area are very large, as the fixed R&D and marketing costs are huge while the marginal cost of producing an additional unit of shrink-wrapped product is vanishingly small. Also, there are strong network exter-nalities (mostly through ease of file sharing) tending to lock users into the dominant product in a class. In the case of operating systems, for example, the enormous jointly sunk costs make mass migration to a new environment an extremely unlikely event.

Worldwide, the packaged software market is valued at approximately US$ 150 bn, with the United States taking a 70 per cent share.[3] The United States is by some distance the leading software exporter, while India has been by far the most successful developing country exporter. As of 2000–2001, India's software exports totalled US$ 6.2 bn, or more than 10 per cent of total exports. Over the previous 5 years, they grew by 62.3 per cent per annum. Most (almost two-thirds) of those exports are destined for the United States, with the United Kingdom another major customer and the remainder of exports spread across some 100 other countries. Currently, more than 185 of the *Fortune 500* companies outsource some of their software requirements to Indian software houses.[4] The Indian software and services industry also served a domestic market worth roughly US$ 2bn in 2000–2001. As of end-2000, total information technology (IT) professional employment in India amounted to 410,000 people[5], with a few of the largest firms employing upwards of 10,000 people each.[6] Software firms are clustered in Bangalore, Chennai, Hyderabad, Mumbai, and New Delhi. Several of the biggest (e.g. Infosys, Wipro) started life as joint-venture partners of foreign computer manufacturers—developing local applications—before the latter withdrew from India in the 1970s; the largest, Tata Consultancy Services (TCS), is part of India's largest private conglomerate.

There is a marked difference in market structure between the Indian domestic and export markets (see Fig. 8.1). Whereas software products and packages make up a negligible portion of the latter, they account for over half of domestic industry sales.

Offshore data entry, programming, and software development began around the early 1980s. India has emerged over the past decade as runaway leader in the software arena, while the Philippines has carved out a niche in data entry

---

[3] It is difficult to find precise estimates of the custom software market, but the global market for all types of software has been put in the range of US$ 300–500bn.

[4] See NASSCOM website: www.nasscom.org

[5] This is roughly 4% of total industrial employment, as reported in the 1997–1998 *Annual Survey of Industries*, published by India's Central Statistical Office.

[6] *Dataquest India*, 11 March 2002.

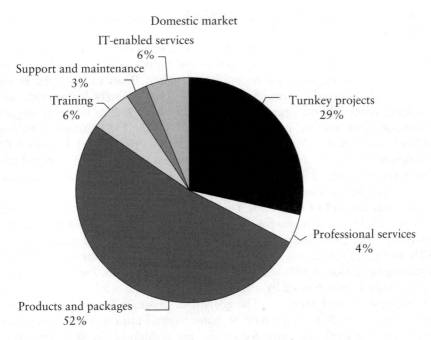

Figure 8.1. *Indian software industry market segments*

and, together with India and a few other locations, has an important market presence in so-called 'IT-enabled services'.[7] The latter include performing back-office functions[8] for major international corporations, operating call centres, providing customer technical support for IT and other companies, maintaining and updating customers' websites, rendering engineering drawings, and transcribing medical records for hospitals and other health care facilities in the industrialized world.[9] In the case of IT-enabled services, time zone differences can be an important factor in making India (and other similar locations) attractive. For example, medical doctors in the United States can have transcribed records of their notes at the start of the next day by sending them electronically to Indian transcription services that start work at the close of the US working day. As of 2000–2001, Indian revenues from these various IT-enabled

---

[7] Defined as 'business processes and services performed or provided from a location different to that of their users or beneficiaries and delivered over telecom networks and the Internet' (NASSCOM). By dramatically lowering international telecommunications rates, technological advance and regulatory reform have combined to make this sort of business economical.

[8] For example, book-keeping, accounting, forms processing, payroll and benefits administration, inventory, and internal auditing.

[9] Numerous players are operating along the entire spectrum in India: data entry (CitiBank), accounting (American Express and British Airways), call centres (Lufthansa), and technical help desks (Microsoft). GE is particularly bullish about India's potential in all these areas, and is active in every one of them.

services amounted to approximately US$ 1bn and the sector employed some 70,000 people.[10]

The Indian software industry has developed, thanks to the production fragmentation alluded to above. The discovery of India's software capabilities by overseas customers (the US semiconductor maker, Texas Instruments, being among the first) owed something to the strong complement of Indian engineers working in their home operations. A key boost to India's software export ambitions came with the partial liberalization, via the 1984 Computer Policy, of hardware imports. A major portion of India's software work has involved migration of software applications across different vendors' hardware and different system configurations (e.g. from minicomputers to PC-based networks) and the maintenance and upgrading of legacy systems.

Towards the end of the 1990s a further boost to India's software exports was provided by code repair for the Y2K rollover, a niche that Indian software companies exploited effectively. For Indian firms facing the prospect of a post-Y2K drought, the dot.com inundation arrived just in time. Having established a strong reputation in managing the millennium transition, Indian firms have increasingly been entrusted by overseas customers with work on development of e-commerce applications.[11] The growth of domestic Internet use in India has provided an additional, if modest, boost to this business. Thus far, the bulk of outsourced work has consisted of the mid-portion of the Waterfall, from low-level design through testing. Rarely is high-level design outsourced, though the ambition of leading offshore software developers is to integrate towards such 'front-end' operations. Ultimately, though, this requires direct involvement in business process re-engineering in client firms, and some have questioned whether this represents a viable strategy for most offshore suppliers (see Arora *et al.*, 2001).

A distinctive feature of Indian software developers has been the adoption of quality practices early in the development cycle, with the pursuit of ISO9001 (International Standard Organization, ISO) certification almost standard industry practice and the achievement of more demanding quality benchmarks (e.g. the Software Engineering Institute's Capability Maturity Model (CMM) Level 5) not uncommon.[12] Commenting on Indian software developers, K. Bhaumik of McKinsey & Co. observes: 'Not only have they been able to reduce the number of bugs per thousand lines of code and increase the percentage of first-pass user acceptance testing, they are able to do it consistently from project to project'.[13] Arora and Asundi (1999) suggest that this may be too generous an interpretation of ISO9001 certification, concluding from an analysis of survey

---

[10] See http://www.nasscom.org/it_industry/it_services_home.asp

[11] *Computerworld*, 2 April 2001.

[12] As of October 2001, thirty-one Indian firms had been assessed at SEI CMM Level 5, out of a reported worldwide total of fifty-eight such organizations; NASSCOM website: http://www.nasscom.org/business_in_india/quality.asp

[13] *Computerworld*, 2 April 2001.

responses from ninety-five Indian software companies that use such certification most as a signalling device for market entry purposes. While it does enable firms to grow faster than otherwise, they charge only a slight premium for their services.[14] Some firms do proceed to institute better-defined software development processes, as suggested by the fact that a large proportion of firms that have obtained CMM certification started out with ISO9001. To the extent that they do so, this may itself reduce the costs of firm growth, for example, by facilitating the integration of new and less experienced staff into project teams (Arora and Asundi, 1999).

As India's software and services (including ICT-enabled services) industry has grown rapidly in recent years, Indian industry leaders have begun to expand abroad, through direct investment and subcontracting. While routinely maintaining a technical support office close to major customers,[15] recent investments have included offshore expansion to other developing countries, mostly with a view to securing sources of low-cost skilled labour as India's own software labour costs have risen steeply. For example, Aptech, a leading software and ICT-enabled service provider, not only has extensive ICT training facilities within India but has also expanded throughout the Asian region and beyond, with a network of training centres spread across dozens of countries. Indian companies Wipro and MindTree Consulting have set up Asia-Pacific headquarters in Singapore. From a Singapore base, some Indian companies are investing in software zones in China. The industry view of China is an ambivalent one, with fear of low-cost competition at least as strong as the perception of collaboration opportunities.[16]

A major deterrent to expansion of domestic e-commerce in India has been the traditional twin constraint on Indian business—poor physical infrastructure and excessive government regulation. The software export industry has been largely insulated from both of these. For example, since 1993, the Software Technology Parks of India (STPI) have offered the only alternative international connectivity to the state telecoms monopoly, VSNL, via earth-to-satellite links to Intelsat; as of 1999, STPI had earth stations in thirteen cities, catering mainly to software exporters and a few other corporations[17] (Wolcott, 1999). The

---

[14] The finding of only a small quality premium associated with ISO certification is consistent with the view expressed in Arora, Gambardella and Torrisi (2001) that follower industries like India and Ireland's software sectors are characterized by rather narrow sources of competitive advantage, hence intense competition among firms that transfer the bulk of benefits to overseas customers.

[15] TCS, India's largest software company, pioneered the establishment of such technical support centres within major markets; it currently has some fifteen centres in the United States and Europe, with the latest addition an Asia-Pacific centre set up in Melbourne, Australia, in early 2002 (website: www.tcs.com).

[16] See *Dataquest India*, 11 March 2002 for a view on the China challenge to the Indian 'software elephant'.

[17] To sustain its software industry's international competitiveness, India also needs to upgrade international bandwidth; by one comparison, China's is five to seven times greater than India's (*Dataquest India*, 11 March 2002).

telecommunications and Internet industries are now also benefiting from deregulation, which should provide a strong boost to their development. In the next few years, at least the major cities of India should be linked by high-speed fibre-optic networks that will stimulate Internet applications and demand. More widespread Internet use depends critically, however, on continued telecoms liberalization at the state level to encourage more competitive pricing of local telephone services (Miller, 2001). Improvements in the electricity grid are also crucial to expanded Internet use and depend also on state-level reforms, namely of the electricity boards. Here again, the software industry has been insulated to some degree from grid-linked power problems via a 5-year tax exemption for electricity generated for self-consumption (Canavan, 2001).

Opinion differs on how large and what sort of an impact India's software industry has had on the domestic economy. The industry employs overwhelmingly highly educated workers, often graduates of the country's network of elite technology and management institutes (Indian Institute of Technology (IIT) and Indian Institute of Management (IIM)). It directly creates little unskilled employment but, while the size of the multiplier on employment and income in construction, personal services, and other less-skilled areas is unknown, it is no doubt sizeable in certain localities. The increased relative demand for skilled programmers has probably served to somewhat widen skilled–unskilled wage differentials. The positive side of this is that skilled workers are almost certainly employed more productively than they would otherwise have been, say, in the government bureaucracy or heavily protected domestic-market-oriented enterprises. Consistent with the O-ring theory of development, the emergence of high-skilled software clusters could thereby raise the overall productivity of India's economy. Whether those skilled software workers capture themselves all the productivity benefits of agglomeration or they spill over to other Indian workers is an area for further empirical investigation.[18] Another difficult-to-measure effect of software industry growth that could be significant in the long run is the reputational capital that it helps India accumulate, as the country becomes known as one capable of supplying high-quality, low-cost technology-intensive goods and services. Many leading world ICT companies are investing in R&D facilities in India (Table 8.1).

India's software industry may still have considerable growth prospects following the tried-and-true model of implementing in code concepts largely developed elsewhere. Yet, it is under growing cost pressure from other locations, notably China but also other countries in South and Southeast Asia, and in any case the major firms would like to be able to break out of relatively low-margin work into more profitable areas. The question then is one of choosing a viable upgrading strategy. The advent of e-commerce has provided

---

[18] Evidence from elsewhere strongly suggests, however, that spillovers can be significant (see Rauch, 1993 for the case of US cities).

Table 8.1. *Major R&D facilities in India by foreign companies*

Company	Date established	Place(s)	Description
Oracle	1994	Bangalore and Hyderabad	The Indian R&D centres work on a range of products covering Oracle's core database, development tools, Web technologies, and e-business application products. The company also has a global consulting group in Bangalore and global product-support centres in Bangalore and Hyderabad.
Sony	February 1998	Bangalore	The two divisions—Architecture lab (engaged in embedded software development for products like AIBO) and systems design—engage in assistance with systems applications.
IBM	April 1998	Delhi (inside the campus of the Indian Institute of Technology)	India Research Laboratory (IRL) is the most recent of IBM's eight research laboratories worldwide. IRL employs seventy-five researchers, of whom approximately half have a Doctorate degree. About a dozen projects in areas such as bioinformatics, intelligent infrastructure, and electronic commerce are currently implemented, some of which are being conducted in collaboration with other IBM research laboratories.
Intel		Bangalore (Multimedia Lab), Delhi (Technology Lab), and Mumbai (Technology Lab; Visual Computing Lab; Microelectronics lab)	

Table 8.1. (*Continued*)

Company	Date established	Place(s)	Description
Microsoft	September 2000	Hyderabad	The two main projects at the India Development Centre are 'Visual J#.NET' (to integrate the java language into the Visual Studio.NET shell, and enable the java language to integrate with the other programming languages supported by the .NET Framework) and 'Services for Unix' (to make Windows NT® operating system and established UNIX environments inter-operable).
Hewlett-Packard (HP)	February 2002	Bangalore	HP Labs India is dedicated to generating usable, economically sustainable technology solutions for the country through understanding the relevant social, cultural, economic, and technological drivers. The research conducted will also help HP's e-Inclusion efforts—a business initiative with a social mission to bridge the digital divide and broaden access to social and economic opportunities in traditionally underserved markets.

Source: Companies' websites.

it with one possible entry point. Whereas before the e-commerce boom the export and domestic markets were largely segmented (as Fig. 3.1 clearly shows), the two are arguably becoming increasingly complementary. In particular, the development of e-commerce applications—some for the domestic market and some for overseas clients—is giving Indian firms greater scope to move into high-level design and conceptualization activities.[19] While the dot.com bubble has burst, it did position the e-commerce survivors—and the developers of e-commerce software applications—to benefit from a more rapid expansion of Internet access. As Ajit Balakrishnan, CEO of leading Indian portal Rediff, notes, India now has a good pool of software project managers and business development managers who will be ready for the next innovative wave in areas like wireless services.[20] Indian software developers have sought to exploit synergies between local e-commerce software development and export markets (Canavan, 2001). In 1999–2000, Indian e-commerce software exports were valued at US\$ 500 m; perhaps the most successful product thus far has been the Infosys-developed BankAway software for Wireless Application Protocol-enabled remote banking (Chandrasekhar, 2000). The e-commerce software market may offer unique opportunities for entrants to develop new products from initial concept, since the dot.com customers are less likely than *Fortune 500* companies to be locked into a long-term relationship with a large US or European IT consulting firm.

Despite their outstanding success in export markets, there is still a risk that, on grounds of supporting industry upgrading, Indian software firms may sue for protection of the domestic market (see Desai, 2000). While the 'learning-by-doing' argument might prove persuasive to some policy makers, the cost to the broader competitiveness of Indian industry could be high indeed, as the Brazilian computer policy of yore suggests. A more attractive strategy for Indian software companies might be to establish partnerships with key US and European companies interested in supplying the Indian and regional markets, combining the former's strong software project management skills with the latter's business process and/or vertical market knowledge. This may involve partnerships with leading IT consultancies: for example, Mumbai-based software developer Mastek recently joined forces with Deloitte Haskins Consulting with a view to competing not just in local but in global IT consulting.[21] It may involve collaboration with industry leaders in areas like banking and financial services. Bangalore-based i-flex provides one example of how such a partnership might evolve. Like Infosys,[22] this company has been

---

[19] It has been suggested, however, that customers for e-commerce applications were interested primarily in India's guarantee of fast turnaround and were willing to trade that for less quality assurance.

[20] www.inomy.com

[21] Leading IT consultancies, Accenture and EDS, have established 'back-end' operations in India.

[22] Infosys remains, however, heavily dependent on service contracts; products provide a minor share of revenue.

successful in designing and making complete software products as opposed to simply providing services. It was set up by Citibank in the early 1990s largely to develop software products for the US bank. With generous parental financial backing, it was able to take the long view and develop financial sector products for clients initially in test-bed areas such as Southeast Asia before turning to Europe and the United States.[23] While riskier and requiring deeper pockets than providing project-by-project customized services (not just for R&D but for marketing and distribution i-flex spends about 12 per cent of revenue on marketing compared with 1 per cent for Infosys), the development of products also holds the prospect of a sustainable long-term revenue stream from patents and copyrights. A sensible upgrading strategy for Indian software companies would be to allow products to emerge naturally from the reusable components that frequently form the basis of project solutions. 'Companies are moving towards this approach inexorably', says Rajendra Pawar, chairman of NIIT, the Delhi-based IT training and software services group. For example, TCS has developed niche software products from the knowledge it has built up working for financial services customers—notably Quartz in wholesale banking and NCS in custody and settlement.[24]

A question frequently posed by developing country policy makers and their advisors is whether India's software success is replicable. There can be no doubt that India enjoys a considerable market lead in software exports over other developing countries. Yet, in some areas like remote IT-enabled services, it is by no means the only supplier. Besides Philippines, several other countries have a significant presence in this sector: Ireland, Singapore, several Caribbean countries, and, more modestly so far, Bangladesh. There, Technosoft Transcription transcribes audio patient record files for medical practitioners in the United States. The 2-year-old company employs twenty-one people with a knowledge of medical terminology, computer and typing skills, and an understanding of American culture and practices. It uses a marketing organization in the United States to secure its contracts and is currently the only company in Bangladesh to contract directly with US clients; other companies obtain subcontracts from India. Clients send their voice files containing dictation of patient records, to a server in the United States, which Technosoft then downloads, promising a 24-h turnaround time (UNCTAD, 2001a).

The examples mentioned are all English-speaking countries serving what is by far the largest market for software and services, namely the United States, the United Kingdom, and the rest of the English-speaking world. Yet, there are other significant markets (e.g. the French-speaking and Spanish-speaking

---

[23] *Financial Times*, India IT Survey 2002.
[24] According to TCS's promotional information, NCS achieves scale economies through automated handling of trade settlement, corporate action administration, registration of securities, billing, and comprehensive client reporting (www.tcs.com/products/ncs/htdocs/ncs_index.htm).

worlds) where similar sorts of services are required and in which low-wage developing countries with large numbers of speakers may enjoy a significant cost advantage, either over a European country or a high-wage Latin American one. Furthermore, it is not yet known how far China will be able to overcome its language barrier to provide competitive software products to overseas (non-Chinese-speaking) markets.[25] The government has identified software as a strategic sector for promotion, announcing a long list of promotional policies in July 2000. For the moment, the size of China's domestic market has absorbed the attention of most local software developers, and the industry is still several years behind India's in terms of quality control.

In summary, the software industry is not a monolith. While Microsoft may have the packaged PC software market largely tied up, there remains a large international market for software development work and programming, some of it one-off (as with Y2K and the digitization of print records) and some of it repeat business. ICT-enabled services are also a growth industry. Indian software firms have captured a large portion of the offshore software business, with ICT-enabled services—heavily dependent on language skills but with a more varied complement of technical skills—more widely spread. The prospects for continued growth in both types of business look good. The Indian industry faces the challenge of upgrading to the most skill-intensive process (high-level design), which is in turn integral with product development capabilities, while many other countries would no doubt like to capture a larger share of the less skill-intensive work. In the Indian case, it may make sense for all but the leading-edge software companies—whether alone or in alliance with leading OECD-based vertical software specialists and systems integrators—to hone their high-level skills by seeking 'front-end' business in a rapidly expanding (and preferably unprotected) domestic market—as well perhaps as in other fast-growing developing countries. The industry leaders may in time be able to specialize in value-added services, including the coordination of the software development supply chain, while subcontracting out much of the routine software production. Likewise, for all but the leading developing country would-be imitators of the Indian model, it may make sense to seek entry into the software and services business via partnerships forged with leading Indian software companies looking for lower-cost locations to perform the 'grunt work'. For a country like the Philippines that already has more than a toehold in the market and a fairly strong entrepreneurial class, an independent strategy may be viable, but without the benefit of anything like India's endowment of human capital.

In conclusion, one can say that the Indian software industry is an example of an industry whose success appears to be driven by two key features. First,

---

[25] Though hardware does not face the same language barrier as software, the rapidity with which China has emerged as one of the largest IT hardware producers in the world should give the sceptics a pause.

software is a digital good, which then fully captures the benefit of Internet so far as the cost of distance is concerned. Second, it is a relatively homogeneous product, for which quality adjustment are readily made. We shall now see that neither of these attributes are present in the examples that we shall be dealing, with daunting consequences on the use of Internet by the poor countries.

8.2. CLOTHING

Increasing levels of import penetration in domestic markets and growing separation of the production process between pre-assembly and assembly activities are the main features of globalization in the textile and, especially, clothing industries. Since the 1960s, in a trend that gained momentum following the imposition of the Multifibre Arrangement (MFA), large parts of the production processes have been relocated to non-OECD countries—eastern Europe and the non-EU Mediterranean region in the case of Europe; Mexico, Central America, the Caribbean, and Asia in the case of the United States.[26] Figure 8.2 reports US clothing imports over the 1990s from the ten top suppliers, showing the dramatic rise of Mexico and only slightly less dramatic one of China. Among the OECD countries, only Canada ranks among the top ten. The source of US apparel imports has changed significantly during the 1980s and 1990s. Substantially less apparel now comes from the Asian Big Three: Hong Kong, Taiwan, and Korea. During this period, there has been an increase in the number of imports from Mexico and Central America and the Caribbean Basin (CB), which are closer to the United States, but also from Association of South East Asian Nations (ASEAN) and China. Today, imports from these regions exceed those from the Asian Big Three in terms of both volume and value. Imports from Mexico are now greater in value than those from China. The relative shift of production for the US market from Asia towards Mexico and the CB no doubt reflects in part preferential trading arrangements of the latter with the United States, but it is likely driven in part by lean manufacturing considerations.

For large clothing producers, subcontracting (including the resort to self-employed artisans and illegal workers to dodge tax and labour laws) has been a traditional feature of the industry even at the domestic level. Italy's industrial districts—geographical clusters of a large number of small firms—are a case in point. In industrial districts the locus of competences and comparative advantage is not the individual firm, but rather the mechanisms of (economic, social, and cognitive) collaboration and cooperation that emerge among them. Despite labour costs well in excess of those in non-OECD countries (see Fig. 8.3), exploiting local knowledge—wool regeneration in the case of Prato, to give just

---

[26] Other international agreements that affect 'North–South' apparel trade include various Association Agreements between the EU and Southern Mediterranean countries, the CB Initiative, NAFTA, and the WTO Agreement on Textile and Clothing, which phases out quotas and limits on tariffs.

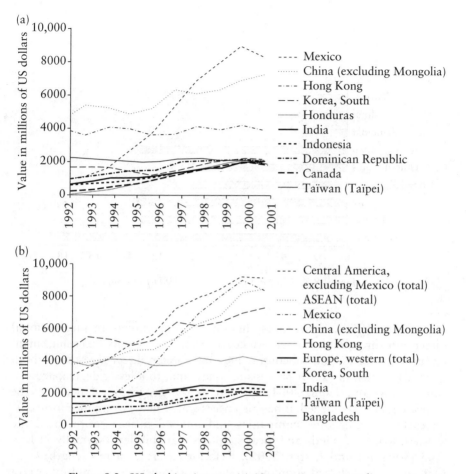

Figure 8.2. *US clothing imports (a) 10-years, top ten suppliers;*
(b) imports from selected countries/regions, 1992–2001

Source: Kavachart servlets from VE.com.

one example—and the tangible and intangible advantages granted by proximity and territorial concentration, they have proved capable of surviving, and indeed of surging ahead. Nonetheless, although labour and capital are relatively mobile within the district, this is not a self-organizing entity. Control over information allows intermediaries to govern the supply chain within the district and direct production as seen appropriate.[27]

---

[27] Analyzing Prato's industrial district, Fioretti (2001) observes that:

production is organised by a special class of agents, herein called the *middlemen*. A middleman can either be one of the larger woollen mills, or a single person who organises the activity of other firms. In this last

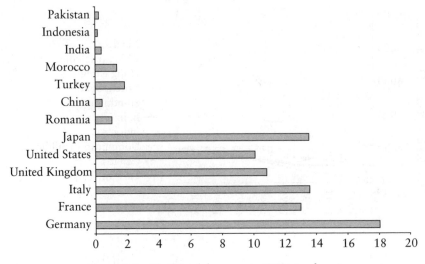

Figure 8.3. *Clothing labour costs (USD per hour)*

Since the 1970s, this process has increasingly taken an international dimension throughout non-equity cooperation agreements (licensing, management contracts, and subcontracting) and foreign direct investment (both greenfield, often in export processing zones, and, to a lesser degree, acquisitions) (Graziani, 1998, 2001). Insofar as the geographical reach of the supply chain has widened, it has also necessitated new governance forms. At an early stage, trading companies and buyers' offices coordinated the Western firms' demands and local suppliers' capabilities, especially in East Asia (Sturgeon and Lester, 2002). Relations were at arm's length: large OECD retailers shifted sourcing at short notice between a multiplicity of potential factories and acted mostly on the basis of cost considerations. Business and social networks played a role in overcoming trade barriers and building trust among the numerous parties engaged along the various steps of the supply chain (Rauch, 2001). In Asia, in particular, middlemen took

case the Pratese jargon employs the specific word *impannatori*. Who wants to buy in Prato, he asks a middleman. If the middleman is a woollen mill, it attempts to fulfill the order with its own productive means. If the order exceeds its productive capacity, or if the middleman is an *impannatore*, it calls several small firms in order to carry out specific production phases. Wares do not need to pass physically through the middleman; on the contrary, they are generally transported directly from a firm to another. However, it is the middleman who decides which wares must be transported where. For a middleman, nothing is more crucial than that the identity of the final buyer remains secret to the firms that he contracts. Otherwise, contracted firms could sell directly to the final buyer (p. 5).

The main feature of a 'leader firm' that comes to influence the whole district is the strong belief in innovation. The risk exists that such firms become 'too large' and impose inflexible, hierarchical obligations on subcontractors that drain the latter's ability to innovate.

advantage of the buyers' lack of information concerning the quality and reliability of suppliers, the state of infrastructure, and more generally the formal and informal norms, values, and regulations governing business.

International vertical fragmentation has been accompanied by horizontal differentiation. While overall OECD consumption growth has started to show signs of stagnation, consumers have increasingly sought a better quality/price relation and price elasticity has also risen in the high end of the market. According to industry experts, 'fashion is increasingly turning into a very individual statement [characterized by] the ability to bring together unique pieces of clothing that somehow, when [brought] together, make a much bolder statement'.[28] In a fashion-oriented business with short production runs, smaller orders, and shorter production-delivery cycles, ICT has played a very important role in the strategic response of the apparel industry in many OECD countries to fight low-cost competition overseas (Abernathy *et al.*, 1999). The use of new technologies makes it easier to implement 'lean retailing' principles: move towards product proliferation and shorter lead times and product life cycles, while reducing inventory carrying costs, stockout costs, and markdown costs. Optoelectronics has permitted the key innovation, the bar code, which tracks demand at the cash register and the status of goods at every earlier stage. That system in turn required computers and software to monitor thousands of prices and millions of items. Retailers already use enterprise resource planning software for human resources, accounting, and inventory management. Developments in computer-aided design and manufacturing (CAD/CAM), layout, and cutting systems have permitted an integration of pre-assembly activities and substantial productivity gains. Production organization has accompanied this shift in demand: in high-wage industrial countries, modular manufacturing is commonly used for high value-added, high fashion, and time-sensitive products.[29]

For brand manufacturers, the emphasis is increasingly on partnerships and long-term relationships with suppliers and on quality management concepts (Feindt, 2001). This results not only from the implementation of lean retailing, but also increasingly from the focus on environment and labour standards and the associated possibility of imposing a premium. As can be expected in a world of horizontal differentiation, certification has become the key for sourcing. This process is complicated, lengthy, and expensive, and the cost of switching away from certified suppliers has increased (Thun, 2000). OECD-based (wholesale

---

[28] See 'No Gap in the market', *Financial Times*, 2/3 March 2002. A telling indicator in this sense is that white shirts now make up less than 15 per cent of all shirts sold in the United States, down from 72 per cent in the early 1960s (McKinsey Global Institute, 2001: 17).

[29] Modular formation consists of grouping tasks, such as the assembly of a collar, and assigning them to a module (a team of 5–30 persons working together). These workers are cross-trained and can, therefore, easily move across tasks. Compensation is based on the module's output instead of that of the individual worker. The key benefit of this method is the reduction in throughput time. However, the costs of switching to this method are very high as extensive training is required.

and speciality) retailers and marketers have developed sophisticated logistics, performance, and trust indicators to interact with suppliers and to govern and coordinate global sourcing networks (Gereffi, 2002). Only a few intermediaries, such as Li & Fung described below, have proved able to upgrade their functions and hence to survive.[30]

Internet developments remain at a very early stage, although some (very optimistic) forecasts are that by 2003 business to consumer (B2C) online clothing sales in the United States will exceed US$ 22.2bn and account for more than 10 per cent of the overall apparel market.[31] There are of course a number of obstacles to e-commerce, including the fact that 'many of the characteristics of a garment that are pivotal in the consumer decision-making process—colour, touch and feel, and fit—are difficult, if not impossible, to communicate virtually' (Hammond and Kohler, 2002). Some front-running companies in this industry are moving towards very sophisticated systems of seamless integration, providing the consumer with customized online catalogues and custom-fit clothing.[32] The use of industry standards to characterize colour and fabric and ensure quality requirements may allow business to business (B2B) trade to rapidly increase its market share and accelerate the migration of production to the developing world.[33]

Insofar as the Internet is open, cheap, and accessible to a host of new and smaller suppliers, such firms may also use the new medium's capabilities to switch from manufacturing apparel to developing their own brand names and opening their own retail stores. Although in clothing, financial, and technological entry barriers to assembly remain low at the same time as retail competition has increased, for most non-OECD countries, upgrading possibilities are limited. The assembly business continues to be dominated by small, family-owned, undercapitalized firms within a very conservative industry culture. Key functions such as product design and sourcing are performed by other firms. These suppliers, in turn, suffer from poor visibility within the supply chain. Despite a tradition of long-term partnerships, many firms are reluctant to pass on information, so that middlemen and importers may tack up to 40 per cent

---

[30] To optimize its use of external resources, Fast Retailing, Japan's largest apparel retailer with over 500 stores under the Uniqlo brand name, similarly entrusts materials procurement and production to trading companies such as Mitsubishi. See 'Fast Retailing: Japan's Biggest Apparel Retailer Goes Global', *Textiles Outlook International*, 97, January 2002.

[31] According to Forrester Research, a market research firm. Innovative attempts are made to fix the problems posed by the need to see how products fit. See 'Finding a Strong Suit', *Red Herring*, 12 June 2001.

[32] Conjoint analysis, for example, allows shoppers to view a series of pairs—say, a plaid flannel shirt and a solid button-down—and select the one they prefer. Based on their choices and some complex mathematical computations, the site generates product recommendations. See, *cit.* 'Finding a Strong Suit', *Red Herring*, 12 June 2001.

[33] But note that for top-quality fashion products standards are far less important. ItalianModa, an exchange portal, provides a 24-h sample service that allows buyers to request rapid delivery of samples of fabrics, leathers, or finished goods before placing a definitive order. See 'European Online Portal Cuts a Dash in Fashion World', *Financial Times-IT Review*, 13 March 2002.

onto the bill. In countries where apparel represents the single largest hard currency earner, like India, for example, the industry is dominated by sweat-shop suppliers who sell to local merchant exporters and, despite enjoying a flexibility advantage, it suffers from severe problems of quality fabrics, trimmings, and accessories (Ramaswamy and Gereffi, 2000; McKinsey Global Institute, 2001).[34] The contrast could hardly be starker with growth-oriented industrial districts that are capable of producing all the inputs (goods and services) needed to compete on global markets. Similarly, in Brazil, considerable investments in the 1990s and persistent cost advantages appear insufficient to make up for other structural problems, such as the lack of strategic alliances and partnerships, the low degree of automation and use of electronic data interchange (EDI) and Efficient Consumer Response (ECR), the dearth of experienced salesmen, and the insufficient effort to increase production and design capabilities (Gorini, 2000).

This does not mean, however, that non-OECD producers cannot aim at upgrading their production mix, as proven by the success of some (especially Asian) in building 'full-package capabilities' to handle all aspects of production and deliver on time a quality finished product at the right price. Buyers can transmit to subcontractors the information and organizational know-how needed to become Original Equipment Manufacturers (OEMs) and Original Brand Name Manufacturers (OBNMs). They can also impose constraints that increase efficiency, for instance, environmental standards (restrictions on the use of carcinogenic dyes and certain chemicals in finishing procedures) that lead to upgrading (see Dolan and Tewari, 2001 in the case of the Tamil Nadu textiles industry). Integrating forward and gaining control over logistics are important strategies and ICT performs a key enabling function in this regard— some Indian manufacturers have indeed used domestically developed systems to track and monitor operations of warehousing facilities established in Europe (Dolan and Tewari, 2001). Smaller suppliers could use (B2B) platforms to bid on requests for proposals posted by OECD-based firms. Though the registration and bidding on RFPs (requests for price) seems the most obvious methodology, an alternative is for member companies of business associations or

---

[34] One important factor is reservations for small-scale industry (SSI) preventing large domestic manufacturers from entering the market and restricting investment in fixed assets to about US$ 200,000 for firms producing more than 50% of their output for the domestic market. This regulation is constraining because setting up even a very basic 500-machine factory (the minimum size required to function effectively) requires a minimum investment of US$ 700,000. As part of the SSI regulation, FDI is limited to 24 per cent in firms that produce over 50 per cent of their output for the domestic market. This results in a limited transfer of skills and knowledge from foreign best practice and reduces technology adoption (foreign investors often provide the cash and insist on adoption of high-tech machinery that the factory would not otherwise bother to invest in). In addition, firms with investments of less than US$ 200,000 are exempt from paying excise duty, which improves their cost position vis-à-vis larger manufacturers. This provides further protection to small-scale plants despite very low productivity. Though SSI reservation in the woven segment of the industry was removed in November 2000, it remains in the knitted and hosiery segments.

industrial chambers, which often lack the bandwidth to access global platforms, to use an OECD-based logistics provider to post sales leads, create online stores, and access logistics.[35]

Information on such trends, let alone quantitative analysis, is still at a very early stage. In terms of the ability to master the potential of the Internet, possibly the most successful strategy has been that of Li & Fung, an old Hong Kong firm that has been exporting traditional commodities (porcelain, silk, bamboo and rattan ware, jade, ivory, handicrafts, fireworks, garments, toys, electronics, and plastic flowers) from China and South-east Asia to the West for almost 100 years.[36] In the 1990s, Li & Fung moved from a traditional vertically integrated business model—owning specialist spinners, dyers, knitters, weavers, finishers, sewers, and printers, as well as wholesalers and retailers across Asia— to using Internet technology to manage production sites, so that each linkage in the supply chain knows what to produce and when. Finding the best suppliers at any given time takes enormous research—criteria include labour and transport costs, quotas, proximity to market, and the ability to forecast, plan, track production, and manufacture apparel quickly and flexibly—and OECD-based companies are increasingly deciding that it no longer pays to do it in-house. Instead, they outsource the knowledge-gathering to Li & Fung that has 61 offices in 37 countries employing 3,600 people roaming for the purpose. The company focuses entirely on optimizing supply chains for other companies and capacity constraints—a ceiling in other industries—are not an issue since Li & Fung has access to 6,000 factories, but does not own any. The real value lies in the power that Li & Fung enjoys to influence factory owners, leaning on them to reserve capacity, monitoring quality, and so forth. The group has recently created a private label division (StudioDirect) to manage the product development process for small- and medium-sized retailers. It uses Net-based applications, such as dynamic image processing and streamlined image production, to optimize supply chain management and reduce the time to market.

Some case studies in Tamil Nadu presented by Ramachandran and Goebel (2002) also offer interesting insights. Quite a few firms reported using software in marketing to find buyers, place bids on orders that were posted, and interface with buyers by sending designs, colours, and patterns electronically. Engineers then download this information into a sophisticated drawing machine that draws out the pattern with perfect precision into life size for the cutters to use.[37] Also, many firms mentioned the use of CAD/CAM for the purpose

---

[35] Canacintra, Mexico's industrial chamber, for example, signed an agreement in October 2000 with 1hemisphere, a United States-based trade portal for the Americas, to provide services to its 33,000 member companies (Curry *et al.*, 2001). The site will allow Canacintra's members to post sales leads, create online stores, and access logistics via 1hemisphere.

[36] This paragraph is based on Sturgeon and Lester (2002) and 'Link in the Global Chain', *The Economist*, 31 May 2001.

[37] The General Sewing Data (GSD) software allows buyers to send a pattern via e-mail for suppliers to analyse and study the garment and identify all stages of production.

of cutting fabric.[38] In one firm the automated cutting of patterns has halved wastage of fabric. Related investments such as the use of voltage regulators have also helped to cut costs. One firm commented that CAD/CAM had enabled it to use 2 m of fabric per shirt, rather than 2.5 m.[39] A disquieting conclusion of this study, however, is that size matters a lot for the adoption of new technologies. For large-sized firms financing equipment upgrades was not a concern; they are so large that the banks are not squeamish about dealing with them and public incentives, such as the Technology Upgradation Fund, can be used for these investments. In the smaller firms interviewed, access to credit limited the use of ICT:

Some firms used computerized accounting methods but many firms we surveyed in the textile and leather sectors did not report any use of IT at all. A senior official at the Cotton Textiles Export Promotion Council pointed out to us that in general, IT was not being adopted by smaller firms. Rather, these firms were focused on trying to purchase power looms, given their limited access to financing. While access to credit is better in Tamil Nadu than many other states, small firms are still very constrained. Small firms need more interaction with product developers, more access to product demonstrations of prototypes, and more investment in skill upgrading, according to the official we interviewed. (Ramachandran and Goebel, 2002: 10–11).

Independently of the location of the production site(s) of the contracting companies, suppliers and subcontractors are likely to be located in close proximity to each other to ensure that quality standards are met and flexibility is achieved in responding to changes in the market. Relocated production facilities are likely to be clustered in a particular region as companies seek to take advantage of local skills that are often geographically concentrated. The Italian industrial districts mentioned above are the best known example, but even in developing countries there is empirical evidence that in the garment industry small clustered firms perform better than dispersed producers. As shown by Visser (1999) in the case of Peru, cost reductions and information spillovers are the dominant type of clustering advantages. They appear to arise mostly at the level of transactions in goods and services and to a lesser extent in the transformation of inputs into output. Participation in global, Internet-mediated networks may increase and diversify the nature of information spillovers and let interfirm cooperation cross local borders.

In conclusion, we see that clothing is almost opposite to software. The industry follows the pattern of lean/flexible production that we analysed in Chapter 7. Far from disappearing, the middlemen who organize the process of vertical disintegration become even more important than before, as they retain critical

---

[38] One project currently underway in one factory attempts to link all the machinery together in an internal network that is tied into the firm's computer system. This producer anticipated greater monitoring of production as a result of this project.

[39] This firm has an electronic time card system; workers are equipped with magnetized ID cards that they swipe when they clock in and out of their jobs. Also, within each major work station there is a computer with Internet access. If a buyer makes a call regarding the status of an order, the director can call up the area supervisor who signs on to the system, and gives real-time feedback to the buyer regarding the status of the order.

information on how best to organize the value chain. From the southern perspective that we adopt in this section, the nightmare scenario is the one that we analysed in Chapter 7 in Box 7.1 dedicated to Zara: in the lean/flexible production context, the benefits of monitoring the production smoothly from the North may overweigh the benefits of producing the goods in the South.

8.3. ORNAMENTAL HORTICULTURE

According to UN Tradestats data, global trade in cut flowers, foliage, and plants in 2000 was equal to US$ 7.7 bn.[40] Roses (on special occasions) and carnations (which last longer) are the main traded cut flowers. Although the United States recently became the world's largest cut flower importer, the European Union as a whole represents the largest market, accounting for three-quarters of world total trade. Some two-thirds of the world's flowers, in particular, are either grown or traded in the Netherlands, generating a total of US$ 5bn a year. In 2000, the United States imported more than 3,700 m. stems, mostly from Colombia and Ecuador. The European Union mostly sources from Africa—Kenya, Morocco, and Southern Africa, in particular—and Israel. Competition has been keen and as volumes of rose exports have increased, prices have been falling on a world-wide basis. French rose imports, for instance, increased 23 per cent in volumes in 1996–2000, but in current value they dropped by 12 per cent. Part of this decline in value of imports is only apparent and is due to the exchange shift between European currencies and the dollar. But the similar increase in volume and drop in value phenomena happened in the United States, where imports in rose stems went up 99 per cent over 5 years, but the value of total rose imports rose only 65 per cent. There are two ways rose-growing costs are being held in check: first, breeders have developed more productive roses, particularly in the 40- and 50-cm lengths destined for the mass markets; and second, growers have lowered costs per stem by increased volume and better management. But, interestingly, there is a floor and a ceiling price at which consumers will buy. If the price is too low, they suspect the rose is old. Thus, consumption of roses has risen not only because of declining pricing, but also because of perceived longer vase life, a wider choice of lengths, and an abundant choice of colours.

Labour represents slightly half of the total cost, interest/depreciation account for a fourth, and other inputs such as seeds, energy, and transport for the remainder (Elshof, 1998). Nonetheless, while manual labour and land costs, daylight availability, and climatic conditions are important factors that benefit non-OECD growers, barriers to entry, such as the need for capital, know-how, and infrastructure, remain considerable. Quality has several dimensions (van Liemt, 1999). Flowers should be free from plagues and diseases and they should be undamaged. These elements can be judged on visual inspection. Other quality aspects, however, are more difficult to judge. For instance, it is hard to see whether flowers have been correctly handled once cut. Yet this is an

---

[40] See 'World Commerce in Cut Flowers and Roses', *FloraCulture International*, April 2002.

Table 8.2. *The distribution of costs and profits in the cut flower chain*

	Cost contribution (per cent)	Gross profit margin (per cent)
Growers	42	NA
Auctions	3	55
Wholesale trade	12	22
Retail trade	43	43

NA: not available.

Source: Rabobank (1992), 'A view of international competitiveness in the floristry industry', cited in Elshof (1998).

important determinant of vase life and whether or not the bud will open. It is the reason why reputation is so important and why growers who have consistently delivered high-quality produce fetch higher prices than little known or irregular suppliers. Strict control of humidity, temperature, and air quality are essential for delivering an attractive product to the market. Even in tropical regions, an increasing number of exporters are now producing 'under plastic' or 'under glass' because this allows them better control over daily (night–day) temperature fluctuations. Growers also rely heavily on an efficient post-harvest chain of handlers, storage, and transport. All this demands investments—about US$ 50,000 per hectare.[41] In Kenya only the three largest companies have their own transport and storage facilities, and other producers are dependent on them. Sulmac, in particular, is the largest grower: it was taken over by Unilever, which then sold it to the Commonwealth Development Corporation in 1998, and it sends most of its flowers to Europe through a distributor.

There are also economies of scale in the purchase and distribution of flowers, including financial liquidity that is an important element for wholesale chain stores that advertise products months in advance and use futures to hedge against climatic and other risks. Before supermarkets entered the picture, importers sold almost exclusively to wholesalers, with very definite lines as to how the chain of distribution was laid out. Recent demand trends in the industry towards low inventory levels, quality control, and strict respect of environment and labour standards also put a premium on the concentration of production (Hughes, 2000). Supermarkets want to buy large quantities of cut flowers through long-term contracts, directly from known producers, and reduce delay (and thus lengthen vase life). Table 8.2 depicts the distribution of costs and profits in the cut flower chain. Growers and retailers each receive around 40 per cent of the final price,[42] a tenth goes to wholesalers, and the auctions get a very small share—but of course trading volumes are huge (see below).

[41] See 'Kenya's Flower Farms Flourish', *BBC News Online*, 14 February 2002.
[42] According to other estimates, however, growers receive a much smaller share: van Roozendaal (1994), for instance, reports that 'Kenyan producers pay around US$ 2 per kilo from Nairobi to Amsterdam (around 50 per cent of the wholesale price)'.

The Dutch have dominated world trade in ornamental horticulture since the sixteenth century. Flower auctions date from about a century ago, when the Aalsmeer growers banded together and formed a cooperative auction. Until then, buyers would play one-off against another, driving down prices. Members must sell all of their production through the auction. In turn, the auction is obliged to sell 100 per cent of its members' products. Of the seven flower auctions in the Netherlands, BVA in Aalsmeer (near Schiphol Airport, one of Europe's largest air cargo hubs) and BVH in Naaldwijk account for 83.7 per cent of sales. The VBA alone handles 19 m flowers and 2 m potted plants a day for a yearly turnover of nearly 1.5 bn Euros.[43] The Aalsmeer indices provide price trends for 'baskets' of the most popular flower and plant groups. Using their daily volumes as a benchmark, short- and long-term future indices allow traders to secure their positions. Nowadays the auctions trade 85 per cent of production through the clock, the rest goes through brokerage firms and cash & carry shops that select, buy, and take away the goods immediately. The brokerage firms are part of the auction and mediate mainly for big companies and for the sale of potted plants. About 50 per cent of potted plants are traded through mediation. The brokered products are not traded at auction, but through contracts. The auction does monitor the sales, however. The brokerage firms provide growers with information on market trends and assist in the sales process. Traders are supplied customized work at the level of product and service in the form of active assistance with the purchasing process.

Markets for all types of perishable goods are highly fragmented, seemingly waiting to be improved by the Internet. A weak point of the auction system is that producers have comparatively little contact with buyers, making it difficult for market signals to pass easily to producers. Jets fly the flowers from Africa to Amsterdam, where they are auctioned to an exporter that repackages and ships them by truck to a wholesaler, who finally sells the blooms to a florist.[44] The process may take a quarter of their month-long lifespan, and middlemen and mark-ups triple the price of a blossom before it reaches the final customer. African producers are capable of producing large volumes and willing to sell directly at an agreed price, making them attractive to supermarkets. However, buying directly and regularly through long-term contracts makes it difficult to source from the Netherlands where growers are obliged to sell their produce through the auctions.

Until the early 1990s BVA used computers in a very traditional way, in the auction hall only.[45] Quality inspectors graded flowers as they arrived in the auction hall and entered information on the flower type, quality, inventory,

---

[43] 'Dutch Flower Auction Blooms', *Financial Times*, 11 October 2001.

[44] All markets within a circle of 800–900 km from Aalsmeer (northern Italy, Austria, Switzerland, Germany, Poland, France, and Belgium) are served by trucks. Destinations further afield are served by air.

[45] The following paragraphs draw on Kambil and van Heck (1996), van Heck and Ribbers (1999), Telematica Instituut (2000), and van Heck (2001).

and grower into the computer. The same information was cross-indexed with bar-code numbers and affixed to each flower lot and flower cart to enable tracking through the auction hall. The computer system was also linked to the buyers' keypad and the clock. It consolidated purchases for payment purposes, and generated summary reports and transaction reports for buyers and sellers. It was also used to schedule and coordinate the many functions of this complex auction, making it run efficiently. With the growth of volume, buyer power, foreign competition, and the need for space, in 1992 EDI was introduced to allow growers and auctions to communicate product, order, and transaction information to each other.

In 1994, BVA began a sample-based auction for trading potted plants. In this auction, growers sent only a sample to the auction house, with the usual data about the product. During the auction, buyers saw only the sample, but were bidding for the entire available quantity. Buyers could specify how to package the product and when to ship it. Growers followed the packaging instructions and shipped it the next day to the buyers in the auction house or to buyer warehouses. For the most part, the expectations of the parties involved were not met. Buyers and auctions expected the number of transactions to increase by separating pricing from product location. Instead, the number of transactions per hour decreased because buyers had to specify the terms of delivery. While the auction had hoped to transact 45 per cent of the supply of potted plants, they transacted only 10 per cent. Thus, the sample-based auction did not effectively reduce storage requirements at the auction house. Furthermore, the buyers perceived that the sample was of better quality than the rest of the lot, so they bid more for the sample and less for the remaining lot, even though it could have been the same type and quality. In addition, incentives to buyers and growers did not materialize. Growers received no extra compensation for modifying packaging and deliveries to accommodate the buyers. Growers also perceived that they got lower prices in a slower auction. In an effort to get higher prices, more and more growers would break a large lot into different sample lots so that the same product would be priced multiple times. There were also no incentives for buyers to transact large lots. Rather the auction maintained rules to favour small lots. In general, there were no significant benefits for buyers or growers to participate in this market and the experiment failed.

A second way of separating logistics from delivery was tested at Naaldwijk through video auctioning, known as the Videfleur experiment. One of the three auction clocks in a room was modified with video screens for product display around the clock. The product was also on display under the clock in the usual manner, giving a second visual display. An auction room solely dedicated to this experiment was not available given the limited space of the auction facilities. Thus the traditional auction was combined with the Videfleur experiment. As a product arrived at the auction, a picture was taken, digitized, and stored in auction computers. These computers transferred the picture to the display screen in the auction hall. Buyers could also see and bid for the flowers on computer screens in their private auction offices. These computers had a representation of the clock. Auctioneers expected this remote video auctioning to provide buyers with better information as they could access their own office computers for purchasing, order, sales, and local inventory information. In addition, auction officials had noticed that buyers often tended to select goods from specific sets of growers rather than inspect the product in great detail. This suggested to them that reputation played a substantial role in shaping buyer purchases. Buyers reacted negatively to screen-based trading. First, they complained that the quality of the auction hall video display was poor. Second, they did not gain any new efficiencies. Buyers trading from their offices also perceived a major informational disadvantage. Buyers on the floor of the auction hall could observe each other and the reactions of large buyers (from supermarket chains, etc.). This non-price information was incorporated into the decision-making of the buyers.

Non-Dutch growers are naturally disadvantaged in terms of the grade and prices they obtain at the auctions (Asea and Kaija, 2000). Moreover, imports have to pay a commission of 21 per cent on gross sales; whereas payments are made in Dutch guilders, loans are given in US dollars, and with currency rates fluctuating, losses are common. Non-OECD farms that do not supply directly to individual wholesalers and/or retailers employ commission agents to sell flowers on their behalf at a fee of 15–20 per cent of the turnover (Hatibu *et al.*, 2000). In 1994 when the share of imports reached significant proportions the Dutch growers thought that they could slow them down by restricting access to their auctions. This action proved futile and was even seen as harmful. The restrictions did little to solve the growers' problems and in 1996, the auctions lifted the restriction on imports again.

In the mid-1990s East African Flowers (EAF)—one of the largest growers of roses, carnations, statices, and other flowers in Kenya—hired Mr. Pol, a Dutch businessman to develop a computerized system allowing buyers to see pictures of flowers and purchase them online.[46] Pol was then running two companies— one supplying bidding systems to auction houses and another selling inventory software to flower buyers and wholesalers. The Tele Flower Auction (TFA) worked but the Aalsmeer authorities tried to ground it by imposing a 20 per cent handling fee. The Africans sued and the European Court of Justice in Luxembourg ruled in their favour. Today, EAF and TFA represent the European interests of nearly fifty top growers of cut flowers located in Kenya, Tanzania, Zimbabwe, Zambia, and Uganda. In 1999, TFA added various rose varieties grown by top Dutch growers to its range of African roses. The catch, however, is that the system is off the open Net and is limited to 100 or so top buyers hooked into Tele Flower's private system. Lacking the resources to expand, in 1999 Pol sold his companies for US$ 5.5 m to a Canadian company (Auxcis)

---

[46] See 'A Flower Crusade that's Going Nowhere', *Business Week*, 23 April 2001.

and stayed on to run its Dutch flower operations. Aucxis already had developed Internet auction software for food industries, cutting out middlemen, and facilitating sales of surplus inventory. Originally, Aucxis had envisioned a direct sales model for flowers still in the ground, but this proved infeasible. Flowers have to be cut when they are in bloom, not just when they are ordered, and shipping the millions of stems in bouquets directly to customers would be ridiculously expensive. The new business model uses the present distribution chain but takes advantage of the Net to streamline it. Instead of sending all their flowers to Dutch auction houses, growers post pictures on a website, and buyers can bid from their offices. Only after flowers have been sold do they move through the Netherlands.

While that is the theory, interest so far is scant. Even though about half of Dutch buyers already use Pol's software to manage their operations, few have signed up for online auctions. Arranging line of credit, foreign exchange, and insurance at various auctions—necessary for selling online—has proven time-consuming and costly. Many also say the clubby atmosphere of Aalsmeer provides them with more security than an open-Internet system could. Only one grower has signed up to sell directly online to wholesalers. Similarly, small florists still prefer the traditional system and very few end customers buy flowers online, preferring to see and feel bouquets in person.

In conclusion, one may say to the least that the business models related to the Internet are not yet fully mature, and *it is still far too early to predict whether e-commerce will lead to greater openness and competition in the ornamental horticulture industry.* As in other industries, network externalities and liquidity needs mean that only few initiatives will survive. If the physical chain, with its interdependency, remains dominant and e-commerce only intensifies pre-existing developments in the industry, the barriers that producers in developing countries have to surmount to directly access consumers remain staggering.

8.4. COFFEE

Coffee is a perennial tree that grows in the tropics only; on the other hand, OECD countries consume most of the world production of tropical beverages.[47] Five types of actors participate in the supply chain: producers, processors/stockists, exporters, importers, and grinders/roasters (Fig. 8.4). Long lead time, resilience to weather disruption, and extreme price variability put a premium on the easy availability of financial capital, not least to invest in insurance protection. In the post-colonial period, state involvement eased the provision of financial and technical inputs to production and marketing, at least as far as export harbours, and led to a dramatic reduction in entry

---

[47] Brazil, the world's largest coffee producer and cocoa's fifth largest, is also an important consumer of both products.

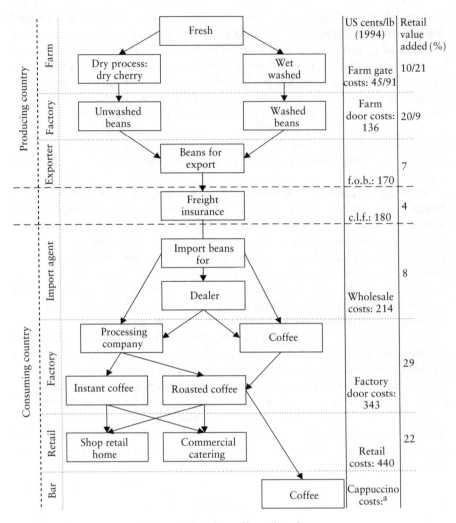

Figure 8.4. *The coffee value chain*

[a] Costs variable but very high. Include: overheads, advertising, other products (i.e. milk), and the 'experience' of the coffee bar. (See breakdown of the price of a cup of coffee.)

Source: Fitter and Kaplinsky (2001).

barriers to the cultivation of tropical crops (Gibbon, 2001*b*). There are, moreover, few economies of scale in planting and harvesting, especially for the most prized coffee varieties that are grown in mountainous areas, such as Colombia's Andes, Jamaica's Blue Mountain, or Kenya's Kilimanjaro. Quality control is also key—coffee berries, for instance, ripen unevenly—and individual picking is therefore widespread. Nonetheless, be they cocoa pods, coffee cherries, or tea leaves, harvesting them does not demand a skilled workforce, which is often made up of uneducated women and children, usually hired on short-term seasonal contracts. The net result of these features is that production is performed by small self-employed farmers, very often near the subsistence frontier. About 70 per cent of the world's coffee is grown by as many as 20 m. smallholders on farms of less than 5 hectares.[48]

Most coffee is exported as green, decorticated, and graded bean. In threshing, warehousing, roasting, transporting, and marketing, there are huge economies of scale. Buyers can purchase tropical beverages either directly at the origin or on spot markets—futures markets do of course exist but they provide hedging against risk rather than being a supply source. What is required to coordinate the chain is not so much proprietary know-how in process and product technology—as in producer-driven chains—or product design, advertising and marketing capabilities, and computer-based supply management systems—as in buyer-driven ones—but rather the ability:

to procure continuously specific volumes and quality mixes for a number of processors [...] Entry barriers to the trading function are very high levels of working capital, accumulated market knowledge, and intangibles like reputation [...] Chain governance by international traders tends to be loose and indirect. Prescriptions on commodity forms are much looser than in retailer/merchandiser-driven ones and while prescriptive grading classifications exist in most cases, these often turn out to have been constructed by larger direct producers rather than having been imposed by traders. (Gibbon, 2001*a*: 351–2)[49]

The incentives are therefore strong for concentration to rise in the trading node of the chain. In the mid-1990s five companies—Neumann, Volcafé, Cargill, Esteve, and ED&F MAN—accounted for almost 50 per cent of world coffee trading, while a third of world roasting was done by four firms—Nestlé, Philip Morris, Sara Lee, and Procter and Gamble. Cargill, Archer Daniels Midland, and Barry Callebaut dominate cocoa trading.

Supply and demand curves are rather inelastic, at least in the short run, and international prices tend to follow a long-term 'boom and bust' pattern linked to the crop cycle. In the second half of the twentieth century, two separate sets of institutions—one country-specific, the other international—have linked up non-OECD producers and OECD consumers. In producing countries, post-independence governments set up marketing boards for individual commodities to provide a single trade channel, often coupled with an administrated price system to insulate producers from the vagaries of international markets. International commodity agreements (ICAs) were also established to reduce

---

[48] 'A Crisis is Brewing in your Coffee cup', *Financial Times*, 11 April 2001.
[49] 'The major coordinating mechanisms linking suppliers with international traders were the simple and inclusive "quality conventions" for the commodities in question, used to differentiate the product into various grades according to national origin and certain crude physical properties of the commodity itself' (Gibbon, 2001*b*: 62).

the great variability of commodity prices that results from the fact that primary products have low supply and demand price elasticities. They worked (relatively) well as long as prices to farmers stood between the cost of growing the crops and the prices they fetched on world markets, but the fiscal crisis of the state in all producing countries made it impossible to fund international agreements. As could be expected, signatories also started cheating and non-ICA producers, for instance African ones in the case of coffee, increased production. A further problem was rising consumer resentment in periods of rising world prices. Spreads increased dramatically because of the asymmetric response of domestic consumer prices to movements in world prices (Morisset, 1997). In all major consumer markets, the transmission of decreases in world commodity prices to domestic consumer prices have been systematically much less than for increases. This asymmetric response, which has been attributed to trade restrictions and bidding processing costs, appears rather to be largely caused by the behaviour of international trading companies.

Quantity demands for homogeneous food commodities show very flat income elasticities and per capita consumption of many agricultural products are approaching saturation levels (OECD, 2001). On the other hand, the elasticities for other food attributes, such as nutrition and health, safety, convenience, and diversity, are quite high (Senauer, 2001). Market developments are dominated by the growth of value-added products and highly refined/processed foods, reflecting the increasing importance that consumers give to health and lifestyle considerations. More efficient forms of delivery from farmers to consumers have resulted in a constant fall in the proportion of households' annual expenditures going to food and, as more income becomes available for non-food spending and female labour participation rates increase, there is an increase in the share of food bought outside of traditional channels (Kinsey and Senauer, 2001). Food marketing in industrial countries has undergone two profound changes over the last few decades that are having profound implications for agricultural producers, *a fortiori* in developing countries. First, concentration has been rising in food and tobacco processing markets and processors' ability to obtain high margins is being eroded by the emergence of large and increasingly concentrated supermarket chains and big discounters à la WalMart specializing in large volumes and low prices. This is an important factor for coffee roasters that has significantly diminished brand loyalties, and hence margins, over the past decade (Gilbert and Ter Wengel, 2000). Also noteworthy is the increasing adoption of supplier-managed inventory that shifts power relations to the advantage of buyers. The rise in the consumption of quality (single origin, fair trade, and organic) products, often taking place out-of-home, is the second major trend of the last quarter of the twentieth century as far as tropical beverages are concerned. Speciality retailers cover niches where convenience, ambience, service, or brand identity count more than price. Starbucks, for instance, is a globally recognized vertically integrated brand that purchases, roasts, and sells high quality whole bean coffee and handcrafted beverages. Eco-labelling has also expanded, partly due to a growing distrust of conventionally produced foodstuffs after a series of food scandals, environmental concerns, and a public perception that organic foods may be fresher and have better taste characteristics.

A third major development has to do with the international governance setting. In the case of tropical beverages, the privatization of marketing boards and the withering of international commodity agreements, when coupled with changes in consumers' demand, have led to greater integration along the entire supply chain. On the one hand, there has been increasing downstream integration and product differentiation[50]—in particular, traders have diversified into secondary processing and coffee roasters into direct retailing—while on the other, traders and specialized retailers have integrated upstream, entering directly into crop production or tightening coordination with large-scale estates to ensure adherence to quality standards.[51]

Despite far from negligible trade barriers, the production of agricultural products, fresh vegetables *in primis*, has been increasingly delocalized to non-OECD countries—African ones in the case of Europe, Latin American ones, including Mexico, for North America—with growing interaction between producers and exporters, on the one hand, and importers and retailers, on the other. Food exports from developing countries increased at a higher rate during the 1990s, or by 5.6 per cent per year on average, than those of developed countries (UNCTAD, 2001*b*). The fastest food export growth occurred in the African region, almost doubling in value between 1990 and 1999. The control of the chain has been through demanding requirements in terms of cost, quality, safety, delivery, product variety, and innovation that have set the entry barriers for farmers, indeed bringing about a concentration of market structure in southern trading partners (Dolan and Humphrey, 2000). In this context, the 1980s and the 1990s have seen a spectacular rise in the resort to contract farming, that is, the vertical coordination between growers of an agricultural product and buyers or processors of that product. Contracts may provide production inputs, credit, and extension services to the grower in return for market obligations on such considerations as the methods of production, the quantity that must be delivered, and the quality of the product.

---

[50] In the case of cocoa, for instance, chocolate manufacturers have specialized in branding and commercialization, 'contracting out to cocoa grinders on a just-in-time basis the supply of dedicated intermediate chocolate products' (Gibbon, 2001*b*: 65). It is not accidental that cocoa international trading is mostly done in undifferentiated form.

[51] As Kherallah and Kirsten (2001) observe, 'the need for increased coordination can also be attributed to the failure of traditional (spot) agricultural markets to deal with this new scenario. Usually, bulk commodities flow through commodity markets to food processors that in turn market standardized products to consumers [who] now demand tailored foods and to ensure that they get them, food companies want more specific farm products. In addition, food safety concerns have brought increased scrutiny and regulation in developed countries. As a result processors/marketers have avoided traditional spot markets and have engaged in more direct market channels such as market and production contracts, full ownership, or vertical integration' (pp. 20–1).

Examples from agribusiness in other resource-dependent economies show that declining terms of trade can be fought through strategies of upgrading and differentiation that permit producers to appropriate a larger share of quality premia and rents. In the case of tropical beverages, these strategies can take various forms, including adding value in producing countries, facilitating producer–consumer communication (including through the use of the Internet, analysed at greater length in the following section), and promoting fair trade and organic consumption (Ponte, 2001: 4416). The Australian wine industry is a very successful example in this sense.[52] In the case of poorer developing countries, however, there are several constraints to trade development. On the one hand, 'contracting with smaller growers involves high transactions costs and, under most circumstances, agro-industrial firms prefer to contract with larger growers. Thus, contract-farming schemes tend to reinforce existing patterns of income stratification' (Warning and Soo Hoo, 2000: 21). On the other hand, after the end of international commodity regimes and the weakening of public-sector institutions in production, marketing, and export, grower organizations and cooperatives have failed to substitute governments in such functions. In Jamaica, one of the few countries that still maintains a centralized system (the Coffee Industry Board that is responsible for exporting the high-quality Blue Mountain variety), big producers' calls for liberalization are resisted, since laxity with quality control risks harming the reputation of the product.[53] Information incompleteness, moral hazard, enforcement problems, and missing markets are also key institutional features of agriculture worldwide (Cook and Chaddad, 2000). In a particularly telling example of lack of information, 'while [coffee] price is broadcast daily on Ethiopian radio, it is broadcast only in the national Amharic language, which [many farmers do] not speak. Even growers who speak Amharic are unlikely to know the price. Only about 2 per cent of coffee growers are estimated to have radios'.[54]

Since the 1970s, a variety of private and public supported electronic exchange mechanisms have emerged both in the United States—in particular TELCOM for cotton and the Egg Clearinghouse—and in Europe, but they generally failed to achieve a significant degree of market penetration (Wheatley *et al.*, 2001). The development of an open architecture system with distributed computing features has opened the way for the establishment of unified electronic platforms that reach beyond business borders, link enterprises in virtual cooperations as well as along production chains, and provide information, communication, and transaction support for both business and market management. In the United States, it is estimated that by 2000 one in

[52] Interestingly, 'the degree of variety of coffee and the variation in taste is at least as great as that of wine' (Fitter and Kaplinsky, 2001: 71). Starbucks sells twenty-four different varieties, including ten single origin coffees from Colombia, Ethiopia, Guatemala, Kenya, Indonesia, and Papua New Guinea.

[53] See 'Blue Mountain Coffee at its Peak', *Financial Times*, 18 October 2001.

[54] See 'Times Turn Hard for Ethiopia's Small-scale Coffee Growers', *Financial Times*, 30 March 2001.

twenty-five farms had already bought or sold agricultural products on the Internet and that e-commerce accounted for 5 per cent of all sales (Mueller, 2000). Some of the earliest farmer-targeted e-commerce websites in OECD countries' sites functioned like electronic brochures ('content providers'), but they soon evolved into virtual 'agribusiness-to-grower' catalogues where farmers and other customers could order pre- and post-harvest supplies and other goods. Many sites now aimed at OECD farmers offer customized soil and market data, weather forecasts, farm and field maps, cropping recommendations, and storage and sales tracking systems. 'Chat' rooms and user fora are increasingly serving as high-tech substitutes for the Old Economy's rural lunch counter.

Despite the common cry by producers of tropical beverages and other so-called 'soft' commodities that trading exchanges are exploitative, the truth is that profit margins in such markets are very thin. The transition of major exchanges such as London's LIFFE to onscreen trading has cut margins, as brokers still earn a fee for providing the screens, but not as much as they would from execution. The pressure to reduce costs and increase efficiency has led to the closing of numerous brokerage business by global trading houses, in particular, in tropical beverages.[55] In view of the saturated market and falling prices, international organizations and donors have urged producers to focus on new marketing initiatives that emphasize quality as a product advantage. In 1997, the International Trade Centre, a joint initiative of the United Nations Conference on Trade and Development and the World Trade Organisation (UNCTAD–WTO) initiative, launched the 3-year Gourmet Coffee Project, with the participation of Brazil, Burundi, Ethiopia, Papua New Guinea, and Uganda. The project tested a range of activities from production methods to marketing tools. The objective was to try new methods of adding value to green coffee, enabling coffee producers to generate premiums. The Internet auction of Brazilian coffees was one of the many activities of the project. Selling coffee via an Internet auction was expected to foster the spirit of competition among growers and to by-pass the existing distribution system and create a closer link between growers and roasters, who could get access to excellent coffees otherwise difficult to find. In October 1999, 315 coffees from different regions in Brazil participated in the 'Best of Brazil' coffee quality contest. In the final round with twenty-four coffees, a group of internationally recognized coffee experts, so-called 'cuppers', selected ten coffees to be offered at the auction. A total of 900 bags of 60 kg each were available for the auction. A Brazilian exporter was appointed to represent all ten farms. The auction was announced on a website well-known within the coffee trade, that of the Specialty Coffee Association of America (SCAA). SCAA's staff and their webmaster helped

---

[55] Even before entering in its well-known and terminal difficulties, ENRON closed its London-based broker (Rudolf Wolff). Also in 2001, Swiss-based André & Cie SA sold its cocoa trading, warehousing, packaging, and distribution operations to Noble Group.

prepare the live website that was to be used for the auction. Twenty-three applicants qualified as bidders. They received samples of all the coffees, detailed instructions on the event, and a password for online participation. In the days up to the auction, the bidders were given the opportunity to participate in a trial bidding just to get familiar with the system—sitting at their screens in the United States, Brazil, Europe, or Japan. The auction started on 15 December 1999 in the morning (in the United States) and lasted for 48 h. The ten coffees were introduced one by one, every 5 min. The auction also closed one by one every 5 min, 48 h later. To no surprise, the real 'fight' for each of the coffees took place during the last hour of the auction. The auction coffees were sold at an average price of US$ 1.73 per lb at a point in time where the New York C-price was approximately US$ 1.00 per lb. Two coffees were sold at prices above US$ 2.00 per lb. The second Internet auction organized by the Brazilian Specialty Coffee Association and sister bodies in Europe and the United States took place in December 2001. Farmers originally submitted 477 samples to a panel of local experts. They were then narrowed down to eighteen by an international panel of sixteen tasters. Anacafé also designed a pilot programme that led to the selection of Guatemala's fifteen best coffees, which in June 2001 was offered at an Internet auction that achieved record prices. Beans from the Los Nubes farm fetched US$ 11 per lb—a record for a coffee auction—and the average price was US$ 3.94—a far cry above the New York ones.[56]

To make a profit with coffee, one cannot deal with small lots; a certain volume is necessary. This challenge becomes doubly difficult when looking for high-quality, gourmet coffee. In the case of this coffee auction, the lot size of the coffees posed a problem from the beginning. Coffees are typically sold by the container, which is 250–300 bags. The lots were on average just below 100 bags. This meant that an importer would either have to piggyback his lot with another Brazilian coffee or would have to pay the shipping on less than a container. Several importers decided not to participate for this very reason. Internet auctions in coffee are for exemplary quality only at the moment and that sometimes comes in very small packages. It is obvious that future auctions will have to address this problem and find cooperative shipping solutions that will be fair to companies of all sizes. The best coffee should not be overlooked simply because the logistics to get it to port are difficult. In the coffee auction, all parties took financial risks, in particular, the farmers. Without putting pressure on the farmers and calling them every day, there would not have been enough coffee for an auction of this kind. The project was asking farmers to take a chance, to hold back selling their coffees in the hope that it would fetch better prices. Shortly before the auction, the farmers sold the coffee to the nominated exporter and a formula to split the premium was worked out. The opening prices were agreed upon and fixed two weeks before the auction. This was not an easy task, as the benchmark prices on the world market were heading up at that point in time.

[56] See 'Guatemala Takes Drastic Steps to Save Coffee Trade', *Financial Times*, 17 July 2001.

Auctions of this kind make it possible to trace rare quality coffees directly among farmers (by conducting a competition) and inform roasters directly. In reality, however, the Brazilian auction could not have happened had the present distribution system not been solidly in place—and left in place for the transactions! Farmers and roasters are seldom equipped to handle intermediary export functions such as transportation, letters of credit, payments, documentation, shipping, and so forth. For this reason, as part of the coffee auction process, a well-respected exporter was nominated to handle all ten coffees—with risks and potential gains from the transactions. Thus the idea that coffee could be sold from a small farmer, directly to a small roaster, was not tested. Skipping the traditional export–import portion of the chain would not have been possible. So in the case of the auction, the coffee moved as it does for ordinary sales: Farmer → Exporter → Importer → Roaster.

In conclusion, one may say that the ultimate impact of e-commerce on the distribution of value added along the supply chain of tropical beverages will depend on the possibility of reducing the cost of operating through the market, increasing its efficiency, and eliminating the friction caused by intermediaries. Given the importance of culture, corporate reputation and relationships with customers, and the cost of establishing them, the Internet does not signal the end of relationships nor level the playing field on which powerful buyers and traditionally weak sellers face off (see also O'Keeffe, 2001).

8.5. TRAVEL AND TOURISM

According to estimates produced by the World Tourism Organization, the travel and tourism (T&T) industry has contributed roughly US\$ 1.4 trillion to the world economy in 2001, or 4.2 per cent of gross world product. The biggest boost to the T&T industry over the past few decades has been the declining cost of air travel, which has been fuelled by a combination of airline industry deregulation, technological improvements in commercial aircraft, and improved 'yield management' to ensure better capacity utilization (the last greatly facilitated by ICT). On the demand side, rising prosperity across the world combined with expanded ranks of retirees—mostly though not only in OECD countries—have been major drivers.

The focus here is on the tourism part of the T&T, though reference is also made to the travel component as the two are closely intertwined. A useful way of decomposing the T&T industry is into retailers, or intermediaries (travel agents, whether traditional or online) and suppliers (airlines, hotels, car rental agencies, etc.). Also crucial are the technology-oriented (software and systems integration) firms that provide the platforms for automated (increasingly web-based) reservation systems. The retailer end of industry has traditionally been highly fragmented, with many small agents; so have portions of the supplier segment (e.g. hotels, restaurants, entertainers, handicraft, and other merchandise vendors, local tour organizers, etc.). The age of 'mass tourism' opened up by cheap air travel has caused major restructuring all along the supply chain. As a result of consolidation, large tour agencies now dominate the major sender markets, offering end-to-end integrated tour packages. Given the economic importance to airlines of filling seating capacity, these large tour operators can negotiate preferential tariffs. The hotel business has also seen extensive consolidation in the past decade, offering tourists comparable standards of accommodation in as many destinations as possible. While comprehensiveness (end-to-end, soup-to-nuts tour management) has become the hallmark of the mass tourism industry, it has fallen short in the provision of flexibility. Packages are still packages, even if there may be more of them from which to choose than ever before. The Internet may change that.

The ICT has long played a central role in the organization of the T&T industry. Almost by definition, the tourism business depends on efficient long-distance communication. Along with telephones and fax machines, mainframe-based reservations systems of the global distribution systems (GDS)—Sabre, Amadeus, Galileo, and Worldspan—remain the workhorses of the industry. Alternative, web-based channels of distribution such as Worldres are fast encroaching in leading markets like the United States and Europe, forcing the entrenched players in the airline, travel agency, car rental, and hotel businesses to adapt. One of the key advantages of web-based systems, from a B2C perspective, is to increase the flexibility of product design. Full customization may at last be affordable. As UNCTAD (2001*a*) explains, 'a tourist may now book online any combination of tourism services with/through any combination of producers or inter/info-mediaries' (p. 9). According to the World Tourism Organization, an estimated 15 per cent of all tourism sales are currently purchased over the Internet. As a share of total online e-commerce, T&T is much larger: in the United States, for example, at its 2001 peak online travel is estimated to have accounted for more than 40 per cent of all online B2C sales (Table 8.3).

The new travel info-mediaries are posing a significant challenge to the traditional T&T industry. Travelocity, Expedia, Priceline, lastminute.com, ebookers, and Dégriftour have modelled themselves as the travel brands of the future, nudging the airline and hotel industries to respond with their own intermediary brands such as airline-backed Orbitz (United States) and Opodo

Table 8.3. *Online consumer sales at US sites (US$ m.; excluding auctions)*

	1Q01	2Q01	3Q01	4Q01	FY01
Total	11,482	12,477	13,300	15,807	53,066
Non-travel	7,755	7,585	7,565	10,804	33,709
Travel	3,727	4,892	5,735	5,003	19,357

Source: Comscore.com.

(Europe), and World.Net, which powers the online content and booking technology for various international tourism bodies.[57]

Dedicated online travel agencies—including budget airlines that operate solely via the web and online booking services like Expedia.com—are encroaching fast on the business of the traditional travel suppliers (airlines, hotels, and car rental companies). In 2001, the former captured 45 per cent of total online bookings, a 22 per cent increase over the previous year, while the latter's share fell by 25 per cent.[58] While, in the US market, online bookings are still under 10 per cent of all leisure travel bookings, they amounted to US$ 14.2 bn in 2001. Projections are for an online leisure travel market of US$ 25–35 bn by 2003.[59] There has been significant consolidation within the online travel industry, with the top five vendors now accounting for two-thirds of the market. They are using their market power to negotiate better deals from T&T service suppliers. Also, whereas most started out principally selling low-cost airline tickets, they have diversified into other products, with Priceline now earning more revenue from selling hotel rooms and car rentals than airline seats.

Acquisitions have been a key element of the airline industry's strategic response to this challenge. For instance, GDS group member Sabre now owns 70 per cent of Travelocity and intends to acquire the rest, while Amadeus has acquired Boston-based e-Travel. Meanwhile, Opodo is owned by the several European airlines that are also served by Amadeus, causing the European Commission to stipulate at the time of Opodo's establishment that Amadeus charge Opodo market rates for access to its central reservation system services and provide access thereto on a non-exclusive basis. Many airlines have, however, given a less-than-enthusiastic embrace to web-based reservations, held back to varying degrees by legacy systems and problems of channel conflict. In particular, they have been reluctant to alienate the travel agents on which they depend so heavily.

Travel agents have had to transform themselves as well to meet the growing online competition that has completely undermined traditional commission and transaction fee structures. The GDS groups and the new travel technology vendors are vying to equip travel agents with online tools. Even if between 80 and 90 per cent of an airline's seat inventory is still sold through traditional travel agents, the possibility for clients to compare prices with those offered via the web exerts considerable cost-cutting pressure. Moreover, under pressure from online agents, some airlines are beginning to shift business from

[57] At the forefront of World.Net's software developments is Travel.World.Net, a product that facilitates business-to-business-to-consumer communication between suppliers, intermediaries, and end-users of T&T products through the operation of Internet-based technologies. The service employs technology developed by World.Net in Australia and offers the possibility of a significant increase in T&T supplier access to local and international markets.

[58] According to Forrester Research, see *Financial Times*, 13 March 2002, supplement.

[59] *Source*: http://www.emarketer.com/estatnews/estats/ecommerce_b2c/20020314_pho.html

traditional agents to their own websites: for example, British Airways is planning to make its cheapest fares available only on its website. A key feature of a web-based system is its capacity for more effective customer profiling and responsiveness to revealed customer preferences. The operator of a full-service travel website can in principle assemble service bundles from a vast array of service providers, tailoring bundles to individual customer requirements. In short, the attraction of a customer-driven one-stop-travel-shop is likely to force even wider collaboration and web-based integration in the B2B realm than currently exists.

The major travel service providers just described are largely OECD based. The GDSs support developing country airline, hotel, and car rental reservations as well, but the leading players in the T&T industry come mostly from the sending countries. They have the most immediate access to the customer base. An important if limited exception is the hotel business, where highly dynamic developing country enterprises have emerged as important regional players (e.g. Mandarin, Oberoi, Shangri-La, and Taj in Asia). Middle-income developing countries and some rapidly growing low-income countries like China and India are now producing growing numbers of international tourists, but so far their numbers are relatively small. So, from a developing country perspective, the principal interface with the global T&T industry in the near term will be one of destination management and marketing. The question then is how industry restructuring under technological innovation will affect the strategies of developing country destination management organizations (DMOs) like tourism promotion boards and tourism authorities, as well as the suppliers themselves—for example, local hotels and chains, car rental agencies, and airlines.

In principle, the relatively low costs of going live with a website make it possible for a small T&T operator in a developing country to establish a global market presence. This does not, however, eliminate all barriers to entry. First, to have a fully functional online reservation system requires a somewhat larger investment—for example, in secure payments software at a minimum. Overcoming reputational barriers can also add to costs, for example, through subscription to an online 'trust sign' or other quality assurance scheme.[60] Participation in an industry association sponsored website may be the lowest cost solution for small operators, in that secure payments software could be shared among multiple members and the association affiliation might also yield reputational benefits. Probably the most effective means of establishing a global presence would be to become integrated into the web-based reservation systems of the major online agents described above. A search

---

[60] Another possibility would be membership in a local 'better business bureau' that could be checked online for any customer reports/complaints filed. Such a solution is imperfect, however, insofar as the BBB may itself suffer from a trust deficit on the part of foreign customers with little or no understanding of how reliable and complete the information provided is.

on Travelocity for a hotel in Hanoi yields only nine properties, all subsidiaries of foreign hotel chains and all serving the middle to high end of the market (lowest price: US$ 45/night). A search on lastminute.com yields only one, also an international chain (price: US$ 90/night). Evidently, local competitors have yet to penetrate this market, though admittedly few have the capacity to meet the standards of service that would appeal to the average rich-country tourist. In other markets, where the local hotel industry is better developed, travel portal representation is not so heavily dominated by foreign chains.

Apart from getting online themselves, travel suppliers (notably of hotel properties) increasingly must ensure that their customers can stay connected. While some destinations are purely leisure destinations, others draw a combination of business and leisure travel. Whereas a beach resort may not need to have state-of-the-art onsite IT equipment, a business-oriented hotel in a major city must. Thus, depending on the market served, hotel operators may have to offer ready Internet accessibility to at least a fraction of guests, and on-call computer technicians may even become an essential competitive feature (e.g. to assist guests in dialling up Internet connections from their laptop personal computers (PCs)).

The average package tourist (including the greying baby-boomers) is probably looking as much for familiarity[61] as for novelty and 'exoticism' in choosing a destination and accommodations. Yet, there is a not insignificant and perhaps growing proportion of tourists—for example, second-generation baby boomers still in the 'backpack' age bracket—who favour 'authenticity of experience' and 'cultural proximity'. It is to these tourists that community-based tourism enterprises in developing countries are likely to have the greatest appeal and the Internet may prove an effective advertising medium for such enterprises and communities to reach this prospective client base.

In summary, the Internet can be a valuable means of advertising the attractions of hitherto undiscovered tourist destinations and even of arranging the logistics of getting and staying there. The competitive disruptions in the T&T industry, however, have been wrought by the emergence of powerful, flexible online travel portals as an alternative to traditional distribution channels. Rents are being redistributed to some extent (away from traditional travel agents) and competed away with the decreased reliance on offline intermediaries. To the extent that T&T are price elastic, this could have the beneficial effect of boosting volumes across the board, including for developing country destinations. It seems unlikely in the foreseeable future that developing country DMOs and intermediaries would be in a position to sell in volume direct

---

[61] See Wharton (2001). In the review of this book, *The Economist* describes the attraction of the Hilton chain of hotels as follows: 'They had air-conditioning, shopping arcades where there was no haggling, and restaurants serving American food. Glass-walled lobbies opened on to historic cityscapes that allowed guests an anxiety-free feeling of participation in a foreign world' (29 November 2001).

to customers in OECD markets, bypassing traditional source-country travel agents and online info-mediaries. To the extent that they are able to penetrate the info-mediary market, the cost could be having to offer discounted prices, though this could well pay off in increased volumes and better inventory management (e.g. higher hotel occupancy and fleet utilization rates).

In conclusion, one sees that trust remains a strong competitive advantage in this business, especially since using the product may expose the consumer to a variety of risks not commonly associated with many other products. At the same time, T&T is preeminently an experience good, with the reputation of a particular destination and of local T&T service providers built up through repeated transmission of experience (often by word-of-mouth but also through trusted brand travel guides, most of which are now available in some form over the Internet). Thus, assuming an obscure T&T service provider—for example, a good value-for-money or unique hotel or restaurant—manages to get discovered—whether by acccident or through effective local publicity—its reputation can spread more quickly and widely than ever before via the Internet.

8.6. MAIN FINDINGS AND POLICY IMPLICATIONS

From the vantage point of the developing country entrepreneur looking beyond the domestic market, what has ICT generally—and the Internet specifically—changed? If we were to venture an answer, it would be that, for the vast majority of them, the answer would be: 'very little'. The daunting policy and institutional constraints on profitable business alluded to above would almost certainly dominate whatever modest benefits adoption of the technology may have to offer them. In this view, addressing obstacles to growth would be the surest way to promote greater global integration of developing economies. To lend some perspective, a recent study of the determinants of rising intra-OECD trade from the 1950s to the late 1980s finds that economic growth *per se* explains two-thirds of the increase, while tariff reductions explain another quarter and falling transport costs 8 per cent of trade growth (Baier and Bergstrand, 2001).[62] This suggests, for developing countries, that strong economic growth is likely to be the dominant driver of trade growth, while further global trade liberalization could have a significantly greater impact on trade opportunities than any technology-induced lowering of transport and transactions costs. That having been said, for specific entrepreneurs and sectors, technology's impact could be relatively important.

---

[62] In terms of the increase in the trade to GDP ratio over this period, tariff reductions explain three-fourths and transport cost reductions only one-fourth. The contribution of income convergence, meanwhile, was trivial, largely because the degree of convergence was so small. The magnitude of the coefficient on the income similarity variable was close to one as Helpman's model predicts, so this variable could prove more significant in explaining trade growth between OECD countries and the rapidly industrializing countries for example.

Moreover, as trade and other policy distortions are gradually diminished, firm-level entrepreneurial decisions are given freer play in shaping competitive outcomes.

Despite differences in structure and governance mechanisms, in all the industries analysed ICT and Internet are affecting the forms of production and exchange, the nature of corporate behaviour, and the terms of competition (Table 8.4). Nonetheless, it is too early to say whether the distribution of costs and profits is changing in a way that is unquestionably supportive of the development process. The relocation of high value-added activities to non-OECD countries is constrained by the differing amenability of processes to outsourcing, in particular remote sourcing from distant locations. The Indian example proves that, provided some basic requirements are met—such as a relatively abundant and well-educated workforce and reliable telecommunications and electricity supplies—the transmission in digital form of codifiable and storable information from remote locations via computer networks is straightforward. Remote outsourcing becomes feasible, although questions remain about its long-term development impact. The situation is different for production-supporting activities that make intensive use of information that requires complex, repeated face-to-face interaction for effective communication. It is not only functions such as R&D that are far from being routinized. The ability to manage efficiently a global supply chain requires skills whose sophistication is directly proportional to the complexity of those chains. Some companies have become specialists in supply chain coordination—recall the case of Li & Fung in textiles and clothing. It is not obvious that the Internet has rendered obsolete the need for such a coordinating agent—at least not in most complex supply chains—though it would appear to render easier the separation of the coordination function from other functions constituting a given chain.

In global supply chains involving agricultural and other commodities, although geography is always likely to be a dominant locational determinant, different capabilities in putting technology to effective use can generate some differentiation, giving one country or region a comparative advantage over others with comparable natural endowments (climate, topography, soil type, etc.). It is in the stages from production to final consumer that the greatest potential for ICT application exists, and to varying degrees the Internet is already being used to coordinate distribution and to auction products to wholesalers and/or retailers in the major importing countries. The effect of these technologies on rent capture by developing country producers and traders is still hard to discern clearly. General trends in industry structure, for example, in the coffee sector, would appear to be quite unfavourable to developing country producers/exporters, but other factors like the entry of major new primary producers would appear to dominate any contribution of technology *per se*. Indeed, the experience of the Internet coffee auctions conducted so far points to the prospect for producers of quality beans to reap a higher premium than was possible in a pre-Internet trading environment. In the case

Table 8.4. *Synthesis of the case studies*

	Software development	Clothing	Cut flowers	Coffee	T&T
Industry characteristics					
Intensity of North–South trade	Medium	Medium-high	High (OECD countries such as Netherlands and Italy remain important players)	Very high (no coffee grown outside of the Tropics)	Medium-high
Governance structure	Buyer-driven	Buyer-driven (retailers)	Buyer-driven (retailers)	Buyer-driven (traders)	Info-mediaries-driven
Degree of fragmentation	High in customized segment of market	High, as retailers increasingly focus on design and marketing, subcontracting production to specialized suppliers	High	High	High
Supply trends		Horizontal differentiation and vertical fragmentation (e.g. The Gap)	Horizontal differentiation and vertical integration (e.g. British supermarkets)	Horizontal differentiation and vertical integration (e.g. Starbucks)	
Impact of ICT					
Degree of digitalization	High	Low	Low	Low	Medium
Use in supply coordination	High	High	Medium-high	Medium-high	
Use of/in auctions	Low	Low	High	High	
Impact on developing countries					
Relocation	Medium	High	Low	Low	High
Rents transfer	Medium	Low	Low	Low	Low
Emergence of 'lead firms'	Low	Low	Low		Low

Source: Text

of cut flowers, the experience to date of Internet's advantages for developing country producers has been less sanguine.

In the travel industry, informational rents are being redistributed away from traditional travel agents to the advantage of emerging online travel portals. For the moment, bypassing traditional source-country travel agents and online info-mediaries to sell in volume directly to tourism customers in OECD markets seems infeasible for most developing country T&T suppliers. If anything, the effect of enlarging the range of destinations on which information is available to prospective travellers may be to increase cost pressures on them. Directly proposing customized travel packages to online consumers in rich countries is unlikely to become a huge market: the very wealthy can afford and will probably continue to rely on 'boutique' travel agents to arrange their T&T packages, while those interested in saving money by shopping on the Internet for exotic destinations are unlikely to be big spenders. If, however, a heretofore 'undiscovered' destination manages to market itself effectively on the Internet, the returns to the local economy of a surge in tourism could be substantial, if possibly short-lived. Beyond the tried-and-true repeat destinations (that have uniquely attractive natural and/or cultural attributes and that have effective means of limiting the adverse effects of mass tourism), the tourism business tends to be rather fickle—with last year the year to 'visit Viet Nam', this year the one to 'visit Cuba', and next year...well, anyone's guess.

Apart from those countries enjoying sizeable endowments of highly educated workers, what does the emergence of Internet-based business and commerce imply for the rest of the developing world? The key point emerging from the case studies is that new technologies do not negate pre-existing sources of comparative and competitive advantage. At both the country and the firm level, access to technology may not be enough if capacity to use it productively demands a certain level of education and skills. Infrastructural bottlenecks in telecommunications, transport, and logistics also remain formidable in many developing countries. Furthermore, underdevelopment is primarily a function of the lack of functioning institutions and non-OECD countries are very likely to fall behind in solving those governance issues— pertaining for instance to consumer protection, security of transactions, privacy of records, and intellectual property—that are crucial to achieve e-business readiness (Goldstein and O'Connor, 2000).

In the meantime, for those countries whose factor endowments consist primarily of natural resources and/or unskilled labour, the impact of the Internet is likely to be felt first and foremost through its use in the management and coordination of global supply chains and in commodity market transactions. Even among non-OECD countries, there are wide variations in ICT performance that are not fully explained by per capita incomes and economic structure. Cross-national differences have to do with the legal system, the stability of institutional and political conditions, and levels of government distortions (Guillén and Suárez, 2001). Simple claims about the links between equity, well-being, and the unhindered development of ICTs are not correct, and may in some cases be dangerously wrong. When new technologies are introduced into a given environment, the diffusion patterns will tend to follow the patterns of the distribution of power, education, and wealth already prevalent in that society. In other words, policies and technologies are embedded in factors unique to each country and the relation between ICT on the one hand, and social inequality on the other, is highly contingent (Rodríguez and Wilson, 2000).

The case material would tend to confirm at the sector level the economy-wide conclusion from econometric studies that declining transport and transaction costs appear to have played a minor role to date in expanding trade prospects of developing countries. Economic growth itself and evolving trade barriers have been more important. The significance of the trade regime is nowhere clearer than in the case of clothing, where patterns of trade have been strongly influenced by preferential trade arrangements between specific OECD countries and either individual developing countries or groupings. Despite its low labour costs, it is improbable that Bangladesh would have emerged as a leading clothing exporter had it not been for the MFA. That having been said, information-technology-induced organizational innovations in the OECD-based clothing retailing sector have forced changes all along the supply chain, favouring—between two locations with comparable production costs—the one closer to the market.

In conclusion, the Internet is becoming a more important—eventually essential—tool for entrepreneurs in developing countries to link into global supply chains (whether or not they are already incumbents). The effect on their individual and collective market power remains ambiguous, and it is certain to be conditioned by various characteristics of the industry concerned, notably, whether it is producing homogeneous or differentiated products. In those many sectors where transaction and coordination costs are a small portion of total costs, the effect of the Internet on cost level and structure is apt to be slight. In sectors where advertising and marketing costs loom large, its effects are potentially more significant, though there is scant evidence to date that Internet advertising is providing a low-cost substitute for traditional media advertising. The Internet does, however, offer the possibility for developing country entrepreneurs in many sectors to establish a direct relationship with prospective rich-country customers, but the advantages of doing so depend again on the nature of the industry—for example, whether the product can be digitized and delivered electronically or must be physically shipped, in which case the individual entrepreneur remains hostage to the state of the country's infrastructure—roads, ports, and logistics—to a greater extent than a 'virtual' product supplier that requires only reliable, low-cost electricity and telecommunications.

The Internet and ICT are often referred to as advanced technologies, the presumption being that only people with advanced education and high levels of skill can make effective use of them. This does not seem plausible, since they are designed to serve a mass market consisting mostly of people with only moderate levels of education. While it is true that average educational attainment in the OECD countries where the technologies are developed is still several years higher than in most developing countries, it is also the case that the highly skilled engineers who design digital products do so with a view to making each new generation easier to use than the last. Thus, beyond basic literacy, it is not obvious that formally acquired skills are crucial to the effective use of the technologies. The fact that young school children are often more adept at using computers and the Internet than their doctorate-toting parents should give pause. In this there is some cause for optimism: the technology itself does not appear to be inherently skill-biased, so modest human capital endowments should not exclude a developing country from enjoying its potential benefits. On the down side, neither is the technology as powerful a leveller as some had originally believed if not hoped. While in many applications using the technologies may not pose insurmountable barriers, apart from the familiar one of affordability of infrastructure and capital equipment, producing the ideas that underlie the major innovations that make up ICT and the Internet is what generates the truly big technological rents; likewise the use of the technologies to support other knowledge production. Moreover, even with widespread Internet access and use, existing market structures and sources of competitive advantage cannot so easily be overturned. There may be welfare changes at the margin, some benefiting developing country entrepreneurs, probably many more benefiting online customers, but if a revolution is in the offing it is at best a gradual one, on the model of previous 'general purpose technologies', whose economic and social impacts have unfolded over decades rather than years.

Appendices

APPENDIX 1

The impact of this new emphasis on quality can be simply formalized using an O-ring production function à la Kremer (1993) and Maskin. Assume that a final good is a composite of an intermediary input and the production of the final plant. Let $0 < q_s < 1$ be the average quality of the input and q_f denote the quality of the organisation of the final producer. The value of the final production is equal to its average quality:

$$y = q_s q_f^{\mu}, \tag{1}$$

where μ is the relative weight of the quality of the last production step in the quality of the final output. Because, the design, the package, and the advertising are crucial to sell a good, we will assume that the quality of the final producer is more essential i.e. $\mu > 1$. Without loss of generality, we assume that $\mu = 2$.

A firm can be a low-quality one q_1 or high-quality one $q_1 < q_2$. The number of low-quality firms is larger than the number of high-quality ones. A firm j can choose to produce the input or the final good. It should be matched with a second firm k in order to produce the complete good. When a match between two firms is realized, they will split the value of the sells according to their outside options, that is, their other potential match. Four states are possible for a high-quality firm: to be the final producer and (1) to work with a high-quality supplier or (2) to use low-quality inputs; to be a supplier and (3) to work with a high-quality final producer or (4) to supply a low-quality final producer.

Because $\mu > 1$, the last state (4) is always sub-optimal. Therefore, three types of production are possible:

$$y_{11} = q_1 \times q_1^2 = q_1^3,$$

$$y_{12} = q_1 \times q_2^2,$$

and

$$y_{22} = q_2 \times q_2^2 = q_2^3.$$

The couples of firms are thus homogeneous (y_{11} and y_{22}) or mixed (y_{12}). At the equilibrium, the high-quality firms (respectively the low-quality ones) will receive the same value. Let us take two low-quality firms and two high-quality firms, their optimal match is either homogeneous or mixed according to the global value of the production; the match is mixed if and only if

$$2q_1 q_2^2 > q_1^3 + q_2^3, \tag{2}$$

that is,

$$q_2 < \frac{1 + \sqrt{5}}{2} q_1. \tag{3}$$

Assume that it is the case. In that initial framework, the high-quality firms are final producers while the low-quality ones are suppliers. Now let us introduce information and communication technology (ICT). Their development implies that the customer is more sensible to the quality. The value of the final good becomes:

$$y' = (q_s q_f^{\mu})^{\alpha}, \tag{4}$$

where $\alpha > 1$ represents the preference of the customers for quality. The parameter α is increasing in the extent of ICT (Internet, etc.). The necessary and sufficient condition for the preservation of the mixed equilibrium becomes:

$$q_2 < \left(\frac{1 + \sqrt{5}}{2}\right)^{\frac{1}{\alpha}} q_1. \tag{5}$$

Now, $((1 + \sqrt{5})/2)^{1/\alpha}$ is increasing in α. Therefore, if α is large enough, then the organization of the supplier–final–producer chain will change. The equilibrium becomes homogeneous: there is a segregation by quality. The high-quality firms will be matched together to produce very-high-quality final goods while the low-quality firms will produce very-low-quality goods. Because of this segregation the difference of revenue between low-quality and high-quality firms should widen. Therefore, if the level of quality can be endogenous for the firm (costly investments, training, etc.), then some low-quality firms should change their organization to reach the high-quality standard.

If this high-quality standard is interpreted as a quality certification (e.g. ISO certification), our simple model predicts that the emergence of the e-world should drive to the development of high-quality value chain and the increase in the number of certified firms. The empirical evidences suggest that these mechanisms hold.

APPENDIX 2: ECONOMETRIC METHOD

Estimating the pattern of Net use conditional on whether the establishment is International Standards Organization (ISO) certified raises serious selection problems. A 'naive' estimation of the impact of ISO certification on the use of web-based technology indicator Y would consist in comparing the rates of technology use for establishments that are ISO certified ($p = 1$) and businesses that are not ($p = 0$). However, differences in technology can result from particular characteristics of companies. Standard methods allowing to correct for such heterogeneity biases have been developed by epidemiologists and labour economists (see Heckman *et al.*, 1999). In this contribution, we implement the so-called Rubin's method of 'causal estimation' or propensy score method. This approach has been used and improved recently by Crépon and Iung (1999) to estimate the impact of innovation on establishments' performance and by Brodaty *et al.* (2001) to estimate the impact of labour policy on employment.

The impact of implementing an ISO norm can be expressed in Rubin's (1974) framework as follows. The use of web technology is described by two probabilities (y_0, y_1) conditional on the realization of the variable P (be or not ISO). Establishment i is thus characterized by the unobservable couple. We only observe y_i:

$$y_i = p_i \cdot y_{1i} + (1 - p_i)y_{0i} \tag{6}$$

The 'causal effect' c_i of P on technology is defined as:

$$c_i = y_{1i} - y_{0i} \tag{7}$$

This parameter is not identifiable because we do not observe simultaneously a realization of y_{0i} and a realization of y_{1i}. With these notations, the 'naive' estimator of c is:

$$\tilde{c} = E(y_i|p_i = 1) - E(y_i|p_i = 0) \tag{8}$$

Again, this estimator is biased because it does not take into account heterogeneity across establishments nor across industries. One way to correct for this bias is to estimate a probit or logit model including P along with all the characteristics of establishments. However, if the 'causal' effect of ISO norms is not homogeneous across the sample,[1] the coefficient associated with P is again biased.

The construction of an unbiased, robust estimator follows Rosenbaum and Rubin's (1983) work. If we want to estimate $E(c_i) = E(y_{1i} - y_{0i})$, we can directly estimate $E(y_{1i} \cdot p_i = 1)$ and $E(y_{0i} \cdot p_i = 0)$ but not $E(y_{1i} \cdot p_i = 0)$ or $E(y_{0i} \cdot p_i = 1)$. The idea is then to find satisfying empirical equivalents for $E(y_{1i} \cdot p_i = 0)$ and $E(y_{0i} \cdot p_i = 1)$. In order to get an empirical distribution for $y_{0i} \cdot p_i = 1$—respectively $y_{1i} \cdot p_i = 0$—one looks for an establishment j who is not certified $(p_j = 0)$—respectively is ISO—and has similar characteristics to that of establishment i. Actually, it is sufficient to compare establishments which have similar propensity score of being ISO (according to their observable characteristics). Crépon and Iung (1999) exploit this principle and give a continuous estimator of the causal effect. This 'weighted' estimator is defined as follows:

$$\tilde{c}_w = E(c_i) = E\left[y_i\left\{\frac{p_i}{\pi(x_i)} - \frac{1 - p_i}{1 - \pi(x_i)}\right\}\right]$$

---

[1] E.g., intuitively, ISO norms might not have the same consequences for manufacturing and for services.

where $\pi(X_i) = P(p_i = 1|X_i)$ is the propensity score of being certified given all the observable characteristics of the establishment *(X)*. Intuitively, this estimator puts higher weights on those companies that are not certified (respectively are ISO) while, because of their individual characteristics, they have to be certified (respectively should not). The crucial point is that this estimator is convergent and unbiased under assumption (9):

$$(y_{0i}, y_{1i}) \perp P \bullet X \qquad (9)$$

that is, when knowing X, the realization of variable P does not provide any information about establishment characteristics but only about their organization. This assumption is obviously never strictly verified; there is always some unobserved heterogeneity. However, given the very detailed nature of our data, the residual information revealed by the fact that an establishment be or not ISO certified should not be decisive, at least as far as its observable characteristics are concerned. We are thus left with the problem of unobserved heterogeneity that cannot be tackled at this point, owing to the lack of adequate instruments and the lack of panel data.

In practice, the estimation method consists of two steps: first, we estimate the probability that a company i be assigned to the work practice P, conditional on its characteristics X_i: $\pi(X_i) = \Pr(p_i = 1 \bullet X_i)$ (using a properly specified logit model); second, we use this estimate to compute $\hat{C}_w$. The estimator $\hat{C}_w$ is asymptotically normal. Its asymptotic variance is the variance of ϕ_i defined as:

$$\phi_i = y_i \left\{ \frac{P_i}{\pi(x_i)} - \frac{1 - P_i}{1 - \pi(x_i)} \right\} - c_0$$

Actually, because the principle of the method is to compare establishments that have similar probability of being certified according to their characteristics but different realization of P, the sample should be restricted to a common support, that is, we exclude certified (respectively non-certified) establishments *i* such that there is no non-certified (respectively certified) business *j* with a $\pi(X_j)$ close to $\pi(X_i)$. Moreover, if the logit of the first step is not properly specified, the results can be jammed. Therefore, we also compute an estimator using a logit excluding variable with the lowest significance (i.e. robustly null at 50 per cent).

Our logit of the first step includes the main characteristics of the establishments (see Appendix 3 for details):

- industry (French classification NAF 16)
- sliced size of the establishment and its mother firm
- dynamics of the establishment (very high, high, stable, negative, and very negative)

- detailed trade union representation
- composition of the workforce (percentages of production workers, managers, clericals, and technicians)
- percentage of workers using computers
- frontiers of the market (local, regional, national, European, and global).

APPENDIX 3: CONTROL VARIABLES OF THE ESTIMATIONS OF PART II

Source: REPONSE survey

Sectoral dummies

1. The reported results are controlled for the NAF 16 (French industrial classification disaggregated into sixteen detailed industries).
2. The survey also provides the industry class of the establishments at level NAF 120 and NAF 700.

Establishment size

Dummies for size class of the workforce (number of workers):

- < 50
- < 100
- < 200
- < 500
- > 500.

Status

We only consider private establishments. Two dummies are introduced taking the value 1 respectively for mono-establishments, and for establishments owned by a firm quoted on a stock market.

Firm dynamism

The employers were questioned on the evolution of the activity of their establishments. Four dummies are introduced, the stability of the dynamics being the reference.

- Strongly increasing activity
- Increasing activity
- Decreasing activity
- Strongly decreasing activity

Geographical market

The survey provides information on the geographical market that operates on the establishment. Five levels are distinguished:

- Local market
- Regional market
- National market
- European market
- International market

Dependence upon the main customer

We also exploit the data on the size of the production dedicated to the main customer. Here again five levels are given:

1. The customers are equal individuals (e.g. for department store)
2. The main customers weights
   (*a*) less than

   - 10% of the shipments
   - 25% of the shipments
   - 50% of the shipments

   (*b*) more than 50% of the shipments

Composition of the workforce

- Percentage of managers
- Percentage of administrative and sales workers
- Percentage of blue-collar workers
- Percentage of technicians

Union representation

A dummy takes the value one when the establishment has a trade union representative.

Personal computer use

Five dummies are built according to the percentage of the workforce that uses personal computers:

- 0
- < 5
- < 20
- < 50
- > 50

Comments

JOHN P. MARTIN

These are very timely and rich chapters. It is timely because, after the collapse of the dot.com bubble, much of the media and public opinion has lost its fascination with the phenomenon variously labelled the 'New Economy', the 'Frictionless Economy', or the 'Weightless Economy'. However, the Internet is continuing to spread its web all over the world and we need to take stock of its current and potential future impacts now that much of the hype has mercifully died down. The report seeks to make a major contribution on this front by assessing the Internet's impact on three separate digital divides, the first between business and consumers within the organization for Economic Cooperation and Development (OECD) countries, the second between firms, and the third between the countries of the North and the South.

I begin my comments with some observations about the general message in the paper. I then turn to the discussion of each of the three digital divides in turn before closing with some remarks about policy implications.

Evolution rather than revolution

The strawman that the paper engages with is the view that the Internet will shift the world closer to the state of perfect competition. It argues that there is only a grain of truth in this view. Far from moving the world economy inexorably to the nirvana of a frictionless world, the Internet may give rise to new entry barriers and frictions. It argues, convincingly in my view, that growing diffusion of the Internet will not solve all informational problems. Indeed, it could even exacerbate some of them given the huge amounts of garbage and inaccurate information littering the Net. Growing use of the Internet will not reduce the importance of *distance*, geography, natural resources, and other traditional determinants of comparative advantage for many economic transactions. It will not resolve existing quality problems for many goods and services and is likely to generate new ones.

Thus far, I would agree with the authors. However, this is more apt as a description of the state of play during 2000–2002 rather than a medium-term prediction. The key issue is surely whether the forces hindering more competition (e.g. unequal access to the Internet, certification procedures, lack of skilled personnel, lack of trust in business to business (B2B) and business to

Director for Employment, Labour and Social Affairs, OECD. I am grateful to Andrea Bassanini and Kurt Larsen for assistance in preparing these comments. The views expressed are my own and cannot be held to represent those of the OECD or its Member Governments.

consumer (B2C) e-commerce, privacy concerns, etc.) are likely to weaken over time or not. The paper is rather coy on this key question. Those who are more bullish about the revolutionary nature of the Internet and the potential of e-commerce would no doubt reply that it is early days yet: e-commerce is only at the beginning of the S-curve that characterizes the evolution of such innovations over time, and its impact on productivity, work organization, value chains, and so on will grow over time. As best as I can judge from the chapters, the authors would probably respond to such an argument with 'perhaps, but it is likely to take a long time'. It would, however, be helpful for the reader if they came off the fence a bit on this question.

The first digital divide: B2C transactions within OECD countries

The authors begin this part of the report by rehearsing a range of arguments that suggest large expected gains in the welfare of consumers from growing B2C e-commerce. At the same time, they draw attention to the fact that B2C transactions are still very small despite many optimistic predictions to the contrary—indeed they poke some gentle fun at an incautious prediction about car sales online made by the OECD a few years ago!

They then review a number of case studies—banks, car retailing, insurance, and the Paris housing market—to see why face-to-face (F2F) commerce appears to be resisting so well the siren songs of B2C e-commerce. They draw attention to the dramatic growth in information made possible by information and communication technology (ICT), which may serve to raise, not lower, information costs. They also highlight the fact that a B2C purchase involves more than just the good or service in question. It also involves a range of complementary attributes, for example, security problems connected to payment online. They rightly emphasize that the 'reputation' of the online seller is often a critical factor. Since reputation building in e-commerce involves endogenous sunk costs (à la Sutton), this could well limit competition in the market.

I particularly liked the case study on the Parisian housing market, especially since I have participated in this one myself using PAP (de Particulier à Particulier). But once again, the reality is a lot less dramatic than the hype: the number of ads placed on the PAP website are not growing rapidly as a share of total transactions nor does there appear to be much of an impact on prices. All that happens to date is that the use of the PAP allows the buyer and seller to split the commission of the intermediary (the 'notaire')—no one other than the notaire will shed tears over this particular outcome!

The second digital divide: between firms

The main point advanced under this heading is that the Internet alone is not sufficient to transform the patterns of competition and the organization of the production chain. Outsourcing, in its traditional format, relies heavily on F2F relationships to ensure that subcontractors meet quality standards in the supply of inputs. The enlargement of the pool of possible subcontractors allowed by the use of the Internet is more nominal than real if the contracting company cannot solve the problem of *quality control*. External *certification* (such as compliance with ISO9000 (International Standards Organization, ISO) norms) becomes therefore, according to the authors, almost the only way to ensure quality standards. The authors argue that acquiring and maintaining certification is a costly process that may create a new production divide to the extent that some firms may not be able to afford the extra cost involved. In brief, it is not true that the Internet induces a frictionless world without entry barriers.

The theoretical argument on the relationships between certification and B2B or B2C e-commerce is compelling though it needs further elaboration (see below). However, the empirical evidence cited in the report to test the hypothesis could be criticized on several grounds.

First, the cross-country bivariate evidence is unconvincing. The positive correlation between the propensity of small- and medium-sized enterprises (SMEs) to trade B2B over the Internet and ISO9000 certification in Fig. 7.2 is driven by an outlier (which country?) in the upper-right corner. Second, the authors test the hypothesis using a representative sample of French firms (REPONSE 98). They also try to adjust for a possible selection bias by using Rubin's 'causal method'. However, the method does not control for either reverse-causality (e.g. recourse to the Internet for B2B sales affecting the probability of adopting ISO norms) or endogeneity due to an omitted variable (e.g. increased competition inducing both greater certification and greater Internet adoption). A few words about each of these issues are in order.

The authors are aware of the reverse-causality problem. Nevertheless, more caution would be desirable when commenting on the results presented in Tables 6–9. There is no reason why the adoption of the Internet should affect the probability of adopting new work practices more than the latter should affect the probability of the former. Indeed, both are more likely to co-evolve and depend on a third factor (e.g. the incidence of just-in-time techniques and access to B2B e-commerce in the pool of possible subcontractors) that is omitted from the regression.

One possible candidate as an omitted variable is that the surge in competitive pressure over the 1990s, by enabling a larger number of firms to compete on a market, has allowed more anonymous transactions and increased the need for both certification and Internet use as a way to gain advantage over other competitors. If this were the case, it would account for a positive evolution of both certification and Internet use driven by product market deregulation.

Now, how might the authors deal with this potential source of bias? They control for industry effects using dummies for sixteen one-digit industries Nomenculature D'Activitiés Française (NAF16 classification). Thus, only competitive pressures *between* industries are controlled for but not competitive pressures *within* each industry. It might well be the case that within each one-digit industry the probability of both adopting ISO standards and the Internet is greater in more competitive sub-industries. In other words, without additional controls and despite the use of Rubin's method, they are not comparing similar firms.

The authors are aware of this problem as well, and they control 'as much as possible' for it on the basis of the proxies for competition that are directly available in REPONSE (whether the firm's market is local, national, or international, and the share of the firm's main customer). The problem is that these controls are at best very crude proxies for competition. Indeed, a firm might operate in a local or regional market and still be under heavy pressure from foreign competitors. However, I believe there is a possibility to solve this problem and test their hypothesis of an independent effect of certification on Internet use against the null hypothesis that the association between certification and Internet use is simply owing to (de)regulation and competition.

In the original data base the industry classification is NAF700 (700 industries) that can be re-aggregated to NAF120 or NAF16. Of course, with a sample of about 2000 firms, the authors do not want to include too many industry dummies since the support of both treatment and no-treatment must be the same to apply Rubin's method. However, by matching REPONSE with other sectoral databases available for France, it should be possible to construct better indicators of competition and regulation (e.g. tariffs and non-tariff barriers using the OECD Indicators of Tariff and Non-tariff Trade Barriers — or import penetration using OECD Foreign Trade Statistics) for very disaggregated industries that could be mapped into NAF. These additional indicators could then be used to improve the control for *within-industry* differences in the competitive environment of the firm, which are not captured by the sixteen industry dummies.

These critical remarks about the econometric results should not detract from the emphasis given in this part of the report to the urgency of solving quality concerns if B2B and B2C e-commerce are to flourish. The authors are absolutely right to insist on this. It is also the case that industrial *certification* could be the route to achieving this though it is less clear to me that the ISO process can best fulfil this goal. Why have the vast bulk of firms engaging in B2B or B2C not opted to go down this route? Is ISO certification possibly just another business 'fad', perhaps a bit like the proliferation of voluntary codes of conduct, often incorporating human rights/core labour standards/environmental norms?

In any event, I would argue that certification alone will not solve all the problems associated with B2B and B2C e-commerce. Consider the case of the so-called e-learning, that is, the delivery of education and training services via the Net. There is much discussion about the potential of this market, particularly for the delivery of higher education courses and training courses, and many universities and some private companies are investing heavily in it. But all commentators agree that concerns about quality loom extremely large in this market.[1] There are major worries about the emergence of 'degree mills', what would be the value of e-learning qualifications at home or on third-country markets, and so on. *Recognition* is as important as certification in this market and it is hindered by the bewildering variety of national quality assurance and accreditation agencies in the higher education field: for example, in the United States alone there are 19 recognized institutional accreditation agencies, many operating on a regional basis. Even within Europe where the problem of accreditation and recognition of higher education qualifications should be easier to solve, little progress has been made.

The third digital divide: between the North and the South

Chapter 8 addresses the question of whether the growing diffusion of the Internet could help close the development gap between the North and the South. It does this through a series of case studies of sectors as diverse as coffee, cut flowers, clothing, software development, and travel and tourism services. While case studies have a bad name with economists through their association with business schools, I found this to be very stimulating of all the chapters. I learned a lot about these sectors and how they have been impacted by e-commerce. This section is rich in factoids—I particularly liked the one about the share of white shirts in total shirt sales in the United States.

The case studies show that ICT/Internet have contributed—together with declining tariff barriers and falling transport costs—to fragmenting production chains and led to outsourcing of specific processes to LDCs. But some sectors are much more affected than others: software development being the leader, followed by clothing and travel and tourism, with the impact on cut flowers and coffee being minimal to date. The effect of these technologies on rent capture by Less Developed Countries (LDC) producers and traders is not very evident in the data.

The key point emerging from the case studies is one that would comfort Ricardo, Heckscher, and Ohlin if they were alive today: the new technologies do not negate pre-existing sources of comparative advantage. Nor will they compensate for the lack of functioning institutions, property rights, and good governance in LDCs. Therefore, I agree with the authors that greater diffusion of the Internet is unlikely to impart a significant new thrust to closing the North–South development gap as compared with better and more consistent application of policies to foster economic growth and development.

---

[1] See the discussion in K. Larsen, J.P. Martin, and R. Morris (2002), 'Trade in Educational Services: Trends and Emerging Issues', *The World Economy*, June, 849–68; and D. van Damme (2002), 'Trends and Models in International Quality Assurance and Accreditation in Higher Education in Relation to Trade in Education Services', OECD/US Forum on Trade in Educational Services, Washington, DC, 23–24 May 2002.

Policy implications

There is little discussion in the paper about the potential role for public policy in promoting productivity, greater transparency, and competition in markets through e-commerce. This is a pity since such a discussion would provide a mouthwatering dessert at the end of Part II. There are many public policies that could have large direct and indirect consequences for fostering e-commerce and ensuring that its potential economic benefits are reaped. The long list includes:

(1) *enabling issues*: network infrastructure, certification, consumer protection, privacy, and so on;
(2) *diffusion*: facilitation/demonstration, training/education, and special policies for SMEs;
(3) *business environment*: competition rules, taxation, trade liberalization, intellectual property rights.

Many of these policies are mentioned in passing in the chapters. But it would have been nice to see some of them developed further. However, I do not want to end on a carping note. I repeat these are very timely and rich chapters on a fascinating topic. What more could one ask for?

JAN SVEJNAR

I am in broad agreement with most of the analysis and findings of this impressive, in-depth study. I wonder, however, about two theses posited by the authors and I will start by voicing my thoughts on these two propositions.

The first proposition is that the world views Internet as creating a frictionless world. My reading of the situation is that while Internet has fundamentally changed the lives of a very large number of people, few claimed or would claim that it produces a frictionless economy. Indeed, although the diffusion of Internet has been faster than that of earlier generations of communications technology, only the most ardent Internet believers during the bubble of the late 1990s would have argued that it was generating a frictionless economy. In the aftermath of the heady days of the late 1990s, the question of whether the Internet revolution has produced a frictionless economy is in my view a bit of a straw horse.

My second reservation relates to the prediction that the Internet revolution would shift the advantage towards the producers and consumers in the poor countries and hence contribute to a reduction in cross-country inequality. As an observer and analyst of the development process, I would a priori not expect this to be necessarily the case. Previous technological breakthroughs that have been developed and first applied in the economically advanced countries (e.g. inventions of the railways and the telephone) have not obviously improved the relative economic position of the poor countries, although the absolute benefits to both rich and poor countries have been substantial. The large producers and market intermediaries in the advanced economies have strong incentives to become leaders in the diffusion of the new technology and thereby limit the diminution of their market power. The fact that the authors find this pattern with respect to Internet-based business is therefore not all that surprising.

In other respects, the study presents very interesting propositions and findings. Documenting the fact that digitizable commodities are most exposed to worldwide market entry and competition is valuable both conceptually and practically. Similarly, the finding that many non-digitizable transactions, such as buying a car or obtaining a house loan, continue to require F2F interaction between the buyers and sellers, with Internet improving the depth and productivity of the F2F interaction rather than replacing it, is intriguing. However, based on the developments such as the availability of online mortgages, I would argue that even in these areas the F2F constraint is being rapidly relaxed or even eliminated. In this respect, the study provides a snapshot of a rapidly moving target.

The finding that Internet quite often raises the complexity of transactions has important policy implications for the developing countries. The prototypical example is one of ordering a book on the Internet and having to rely on complex logistics and security of transactions and delivery compared to buying the book for cash by strolling casually into a local bookstore. In advanced countries, the 'complex' Internet transactions are now routine and from the consumer standpoint the online purchase of a book may be cheaper and have a lower opportunity cost of time than making a special trip to a bookstore. Consumers in the poor countries where the logistics and security issues are unresolved may of course be better off visiting the local bookstore, provided there is one in their area and has the given book in stock. Outside of the capitals of developing countries, neither approach to obtaining books may be easy and public policies oriented towards Internet availability and institutional development in the areas of law, security, and communications may enable the poor areas to leapfrog, at least in part, the traditional approach to purchasing books and other commodities. One already observes that the emerging market economies (those undertaking major market-oriented reforms, institutional development, and infrastructure investment) move faster ahead in introducing Internet on a large scale than the more traditional less developed countries. With further globalization, I expect the 'complexity constraint' of the Internet to be increasingly overcome in the former but remain binding in the latter set of countries. If this conjecture turns out to be correct, we will observe Internet-related polarization within the developing world.

The authors' related proposition that Internet reduces the barrier to entry for outsiders by providing a cheap way of communicating but that it simultaneously restores the barrier by increasing the need for higher standard in reputation, is truly intriguing. The authors muster evidence that branded B2C Internet retailers and B2B suppliers can charge a premium over their respective unbranded counterparts. This is important but a question arises as to whether this demand for higher standard in reputation, including certification, is brought about by Internet *per se* or whether it is an outcome of globalization, increased competition, and technological progress. Put differently, would this tendency for increasing reputation and the associated price premium for brand not be observed even in the absence of Internet? After all, the emphasis on ISO norms and other forms of certification has been growing even before the spread of Internet and has continued during the Internet era even in countries that have been relatively slow to switch to Internet on a large scale (e.g. France and Italy). There is hence a question for future research about the extent to which Internet drives the growing demand for expensive certification. What is clear is that producers in poor countries are increasingly worse off as pricey certifications become the prerequisite for doing business with advanced economies.

Given that Internet appears to bring both benefits and costs that are unequally distributed around the world, the question that obviously needs to be answered is whether Internet enhances consumers' welfare through lower prices. The study presents a variety of findings and the evidence seems to suggest that prices decline at least mildly with Internet availability. However, the benefit of low prices seems to go primarily to the consumers in rich countries and to the middle and upper classes in the less developed economies. The poor people in poor regions of the world appear to have been largely left out. The challenge for public and private policy is how to bring the benefits of Internet, and the ICT in general, to these people. I view this as a serious challenge despite the claim of the present study that reducing income and wealth inequality between the rich and poor countries may be better achieved by stimulating economic growth and reducing trade barriers than by lowering transport and transaction costs through the introduction of Internet. This is because assigning relative priorities of this type is questionable since widespread introduction of Internet into an economy may itself be an important source of economic growth.

References

Abernathy, Frederick H., John T. Dunlop, Janice H. Hammond, and David Weil (1999), *A Stitch in Time*, Oxford and New York, NY: Oxford University Press.

Abowd, J., B. Crépon, and F. Kramarz (2001), 'Moment Estimation with Attrition', *Journal of the American Statistical Association*, 96(456), 1223–31.

Abraham K.G. and S.K. Taylor (1996), 'Firm's Use of Outside Contractors: Theory and Evidence', *Journal of Labor Economics*, 14, 394–424.

Amsden, Alice (2001), *The Rise of 'The Rest'. Challenges to the West from Late-Industrializing Economies*, Oxford and New York, NY: Oxford University Press.

Arndt, Sven W. (1996), 'Globalization and the Gains from Trade', in K. Jaeger and K.-J. Koch (eds.), *Trade, Growth, and Economic Policy in Open Economies*, New York: Springer Verlag.

Arora, Asish and Jai Asundi (1999), 'Quality Certification and the Economics of Contract Software Development: A Study of the Indian Software Industry', NBER Working Paper no. 7260.

——, V.S. Arunachalam, Jai Asundi, and Ronald Fernandes (2001), 'The Indian Software Services Industry', *Research Policy*, 30(8), 1267–87.

——, A. Gambardella, and S. Torrisi (2001), 'In the Footsteps of the Silicon Valley? Indian and Irish Software in the International Division of Labour', Stanford Institute for Economic Policy Research, Discussion Paper no. 00-41.

Asea, Patrick and Darlison Kaija (2000), 'Impact of the Flower Industry in Uganda', Sectoral Activities Programme, Industrial Activities Branch, ILO, Working Paper no. 148.

Baier, S. and J.H. Bergstrand (2001), 'The Growth of World Trade: Tariffs, Transport Costs, and Income Similarity', *Journal of International Economics*, 53(1), 1–27.

Bailey, J. (1998), *Intermediation and Electronic Markets: Aggregation and Pricing in Internet Commerce*, Ph.D thesis, MIT.

Borenstein, S. and G. Saloner (2001), 'Economics and Electronic Commerce', *Journal of Economic Perspectives*, Vol. 15(1), 3–12.

Brynjolfsson, Erik and Lorin M. Hitt (2000), 'Beyond Computation: Information Technology, Organizational Transformation and Business Performance', *Journal of Economic Perspectives*, 14(2), 23–48.

—— and M. Smith (2000), 'Frictionless Commerce: A Comparison of Internet and Conventional Retailers', *Management Science*, 46(4), 563–85.

——, Thomas Malone, Vijay Gurbaxani, and Ajit Kambil (1994), 'Does Information Technology Lead to Smaller Firms?', *Management Science*, 40(12).

Brodaty, T., B. Crépon, and D. Fougère (2001), 'Using Matching Estimators to Evaluate Alternative Youth Employment Programs', in M. Lechner and F. Pfeiffer (eds.), *Econometric Evaluation of Market Policies*, Berlin: Springer Verlag, pp. 85–123.

Brown, J.R. and A. Goolsbee (2000), 'Does the Internet Make Markets more Competitive', NBER Working Paper no. 7996.

Cairncross, F. (2001), *The Death of Distance*, Harvard: Harvard Business School Press.

Canavan, T.H. (2001), 'Factors Affecting the Competitive Position of the Indian Software Industry', *Industry Trade and Technology Review*, January.

Chandler, Alfred D. (1962), *Strategy and Structure*, Cambridge, MA: MIT Press.

Chandrasekhar, C.P. (2000), 'ICT in a Developing Country Context: An Indian Case Study', HDR 2000 Background Paper, UNDP, NY, Processed.

Clark, Gregory and Robert Feenstra (2001), 'Technology in the Great Divergence', NBER Working Paper no. 8596.

Clay, K., R. Krishnan, E. Wolff, and D. Fernandes (2000), 'Retail Strategies on the Web: Price and Nonprice Competition in the Online Book industry', *Journal of Industrial Economics*, forthcoming.

——(2001), 'Prices and Price Dispersion on the Web: Evidence from Online Book Industry', NBER Working Paper no. 8271.

Clemmer, Kenneth, David Weisman, Gillian DeMoulin, and Todd Eyler (2000), 'Insurance's Researched Future', *The Forrester Report*, March.

Clemons, Eric K., Il-Horn Hann, and Lorin M. Hitt (2002), 'Price Dispersion and Differentiation in Online Travel: An Empirical Investigation', *Management Science*, 48(4), 534–9.

——and Michael Row (1992), 'Information Technology and Industrial Cooperation: The Changing Economics of Coordination and Ownership', *Journal of Management Information Systems*, 9(2).

——, Hann, I.-H. and Hitt, L.M. (1998), '*The Nature of Competition in Electronic Markets: An Empirical Investigation of Online Travel Agent Offerings*', Working Paper, The Wharton School of the University of Pennsylvania.

Cook, Michael L. and Fabio R. Chaddad (2000), 'Agroindustrialization of the Global Agrifood Economy: Bridging Development Economics and Agribusiness Research', *Agricultural Economics*, 23(3), 207–18.

Coase, R.H. (1937) 'The Nature of the Firm' *Economica*, 4(16), 386–405.

Crépon B. and N. Iung (1999), 'Innovation, emploi et performances', Institut national des enquêtes et études économiques, Direction des études et synthèses économiques, *Working paper* no. G9904.

Curry, James, Oscar Contreras, and Martin Kenney (2001), 'The Internet and E-commerce Development in Mexico', BRIE Working Paper no. 144.

Danzon, P. and M. Furukawa (2001), 'e-Health: Effects of the Internet on Competition and Productivity in Health Care.' In *The Economic Payoff from the Internet Revolution*, The Brookings Task Force on the Internet. Brookings Institution Press.

Davis, Donald R. and David E. Weinstein (2001), 'Bones, Bombs and Break Points: The Geography of Economic Activity', NBER Working Paper no. 8517.

Deardorff, Alan V. (1998), 'Fragmentation in Simple Trade Models', University of Michigan, Department of Economics, Working Paper no. 98–11.

——(2001), 'Trade and Welfare Implications of Networks', Prepared for the Murray S. Johnson Conference on International Economics, University of Texas, April 28–29.

Desai, A.V. (2000), 'The Peril and the Promise: Broader Implications of the Indian Presence in Information Technologies', Center for Research on Economic Development and Policy Reform, Stanford University, Working Paper no. 70.

Dolan, Catherine and John Humphrey (2000), 'Value Chains and Upgrading: The Impact of UK Retailers on the Fresh Fruit and Vegetables Industry in Africa', *Journal of Development Studies*, 37(2), 146–76.

——and Meenu Tewari (2001), 'From what we Wear to what we Eat: Upgrading in Global Value Chains', *IDS Bulletin*, 32(3), 94–104.

Dore, Ronald (1987), *Taking Japan Seriously*, Stanford, CA: Stanford University Press.

E-marketer (2001), The *eCommerce B2B Report*, Executive summary.

Eaton, C. and R. Lipsey (1989), 'Product Differentiation', in R. Schmalensee and R. Willig (eds.), *Handbook of Industrial Organisation*, Amsterdam: North-Holland.

Elshof, Paul (1998), 'The Dutch Flower Sector: Structure, Trends and Employment', ILO, Sectoral Activities Programme, Industrial Activities Branch, ILO Working Paper no. 120.

Eurostat (2001), *Towards a European Research Area. Key Figures 2001*. Luxembourg: Office for Official Publications of the European Communities.

Feenstra, Robert C. (1998), 'Integration of Trade and Disintegration of Production in the Global Economy', *Journal of Economic Perspectives*, 12(1), 31–50.

Feindt, Sylvie (2001), 'Textile Clusters and the Development of E-business: Embracing the New Challenge?', Socio-Economic Trends Assessment of the Digital Revolution (STAR) Project, Issue Report, no. 19.

Fioretti, Guido (2001), 'Structure and Behaviour of a Textile Industrial District', International Center for Economic Research, Working Paper no. 2/01.

Fitter, Robert and Raphael Kaplinsky (2001), 'Who Gains from Product Rents as the Coffee Market Becomes More Differentiated? A Value Chain Analysis', *IDS Bulletin*, 32(3), 69–82.

Friberg, R., M. Ganslandt, and M. Sandström (2001), 'Pricing Strategies in E-Commerce: Bricks vs. Clicks', The Research Institute of Industrial Economics, IUI, Working Paper no. 559.

Garricano, L. and S. Kaplan (2000), 'The Effects of Business-to-Business E-commerce on Transaction Costs', NBER Working Paper no. 8017.

Garven, James R. (2000), 'On the Implications of the Internet for Insurance Markets and Institutions', *mimeo*, Louisiana State University.

Gereffi, Gary (2002), 'The Impact of the Internet on Global Value Chains', in Andrea Goldstein and David O'Connor (eds), *Electronic Commerce for Development*, Paris, OECD.

Gibbon, Peter (2001*a*), 'Upgrading Primary Production: A Global Commodity Chain Approach', *World Development*, 29(2), 345–63.

—— (2001*b*), 'Agro-Commodity Chains', *IDS Bulletin*, 32(3), 60–8.

Gilbert, Christopher and Jan ter Wengel (2000), 'Commodity Production and Marketing in a Competitive World', mimeo, Vrije Universitiet, http://www.feweb.vu.nl/medewerkers/cgilbert/UNCTAD_paper.PDF.

Goldstein, Andrea and David O'Connor (2000), 'E-commerce for Development: Prospects and Policy Issues' (with D. O'Connor), OECD Development Centre, *Technical Paper*, no. 164.

Gorini, Ana Paula Fontanelle (2000), 'Panorama do setor têxtil no Brasil e no mundo: reestructuração e perspectivas', mimeo, BNDES.

Graziani, Giovanni (1998), 'Globalization of Production in the Textile and Clothing Industries: The Case of Italian Foreign Direct Investment and Outward Processing in Eastern Europe', in John Zysman and Andrew Schwartz (eds.), *Enlarging Europe: The Industrial Foundations of a New Political Reality*, IAS-University of California at Berkeley, CA.

—— (2001), 'International Subcontracting in the Textile and Clothing Industry', in Sven W. Arndt and Henryk Kierzkowski (eds.), *Fragmentation: New Production Patterns in the World Economy*, Oxford University Press.

Greif, Avner (1997), 'Contracting, Enforcement, and Efficiency: Economics Beyond the Law', in Michael Bruno and Boris Pleskovic (eds.), *Annual World Bank Conference on Development Economics*, Washington: World Bank.

Grossman, Gene and Elhanan Helpman (2002*a*), 'Outsourcing in the Global Economy', NBER Working Paper no. 8728.

—— (2002*b*), 'Integration versus Outsourcing in Industry Equilibrium', *Quarterly Journal of Economics*, 117(1), 85–120.

——, Hart, O.D. (1986). 'The costs and benefits of ownership: A theory of vertical and lateral integration', *Journal of Political Economy*, 94(4), 691–719.

Guillén, Mauro F. and Sandra L. Suárez (2001), 'Developing the Internet: Entrepreneurship and Public Policy in Ireland, Singapore, Argentina, and Spain', *Telecommunications Policy*, 25(5), 349–71.

Hammond, Janice and Kristin Kohler (2000), 'E-commerce in the Textile and Apparel Industries', in *Tracking a Transformation: E-commerce and the Terms of Competition in Industries*, Washington, DC: Brookings Institution Press.

Hatibu, Haji, Haji Semboja, Rhoda Mbelwa, and Charles Bonaventura (2000), 'The Cut Flowers Industry in Tanzania', Sectoral Activities Programme, Industrial Activities Branch, ILO, Working Paper no. 152.

Heckman J., R. Lalonde, and J.A. Smith (1999), 'The Economics and Econometrics of Active Labor Market Programs', in Orley Ashenfelter and David Card (eds.), *Handbook of Labor Economics*, New York: Elsevier, pp. 1865–2097.

Hitt, Lorin M. (1999), 'Information Technology and Firm Boundaries: Evidence from Panel Data', *Information Systems Research*, 10 (2), 134–49.

—— and F.X. Frei (2002), 'Do Better Customers Utilize Electronic Distribution Channels? The Case of PC Banking,' *Management Science* 48: 6 (June), pp. 732–48.

Hughes, Alex (2000), 'Retailers, Knowledges and Changing Commodity Networks: The Case of the Cut Flower Trade', *Geoforum*, 31, 175–190.

Italian Banking Association (2001), 'Bank's Initiatives in B2B Digital Marketplaces', WPIE ad hoc Technical Expert Group, Electronic Commerce Business Impacts Project.

Jones, Ronald W. and Henryk Kierzkowski (1990), 'The Role of Services in Production and International Trade: A Theoretical Framework', in Ronald W. Jones and Anne O. Krueger (eds.), *The Political Economy of International Trade: Essays in Honor of Robert E. Baldwin*, Cambridge: Blackwell, pp. 31–48.

Kambil, Ajit and Eric van Heck (1996), 'Re-engineering the Dutch Flower Auctions: A Framework for Analyzing Exchange Organizations', New York University, Center for Research on Information Systems, Working Paper Series no. IS-96-24.

Kherallah, Mylène and Johann Kirsten (2001), 'The New Institutional Economics: Applications for Agricultural Policy Research in Developing Countries', Markets and Structural Studies Division, International Food Policy Research Institute, Discussion Paper no. 41.

Kinsey, Jean and Ben Senauer (1996), 'Food Marketing in an Electronic Age: Implications for Agricultural Producers', The Retail Food Industry Center, Working Paper no 96-02, http://agecon.lib.umn.edu/mn/tr96-02.pdf.

Klauber, Adam (2000), 'Insurance on the Internet', *Risk Management and Insurance Review*, 3(1), 45–62.

Kremer, Michael (1993), 'The O-Ring Theory of Economic Development', *Quarterly Journal of Economics*, 98(3), 551–76.

Kuhn, P. and M. Skuterud (2000), 'Job Search Methods: Internet Versus Traditional', *Monthly Labor Review*, October, 3–11.

Kwoka, J. (1984), 'Advertising and the price and quality of optometric services', *American Economic Review*, 74(1), 211–16.

Latzer, M. and S. Schmitz (2001), 'B2C E-commerce: A Frictionless Market is not in Sight—argument and Policy Implications', mimeo, Research Unit for Institutional Change and European Integration, Austrian Academy of Sciences, Vienna.

Learner, Edward E. and Michael Storper (2001), 'The Economic Geography of the Internet Age', NBER Working Paper no. 8450.

Lee, H.G. (1998), 'Do Electronic Marketplaces Lower the Price of Goods?', *Communications of the ACM*, 41(1), 73–80.

Lesne, J.P. and J. Mairesse (2001), 'The beginnings of internet for the Small French Manufacturing Firms: To Connect or not to Connect?'.

Lindert, Peter H. and Jeffrey G. Williamson (2001), 'Does Globalization Make the World More Unequal?', Presented at the NBER Conference Globalization in Historical Perspective, Santa Barbara, 3–6 May.

Litan, Robert and Alice Rivlin (2000), 'The Economy and the Internet: What Lies Ahead?', Conference Report Brookings Institutions no. 4, December, Washington, DC.

Luckin-Reilly, D. and D. Spulber (2000), 'Business-to-Business Electronic Commerce', Vanderbilt University, Working Paper no. 00-W16.

Markusen, Ann, Karen Chapple, Greg Schrock, Daisaku Yamamoto, and Pingkang Yu (2001), 'High-Tech and I-Tech: How Metros Rank and Specialize', Humphrey Institute of Public Affairs, August, http://www.hhh.umn.edu/gpo/degrees/murp/htmetros.pdf.

McKinsey Global Institute (2001), *India: The Growth Imperative. Apparel Case study.*

MediamétrieeRatings.com (2001), Infos Panel no. 3.

Miller, R.R. (2001), 'Leapfrogging? India's Information Technology Industry and the Internet', World Bank Group, IFC Discussion Paper no. 42.

Milyo, J. and J. Waldfogel (1999), 'The Effect of Price Advertising on Prices: Evidence in the Wake of 44 Liquormarts', *American Economic Review*, 89(5), 1081–96.

Morisset, Jacques (1997), 'Unfair Trade? Empirical Evidence in World Commodity Markets over the Past 25 Years', The World Bank, Policy Research Paper no. 1815.

Mueller, Rolf A.E. (2000), 'Emergent E-commerce in Agriculture', University of California, Davis, AIC Issues Brief no. 14.

Nelson, Phillip (1970), 'Information and Consumer Behavior', *Journal of Political Economy*, 78(2), 311–29.

O'Keeffe, Michael (2001), 'Myths and Realities of E-commerce in the Perishable Foods Industries: Unleashing the Power of Reputation and Relationship Assets', *Supply Chain Management*, 6(1), 12–15.

OECD (1999), *The Economic and Social Impact of Electronic Commerce. Preliminary Findings and Research Agenda.* Paris: OECD.

——(2000), *A New Economy? The Changing Role of Innovation and Information Technology in Growth.* Paris: OECD.

——(2001a), *OECD Agricultural Outlook: 2001–2006.* Paris: OECD.

——(2001b), *Understanding the Digital Divide.* Paris: OECD.

Oliveira Martins, Joaquim (1994), 'Market Structure, Trade and Industry Wages', *OECD Economic Studies*, 22(Spring), 131–54.

Pohjola, Matti (ed.) (2001), *Information Technology, Productivity, and Economic Growth—International Evidence and Implications for Economic Development,*

WIDER Studies in Development Economics, Oxford and New York, NY: Oxford University Press.

Ponte, Stefano (2001), 'Behind the Coffee Crisis', *Economic and Political Weekly*, 24 November, 4410–17.

Ramachandran, Vijaya and Jeffery Goebel (2002), 'Linkages Between the Information Technology Sector and "Traditional" Sectors in Tamil Nadu', Center for International Development, Harvard University.

Ramaswamy, K.V. and Gary Gereffi (2000), 'India's Apparel Exports: The Challenge of Global Markets', *The Developing Economies*, 38(2), 186–210.

Rauch, James E. (1993), 'Productivity Gains from Geographic Concentration of Human Capital: Evidence from the Cities', *Journal of Urban Economics*, 34, 380–400.

—— (2001), 'Business and Social Networks in International Trade', *Journal of Economic Literature*, 39(4).

Rodríguez, Francisco and Ernest J. Wilson, III (2000), 'Are Poor Countries Losing the Information Revolution?', University of Maryland at College Park.

Rosenbaum, Paul and Donald Rubin (1983), 'The Central Role of the Propensy Score in Observational Studies for Causal Effects', *Biometrika*, 70(1), 41–55.

Rubin, Donald (1974), 'Estimating Causal Effects of Treatments in Randomized and Non Randomized Studies', *Journal of Educational Psychology*, 66, 688–701.

Sako, Mari and Fiona Murray (1999), 'Modules in Design, Production and Use: Implications for the Global Automotive Industry', Prepared for the International Motor Vehicle Program (IMVP) Annual Sponsors Meeting, 5–7 October, Cambridge, MA.

Scott Morton, F., F. Zettelmeyer, and J.S. Risso (2000), 'Internet Car Retailing', NBER Working Paper no. 7961.

Senauer, Ben (2001), 'The Food Consumer in the 21st Century: New Research Perspectives', The Retail Food Industry Center, Working Paper no. 01–03, http://agecon.lib.umn.edu/mn/tr01-03.pdf.

Soresen, A. (2000), 'Equilibrium Price Dispersion in Retail Markets for Prescription Drugs', *Journal of Political Economy*, 108(4), 833–50.

Sturgeon, Timothy J. (2001), 'How do we Define Value Chains and Production Networks?', *IDS Bulletin*, 32(3).

—— and Richard K. Lester (2002), 'Upgrading East Asian Industries: New Challenges for Local Suppliers', MIT Industrial Performance Center, Working Paper no. 02-001.

Sutton, J. (1991), *Sunk Cost and Market Structure*. Cambridge, MA: MIT Press.

—— (1998), *Technology and Market Structure*. Cambridge, MA: MIT Press.

Telematica Instituut (2000), 'Perspectives of Electronic Commerce: The Flower Sector in the Netherlands', Prepared for the OECD Electronic Commerce Business Impact Project.

Thun, Eric (2000), 'Growing Up and Moving Out: Globalization in the Taiwanese Textile/Apparel and Automative Sectors', MIT Industrial Performance Center, Working Paper no. 00-007.

UNCTAD (2001a), *Electronic Commerce for Development Report*.

—— (2001b), 'Ways To Enhance the Production and Export Capacities of Developing Countries of Agriculture and Food Products, Including Niche Products, such as Environmentally Preferable Products', Trade and Development Board, Commission on Trade in Goods and Services, and Commodities, Geneva, 16–18 July.

van Heck, Eric (2001), 'Innovative Electronic Auctions in Supply and Demand Chains: Empirical Research in the Flower Industry', *Journal on Chain and Network Science*, 1(1), 65–76.

van Heck, Eric and Pieter Ribbers (1999), 'Experiences with Electronic Auctions in the Dutch Flower Industry', in Christopher Westland and Ted Clark (eds.), *Global Electronic Commerce: Theory and case studies*, Cambridge, MA, MIT Press, pp. 355–66.

van Liemt, Gijsbert (1999), 'The World Cut Flower Industry: Trends and Prospects', ILO, Sectoral Activities Programme, Industrial Activities Branch, ILO, Working Paper no. 139.

van Roozendaal, Gerda (1994), 'Kenyan Cut Flower Export Blooming', *Biotechnology and Development Monitor*, 21.

Varian, Hal R. (2002), 'A New Economy with No New Economics', *The New York Times*, 17 January.

Venables, Anthony J. (2001), 'Geography and International Inequalities: The Impact of New Technologies', Prepared for World Bank Annual Conference on Development Economics, Washington, DC, May.

Visser, Evert-Jan (1999), 'A Comparison of Clustered and Dispersed Firms in the Small-scale Clothing Industry of Lima', *World Development*, 27(9), 1553–70.

Warning, Matthew and Wendy Soo Hoo (2000), 'The Impact of Contract Farming on Income Distribution: Theory and Evidence', Paper Prepared for Presentation at the Western Economics Association International Annual Meetings, http://www.ups.edu/econ/working_papers/00-6.pdf.

Wharton, Annabel Jane (2001), *Building the Cold War: Hilton International Hotels and Modern Architecture*, Chicago, IL and London: University of Chicago Press.

Wheatley, Parker W., Brian Buhr, and Dennis DiPietre (2001), 'E-commerce in Agriculture: Development, Strategy, and Market Implications', University of Minnesota, Department of Applied Economics, Staff Paper P01-6.

Wolcott, P. (1999), 'The Diffusion of the Internet in the Republic of India: An Update', *The Global Diffusion of the Internet Project*.

World Bank (2001), World Development Indicators.

Yin, R. (1994), *Case Study Research: Design and Methods* (2nd edn), Thousand Oaks, CA: Sage Publishing.

Final Remarks

GØSTA ESPING-ANDERSEN

The two main contributions to this conference tackle, respectively, the equality and the efficiency side of the information and communication technology (ICT) economy. Surprisingly, there has been little attention to how the two sides are connected, and it is to this issue that I address my comments. On admittedly speculative grounds, I argue that long-term efficiency dividends are likely to require a far more equal distribution of human capital than is presently the case in most countries.

My reading of Part I by Bartelsman *et al.* is that ICT may help economies prosper through productivity gains if, that is, the institutional conditions are favourable. Among the potential obstacles, they highlight restrictive labour and product market regulation. Their analysis is far less attentive to demand-side factors, perhaps because they principally focus on how ICT is adopted into the firms' production process as productivity enhancing technologies. But, inattention to aggregate demand means that the productivity–growth horizon they operate with is fairly short. I would imagine that the growth momentum of the new information economy must, in the long haul, depend on whether the consumer masses can and will shift their preferences in favour of ICT-based transactions and products. To be sure, ICT investments are in large part a means to lower production and distribution costs of traditional consumer goods, be it cars, books, or vacations. Nonetheless, inherent in the ICT economy itself is the notion that the act of consumption *per se* will change, arguably to the benefit of the consumer. The Internet should empower the public; ICT products are in large measure potential household labour and time-saving technologies. I would imagine that the really powerful growth potential from ICT first begins when the millions of families that consume it multiply into the trillions.

Part II by Amable *et al.* is, in turn, mainly addressed to the digital-divide debate. They look at the inequality side of the coin, providing excellent evidence for why the naive view of ICT as the Great Leveller is, yes, naive. Just like the transportation revolution, ICT also may result in concentration within as well as between nations. Their analysis is predominantly directed at the Global impact—will poor countries benefit, or not? The answer to this depends on macroeconomic factors, such as trade barriers, but also on microeconomic conditions. Like Part I, the focus is on the producers and not the consumers. So, if *Zara* can gain markets in New York, additional textile jobs will be created in Mexico. The one great 'micro' question, namely what it takes to effectively make use of advanced communication technologies is, in Part II, unproblematic. They assume (page 5) that the barriers to entry in the Internet or in ICT technologies are almost non-existent, requiring virtually no special skills. They cite the embarrasing fact that our kids are better at using computers than are we, distinguished professors and all. Unfortunately, this is one big assumption. For one, the smart computer-whizz kids are typically *our* kids who, moreover, have access to the Internet both at home and in school. Even mass-produced, low-level ICT products like Pokémon are not very widespread among working class kids, and they are probably unheard of in the barrios of Lima. For another, if ICT is supposed to level individual life chances and global inequalities, we would clearly need to differentiate between the kinds of ICT uses. One thing is to log on to play video games or to watch porno, another is to access the Internet actively and creatively so as to enhance one's knowledge, opportunities, and welfare.

This is where I arrive at my modest contribution to the conference. If ICT is to move us towards a superior Pareto-frontier, it will have to deliver, at once, a sustainable growth dividend *and* more equality. How? I fear that we require additional data in order to provide any answers to this question. If long-term, sustainable growth is to be reaped from ICT we need, according to my argument, a *growing* mass public willing to, and capable of, using it productively. If ICT is also meant to level the playing field, both domestically and globally, these abilities and capabilities would have to be democratized. Oversimplifying, we might easily imagine two contrasting scenarios. The first we might describe as a world of 'islands of excellence in a sea of ignorance'. The case of India may approximate this model, but considering the huge proportion of functional illiterates in the United States (see below), not even the World's most advanced economy is automatically guaranteed long-term sustainable ICT-based growth. The second might be described as 'a tranquil duckpond without swans', a society without scores of Nobel prize winners but neither of illiterate masses. Here, the Nordic countries come to mind. We can actually arrive at rough measures of the ICT and Internet consumer potential for the decades to come by examining the incidence and distribution of basic cognitive abilities among today's young citizens. This assumes, of course, that there exists a direct relationship between cognitive abilities and, say, ability to utilize Internet. From the international programme for international student assessment (PISA) data on 15–16-year-olds we can regress computer abilities on youths' scholastic aptitudes. The former variable is an 'ability scale' (-3 to $+3$), while cognitive scores can range from 0 to 915.[1] Using the US data file, the simple bivariate regression yields a $B = 0.002$ ($t = 12.20$). Without proper controls, this is obviously not the true elasticity but were we to accept it as such, an improvement

---

[1] Scores below 407 are, in the PISA study, considered cognitively problematic, signalling very poor comprehension of all but rudimentary information.

of one standard deviation in cognitive aptitudes should roughly double a person's computer skills. Another way of examining the relationship is to compare the computer-skill scores of the bottom quintile of cognitive abilities to the median. In the case of the United States, the Q1/median ratio is 0.21—in other words, a rather massive gap. We certainly cannot put our faith in the assumption that kids today are naturally and easily computer literate. Indeed, one interesting finding from the PISA data is that a noticeable jump in computer abilities occurs just about when we arrive at median-level cognitive scores. In fact, the data point to a rather bipolar distribution of computer skills among today's youth.

Children are perhaps not the best to study if we wish to get at a nation's potential for mass ICT consumption, and I therefore move to the International Adult Literacy Survey (IALS) data which, likewise, monitor the distribution of cognitive abilities on three dimensions: prose, document, and quantitative skills, all obviously of direct importance for any serious ICT use. Akin to the PISA study, those falling into the lowest literacy level (I) can be defined as unable to master more than absolutely rudimentary information. From the IALS, I present data for the age group 20–29, a group that ought to be at the pinnacle of ICT literacy and use (see Table 1).

The distribution and incidence of intellectual abilities may matter relatively little for the phase of developing national ICT production. At this stage, the

Table R.1. *The potential consumer limits of the ICT economy*

	Percentage of 20–29-year-olds with insufficient cognitive abilities (IALS data)[a]	Cognitive Gini coefficients (20–29-year-olds) (IALS data)	Internet users per 1000 inhabitants[b] (2000)
United States	28	0.15	450
United Kingdom	18	0.12	301
Germany	5	0.09	292
Italy	17	0.10	230
Denmark	2	0.07	366
Finland	4	0.07	372
Sweden	4	0.09	456
Hungary	25	0.11	71
Poland	35	0.14	72
Russia			29
Chile	44	0.13	166
Brazil			29
Mexico			27

[a] Corresponding to IALS level 1.
[b] Data from international telecommunication union (ITU) (www.itu.int/ITU-D/ict/statistics).

Sources: IALS, second wave, and OECD's PISA study.

'islands of excellence' society ought to perform well, and any shortage of appropriate human capital can easily be remedied with economic incentives. But for the phase of mass ICT consumption, one would expect that the 'tranquil duckpond' would prove more dynamic. For an economy like the American or German, the long-term ICT accelerator will depend on, first, how many American and German citizens actively log on and conduct their economic transactions through ICT technology and, more removed, how many citizens throughout the rest of the world can be reached. The Finns and Swedes are highly reachable because they are homogeneously quite ICT-literate, but they represent tiny markets. There exist large markets with a favourable cognitive profile, like Germany and Japan, and others with rather unfavourable ones, like Brazil, Mexico, Poland, and Russia.[2] With roughly 50 million functionally 'illiterate' adults, the potential limits to ICT consumption seem, in the United States, also comparatively narrow.[3]

I no doubt exaggerate my cognitive skills story. Yet, I believe there is a broader case to be made for the salience of inequalities in any long-term ICT-based growth scenario. It is by now quite well established that levels of cognitive and educational inequalities coincide with overall societal inequalities, including the strength of intergenerational social inheritance.[4] If so, any sustained growth momentum from ICT might require some kind of revamped Keynesean intervention, aimed not so much at citizens' purchasing power as at their intellectual capacities.

PAUL A. GEROSKI

Introduction

I have been asked to comment on Parts I and II included in this volume, as well as to provide a perspective on some of the broader issues that arise in the so-called new economy. Given how much territory the two parts cover—as well as the thoroughness with which they cover that territory—I think that I can only make rather general remarks, and I will confine myself to four, to be discussed under the following headings:

- Market experimentation
- Competition and innovation
- The Internet and competition
- Which new economy?

---

[2] Unfortunately, we do not have IALS data for Brazil, Mexico, or Russia. The PISA data do. The percentage 15-year-olds falling into the 'dysfunctional' cognitive level in Brazil is 59%, in Mexico, 39%, and in Russia, 25%.

[3] Over the entire adult population, the percentage Americans at IALS level 1 is a bit more than 20%.

[4] See, for example, M. Corak (2001), 'Are the Kids all Right? Intergenerational Mobility in Canada', *Family and Labour Studies, Statistics Canada*, Working Paper no. 171.

Market experimentation

As I understand it, Part I by Bartelsman *et al.* argues that the recent growth performance of the United States (and some smaller countries) is due to the production and usage of information and communications technology (ICT). This, the authors suggest, is due to at least two things: market experimentation, and the degree of competition in the markets of these economies. Let me concentrate on the first of these arguments here, and return to the second in a moment.

The market experimentation argument seems to turn on three observations: in the United States, entrants are small relative to industry size; they display a low initial level but a high initial variance of productivity; and those who are successful generate very strong employment growth. This, it is argued, is what you might expect to see in a market experimentation process: high variance (owing, say, to various types of mutations) generates grist for the selection mill that grinds on in competitive markets, and, when the least fit have been weeded out, those who remain display high mean productivity growth. This is a rather seductive argument, and it may or may not be true of what is happening in the United States. Let me step back from the facts in this particular case however, and make three general observations on the process of market experimentation:

In the first place, we know that market experimentation processes like that alluded to in Part I happen in markets, and we know that they particularly happen in very young markets. The early pre-history of most markets is very interesting: it sees massive waves of entry, a sometimes enormous proliferation of different product and process innovations, and then a shake-out that drastically reduces the number of firms and shrinks the range of products available on the market into those that use one or more 'dominant designs' as basic platforms. I think that much of what the authors have observed in ICT is something that happens in virtually all very young markets, and they are right to highlight its importance.

Given this, it is interesting to ask a question: namely why is it that we need market experimentation processes? why cannot the same things happen in R&D labs or in product design studios? Is it really the case that this kind of market turbulence is the best way to develop and extend the usage of a new technology? I think that there are at least two reasons why market experimentation is necessary. First, firms are not good places in which to undertake experiments. Firms are large, complex organizations that are devoted to doing one or more things as well as they can. The kind of inquiring and questioning mindset that is the lifeblood of proper experimentation just does not often prosper, much less function well, within corporate boundaries. Second, market leaders usually have something to protect—something to defend—that makes them very reluctant to generate or introduce new products or processes that displace their existing—and very successful—products and processes. In these circumstances, it is probably not wise to leave control of the whole of the innovation process in their hands.

This, in turn, leads to a third observation: namely, what, if anything, is the role that policy makers might play in all of this? Here I think that we come up against one of the major challenges in policy that confronts us. Just how does one encourage people to be imaginative, to make experiments, to take risks, and to just try something new? And, even if that problem is cracked, just how does one deal with the moral hazards that such a policy inevitably creates? One might, I think, reply to these gloomy observations by saying that the best that policy can do is to free up entry restrictions (one might, indeed, say that this is all policy needs to do). This might be right, but it leaves me wondering whether it really is more efficient to create new enterprises and let them loose on unsuspecting consumers, rather than making existing enterprises more flexible.

Innovation and competition

The second argument in Part I that I want to comment on has to do with the relationship between innovation and competition. They argue that stringent regulation may hinder the development and uptake of new technologies, largely because it hinders entry and reduces (some might say displaces) competition. They point to the regulatory structure of the United States as being one of the reasons why the United States leads in the production and usage of ICT. This may or may not be true, but what is indisputably the case is that the regulation or promotion of entry is not anything like the whole story of how government policies (including regulation) affect innovation.

For a start, it is the case that many government policies actually stimulate competition. Competition policy is one obvious example, and, in Europe at least, it is an activity that is growing in importance. Anything that makes markets more competitive is, I think, likely to stimulate either the production or the uptake of new technologies (or both). Governments also stimulate innovation much more directly through the use of R&D subsidies, subsidies to Universities and basic scientific institutes, and through the judicious application of procurement policy. No one who has understood the history of the computer industry (or semiconductors or aircraft or agriculture...) can have missed the often key role that government policies have played in stimulating the development of these sectors. It is, I think, no accident that ICT was first developed in the United States, and I think that everyone knows just how key US government institutions like defence advanced research projects agency (DARPA) (plus large dollops of cash) were in the development and take up of these technologies. Let me also add that regulation does not always inhibit innovation. When governments get involved in setting or enforcing standards (technical standards, or environmental and/or product safety standards that all producers must meet), they usually stimulate the development and uptake of new technologies (even if this sometimes occurs by accident, and in unexpected ways). Not all of these interventions have turned out to be for the good, but a dispassionate reading of the evidence suggests, I think, that not all of them have turned out for the bad. In the area of ICT, a particularly important form of government regulation is through the development and enforcement of intellectual property rights laws. Here the recent record suggests that attempts to stimulate innovation through ever more rigorous intellectual property rights laws may sometimes actually retard the rate of advance. We shall see.

All of this said, it must also be said that ICT is hardly a showcase for the range of government policies that are usually grouped under the heading of 'industrial policy'. Indeed, the 'new economy' seems to have led industrial policy design as often as it has followed it. The current public policy focus on forming industrial clusters has arisen from the palpable success of Silicon Valley, something which, in turn, owes its success to no policy maker. More generally, much of ICT has clearly arisen from private sector activity, and it's growth and expansion has been the result of the midwifery of private sector agents, and not enlightened public policy makers. This is, I think, an interesting observation because the whole ICT sector is based on knowledge, and the production and commercialization of knowledge is exactly the kind of activity which one might have thought was most prone to 'market failure'. In the case, of ICT, however, the need for an industrial policy to correct such market failures has turned out to be more apparent than real.

Let me make one final observation, and that is on the relation between innovation and competition. This is an old chestnut, and economists since Schumpeter have enjoyed roasting it in different ways, and over different fires. I myself have come to be persuaded that in all but a few cases the common misrepresentation of Schumpeter—namely that monopoly stimulates innovation—is, quite simply, wrong. Further, I think that the weight of the evidence is against it. While it seems clear that monopolists may have the ability to innovate more effectively than small firms in very competitive markets—they have access to finance, they can build big labs and undertake big risky projects, and they are more likely to be able to appropriate the benefits of the innovations that these labs produce—the simple fact is that their incentive to take advantage of these advantages is often sadly lacking. Documenting these assertions is a task that I will not undertake here, but it is at least worth pointing out that the development of ICT is an achievement that owes very little to monopoly and quite a lot to competition understood in the old fashioned and classical sense of lots of small firms striving against each other to gain competitive advantage through the use of new technologies in the market. My sense is that the authors and I see more or less eye to eye on this.

The Internet and competition

Part II by Amable *et al.*, focuses on possibly the most obvious manifestation of the new ICT sector, namely the Internet. This paper is a careful and thought provoking evaluation of just what the Internet is all about. I am going to add a few small footnotes to what they have said, focussing largely on the relationship between the Internet and competition.

The authors rightly suggest that we need to be cautious about concluding that a device like the Internet, which greatly facilitates communication, will, for that reason, necessarily increase competition. For a start, the Internet will only facilitate certain types of transactions. The authors cover this ground well, but I want to briefly re-cover part of it using a different language. It is common to make a distinction between 'search' and 'experience' goods. The former are those goods that can be completely valued prior to purchase; experience goods, by contrast, must be consumed to be evaluated and are, therefore, a much more risky purchase for consumers. The Internet will clearly be a device that will facilitate the development of transactions involving search goods, but it seems to me that it will only do so for certain kinds of search goods, namely those that can be experienced prior to purchase over the Internet. For me, this is a significant restriction. I buy books all the time over the Internet, but I rarely buy works of art, or curtains, or wallpaper. These are all search goods, but they are not as easy to 'search' over the Internet as they are in other settings (like retail outlets or in your home).

The Internet is all about transmitting information, but even here I think that it is clear that the possibilities offered by the Internet are distinctly limited. It is common to make a distinction between knowledge that is codified and that which is tacit. The former is easy to transmit—the Internet, for example, is almost perfect for much knowledge of this kind. Tacit knowledge, however, is usually much trickier to transmit, and often must be done on a face-to-face basis. It is just not clear whether the Internet is ever going to be a place where much tacit information is transmitted, much less bought and sold.

Let me add one very small observation to everything that the authors have said on this subject, and that is that while it may be the case that the Internet will stimulate competition in certain markets, the amount of competition that it stimulates depends on how it develops. And, this in turn, depends on who—if anyone—owns it, and on how it is regulated. The Internet that we know has emerged from a fairly competitive market cauldron, and it has done so in the absence of regulation. It is, however, a valuable technology and a potentially revolutionary one. That it is valuable means that people will make an effort to control and dominate it; that it is potentially revolutionary means that many governments are going to find it hard not to get involved in regulating it. What all this means for the future is anyone's guess, but I think that pretty much everyone agrees that it is the important issue facing the Internet as it grows and develops.

Which new economy?

Whenever I read the phrase 'the new economy', I find myself wondering just what the people who are using it are talking about. For a start, there are two major technologies which are currently transforming our world in a profound and irreversible way, and either of them might be regarded as the harbinger of the 'new economy'. The first is ICT, based on digital technologies that facilitate the encapsulation, transmission, and display of information. For some, this technology has led to a series of product innovations—computer games, e-mail, and so on. For most, however, ICTs are process innovations which reduce transactions costs, (possibly) improve managerial effectiveness, and (probably) increase competition in a range of markets by facilitating the entry of new types of competitors (think of retailing, for example). ICT is inducing a convergence between telecommunications, computing, and entertainment, and has seen the growth of several new, enormous businesses (for example, various types of computer software, mobile communications, and, perhaps, digital television).

The other candidate technology that might be the harbinger of the 'new economy' is that which is sometimes referred to as 'life sciences' technologies (LST). These technologies are based on new developments in genetic engineering, and they seem to be affecting most businesses that deal with living things or organic compounds. For some, one of the important potential outputs of this technology may be a product innovation such as 'agri-ceuticals', foods with desirable therapeutic properties that both nourish and also treat specific ailments. At the moment, however, this technology seems to be having an impact mainly as a process innovation, introducing new methods of medical diagnosis, new pest-resistant seeds, and so on. LST is inducing a convergence across sectors like chemicals, pharmaceuticals, agriculture, and food processing industries.

Although it is very tempting to argue about which of these two technologies is *the* basis of the 'new economy'—to try to identify which is likely to have a bigger effect on the workings of the economy or, more generally, on our lives and those of our children—doing so would miss the important point that these two technologies have much in common. Let us pause just for a moment, and identify a number of their (trivial and non-trivial) similarities:

1. They are both based on code: in the case of ICT, it is a binary code, while in the case of LST, the alphabet of the code contains four letters. Either way, the breakthroughs in both areas can often be succinctly expressed in easily communicable (although perhaps not so easily understandable) formulas.
2. Both technologies are still rapidly evolving, and some of the breakthroughs that are being achieved are still very surprising. Moore's Law has delivered a set of portable computers that are unimaginably more powerful than the mainframe that transformed our lives 20–30 years ago, while the Human Genome project has mapped out vast tracts of our genetic make-up, yielding medical advances that are reported on almost a daily basis.
3. In the sectors that both technologies have touched, market structures are often initially very fluid, with massive waves of entry followed by major shake-outs. Entry has often turned out to be a vehicle for the arrival of new techniques or products using both of these technologies; substantial incumbent firms have been swept aside in many of the markets touched by these technologies.

4. In both sectors, geographical clustering has been a principal form of economic development. Local agglomerations of firms using similar technologies have developed, often in the most unlikely of places, and these 'growth poles' have attracted other, related firms. Silicon Valley is the most famous of these, but there are others.

5. Both sectors have seen new forms of business organizations develop, often built up around alliances between companies with quite different skill sets who produce products that are complementary from the point of view of consumers downstream. As with almost every other aspect of the market structures of these sectors, these alliance structures are very fluid and can change rapidly when new technological advances appear on the market.

6. Issues of ethics (largely in LST) and access (in both ICT and LST) are looming large as areas of major policy concern, making it very unlikely that public policy towards either sector will have the same narrow economic basis that has typically been the case in many 'old economy' sectors.

These several common features of ICT and LST appear to be a consequence of a much deeper seated similarity between these two technologies. This is the fact that firms involved with both technologies have come to regard knowledge as a key source of competitive advantage. To be a player in any of the markets that ICT or LST is transforming, one needs to keep up with the ever expanding frontier of knowledge on which these technologies are based. Indeed, it is now widely regarded as a truism that the 'new economy' is a knowledge based economy, that those who have access to this knowledge (and know what to do with it) will always prosper at the expense of those who do not.

It is, however, important to be careful about just what all of this really means. There is, in a sense, something deeply wrong with any proposition, which asserts that knowledge is now, for the first time ever, a key competitive asset for firms. The simple fact of the matter is that knowledge has always mattered, and it has always powered economic growth and development. We have always lived in a knowledge-based economy, even if the particular nature of that knowledge base has shifted over time. Further, there is nothing new about how the knowledge embodied in ICT and LST is transforming our economy, even if the particular bytes of knowledge embodied in ICT and LST are new. New technologies always generate fluid market structures, and induce convergence between hitherto unrelated sectors. If the 'new economy' really is new in the sense of being a 'knowledge-based economy', it must be because of the type of knowledge that it relies on.

There are two possible differences worth noting between the knowledge base of 'new economy' and that which formed the basis of the 'old economy'. First, 'know-how' has always been the key to competitive success in all industries and all economies, but knowledge in the 'new economy' is more than know-how: as we have seen, it tends to be codified and very portable. It has powered the entry of many new firms into sectors where it is applied, and it often seems to elude the control of its producers and users—at least more easily than 'know-how' and tacit knowledge has traditionally done. This observation suggests that it is the portability of knowledge that may distinguish the knowledge base of the 'new economy' from that of the 'old economy', and not the fact that knowledge *per se* matters. Second, much of the knowledge that is powering the 'new economy' comes from many sources; it has not been sponsored or controlled by a small group of firms or research institutes. Much of this knowledge has appeared in the public domain and, to a large extent, has stayed there, making it all the more difficult for firms who use ICT or LST to gain a long-term competitive advantage by controlling valuable knowledge or knowledge generation procedures. Everything always seems to be up for grabs in 'the new economy'. As a consequence of this, firms have become more interested in claiming property rights and using them to defend their market positions, which has been the case in the past. Firms have also physically moved themselves towards knowledge sources and clustered around them, and taken advantage of the rich traffic of knowledge transmission available to anyone 'in the loop'.

I am not quite sure where all of this leads us, but two observations seem to be worth making. First, insofar as ICT is regarded as a major disruptive innovation that is transforming vast chunks of the economy, it must be added that it is only part of the story of the technologically driven transformations, which are driving the economy forward, and possibly not the most important one. Second, what is happening today is 'new' mainly in the sense that it is happening today. As Parts I and II—and many other papers—show, what the so-called 'new economy' is doing to our lives is not dissimilar to what the 'old economy' did when it was new. Further, it is perfectly possible to understand the workings of the 'new economy' by applying what we have learned by studying the 'old economy'. In this one sense at least, there is nothing new about the new economy.

Index

f. indicates a figure, n. a footnote and t. a table